THE CIVIL WAR
OPPOSING VIEWPOINTS®

Other Books in the American History Series:

THE CIVIL WAR
OPPOSING VIEWPOINTS®

David L. Bender, *Publisher*
Bruno Leone, *Executive Editor*

William Dudley, *Series Editor*
John C. Chalberg, Ph.D., professor of history,
Normandale Community College, *Consulting
Editor*

William Dudley, *Book Editor*

AMERICAN HISTORY SERIES

Greenhaven Press, Inc.
San Diego, California

Cover illustrations, clockwise from top: 1) Currier & Ives engraving of the Battle of Gettysburg (Library of Congress); 2) front page of the *Charleston Mercury*, December 20, 1860 (The Bettmann Archive); 3) photograph of black soldiers at Fort Stevens, Washington, D.C. (Library of Congress); 4) photograph of Abraham Lincoln (Library of Congress)

Library of Congress Cataloging-in-Publication Data

The Civil War : opposing viewpoints / William Dudley, book editor.
    p.   cm. — (American history series)
    Includes bibliographical references and index.
    ISBN 1-56510-225-8 (lib.) — ISBN 1-56510-224-X (pap.)
    1. United States—History—Civil War, 1861-1865—Sources.
2. United States—History—Civil War, 1861-1865. I. Dudley, William, 1964-   . II. Series: American history series (San Diego, Calif.)
E464.C53   1995   94-9510
973.7—dc20   CIP

"America was born of revolt, flourished in dissent, became great through experimentation."

Henry Steele Commager, American Historian, 1902-1984

Contents

Foreword

Aboard the *Arbella* as it lurched across the cold, gray Atlantic, John Winthrop was as calm as the waters surrounding him were wild. With the confidence of a leader, Winthrop gathered his Puritan companions around him. It was time to offer a sermon. England lay behind them, and years of strife and persecution for their religious beliefs were over, he said. But the Puritan abandonment of England, he reminded his followers, did not mean that England was beyond redemption. Winthrop wanted his followers to remember England even as they were leaving it behind. Their goal should be to create a new England, one far removed from the authority of the Anglican church and King Charles I. In Winthrop's words, their settlement in the New World ought to be "a city upon a hill," a just society for corrupt England to emulate.

A Chance to Start Over

One June 8, 1630, John Winthrop and his company of refugees had their first glimpse of what they came to call New England. High on the surrounding hills stood a welcoming band of fir trees whose fragrance drifted to the *Arbella* on a morning breeze. To Winthrop, the "smell off the shore [was] like the smell of a garden." This new world would, in fact, often be compared to the Garden of Eden. Here, John Winthrop would have his opportunity to start life over again. So would his family and his shipmates. So would all those who came after them. These victims of conflict in old England hoped to find peace in New England.

Winthrop, for one, had experienced much conflict in his life. As a Puritan, he was opposed to Catholicism and Anglicanism, both of which, he believed, were burdened by distracting rituals and distant hierarchies. A parliamentarian by conviction, he despised Charles I, who had spurned Parliament and created a private army to do his bidding. Winthrop believed in individual responsibility and fought against the loss of religious and political freedom. A gentleman landowner, he feared the rising economic power of a merchant class that seemed to value only money. Once Winthrop stepped aboard the *Arbella*, he hoped, these conflicts would not be a part of his American future.

Yet his Puritan religion told Winthrop that human beings are fallen creatures and that perfection, whether communal or individual, is unachievable on this earth. Therefore, he faced a paradox: On the one hand, his religion demanded that he attempt to live a perfect life in an imperfect world. On the other hand, it told him that he was destined to fail.

Soon after Winthrop disembarked from the *Arbella*, he came face-to-face with this maddening dilemma. He found himself presiding not over a utopia but over a colony caught up in disputes as troubling as any he had confronted in his English past. John Winthrop, it seems, was not the only Puritan with a dream of a heaven on earth. But others in the community saw the dream differently. They wanted greater political and religious freedom than their leader was prepared to grant. Often, Winthrop was able to handle this conflict diplomatically. For example, he expanded, participation in elections and allowed the voters of Massachusetts Bay greater power.

But religious conflict was another matter because it was grounded in competing visions of the Puritan utopia. In Roger Williams and Anne Hutchinson, two of his fellow colonists, John Winthrop faced rivals unprepared to accept his definition of the perfect community. To Williams, perfection demanded that he separate himself from the Puritan institutions in his community and create an even "purer" church. Winthrop, however, disagreed and exiled Williams to Rhode Island. Hutchinson presumed that she could interpret God's will without a minister. Again, Winthrop did not agree. Hutchinson was tried on charges of heresy, convicted, and banished from Massachusetts.

John Winthrop's Massachusetts colony was the first but far from the last American attempt to build a unified, peaceful community that, in the end, only provoked a discord. This glimpse at its history reveals what Winthrop confronted: the unavoidable presence of conflict in American life.

American Assumptions

From America's origins in the early seventeenth century, Americans have often held several interrelated assumptions about their country. First, people believe that to be American is to be free. Second, because Americans did not have to free themselves from feudal lords or an entrenched aristocracy, America has been seen as a perpetual haven from the troubles and disputes that are found in the Old World.

John Winthrop lived his life as though these assumptions were true. But the opposing viewpoints presented in the American History Series should reveal that for many Americans, these assumptions were and are myths. Indeed, for numerous Americans, liberty has not always been guaranteed, and disputes have been an integral, sometimes welcome part of their life.

The American landscape has been torn apart again and again by a great variety of clashes—theological, ideological, political, economic, geographical, and social. But such a landscape is not necessarily a hopelessly divided country. If the editors hope to prove anything during the course of this series, it is not that the United States has been destroyed by conflict but rather that it has been enlivened, enriched, and even strengthened by Americans who have disagreed with one another.

Thomas Jefferson was one of the least confrontational of Americans, but he boldly and irrevocably enriched American life with his individualistic views. Like John Winthrop before him, he had a notion of an American Eden. Like Winthrop, he offered a vision of a harmonious society. And like Winthrop, he not only became enmeshed in conflict but eventually presided over a people beset by it. But unlike Winthrop, Jefferson believed this Eden was not located in a specific community but in each individual American. His Declaration of Independence from Great Britain could also be read as a declaration of independence for each individual in American society.

Jefferson's Ideal

Jefferson's ideal world was composed of "yeoman farmers," each of whom was roughly equal to the others in society's eyes, each of whom was free from the restrictions of both government and fellow citizens. Throughout his life, Jefferson offered a continuing challenge to Americans: Advance individualism and equality or see the death of the American experiment. Jefferson believed that the strength of this experiment depended upon a society of autonomous individuals and a society without great gaps between rich and poor. His challenge to his fellow Americans to create—and sustain—such a society has itself produced both economic and political conflict.

A society whose guiding document is the Declaration of Independence is a society assured of the freedom to dream—and to disagree. We know that Jefferson hated conflict, both personal and political. His tendency was to avoid confrontations of any sort, to squirrel himself away and write rather than to stand up and speak his mind. It is only through his written words that we can grasp Jefferson's utopian dream of a society of independent farmers, all pursuing their private dreams and all leading lives of middling prosperity.

Jefferson, this man of wealth and intellect, lived an essentially happy private life. But his public life was much more troublesome. From the first rumblings of the American Revolution in the 1760s to the North-South skirmishes of the 1820s that ultimately produced the Civil War, Jefferson was at or near the center of American political history. The issues were almost too many—and too crucial—for one lifetime: Jefferson had to choose between supporting or rejecting the path of revolution. During and after the ensuing war, he was at the forefront of the battle for religious liberty. After endorsing the Constitution, he opposed the economic plans of Alexander Hamilton. At the end of the century, he fought the infamous Alien and Sedition Acts, which limited civil liberties. As president, he opposed the Federalist court, conspiracies to divide the union, and calls for a new war against England. Throughout his life, Thomas Jefferson, slaveholder, pondered the conflict between American freedom and American slavery. And from retirement at his Monticello retreat, he frowned at the rising spirit of commercialism he feared was dividing Americans and destroying his dream of American harmony.

No matter the issue, however, Thomas Jefferson invariably supported the rights of the individual. Worried as he was about the excesses of commercialism, he accepted them because his main concern was to live in a society where liberty and individualism could flourish. To Jefferson, Americans had to be free to worship as they desired. They also deserved to be free from an over-reaching government. To Jefferson, Americans should also be free to possess slaves.

Harmony, an Elusive Goal

Before reading the articles in this anthology, the editors ask readers to ponder the lives of John Winthrop and Thomas Jefferson. Each held a utopian vision, one based upon the demands of community and the other on the autonomy of the individual. Each dreamed of a country of perpetual new beginnings. Each found himself thrust into a position of leadership and found that conflict could not be avoided. Harmony, whether communal or individual, was a forever elusive goal.

The opposing visions of Winthrop and Jefferson have been at the heart of many differences among Americans from many backgrounds through the whole of American history. Moreover, their visions have provoked important responses that have helped shape American society, the American character, and many an American battle.

The editors of the American History Series have done extensive research to find representative opinions on the issues included in these volumes. They have found numerous outstanding opposing viewpoints from people of all times, classes, and genders in American history. From those, they have selected commentaries that best fit the nature and flavor of the period and topic under consideration. Every attempt was made to include the most important and relevant viewpoints in each chapter. Obviously, not every notable viewpoint could be included. Therefore, a selective, annotated bibliography has been provided at the end of each book to aid readers in seeking additional information.

The editors are confident that as this series reveals past conflicts, it will help revitalize the reader's views of the American present. In that spirit, the American History Series is dedicated to the proposition that American history is more complicated, more fascinating, and more troubling than John Winthrop or Thomas Jefferson ever dared to imagine.

John C. Chalberg
Consulting Editor

Introduction

"The central issues of the Civil War . . . went to the core of America's identity as a nation of freedom."

In 1869 retired Harvard University professor George Ticknor wrote that the American Civil War, which had concluded four years earlier, had created a "great gulf between what happened before in our century and what happened since, or what is likely to happen hereafter. It does not seem to me as if I were living in the country in which I was born." Most scholars of American history have agreed with Ticknor in naming the Civil War as the single most important and influential event in the story that is America's history. It has retained an interest for many Americans besides historians—indeed, a revealing element of its influence has been its continuing hold on the American imagination. The Civil War has been the subject of tens of thousands of books and of innumerable motion pictures. Hundreds of parks and historical landmarks commemorate former battlefields. Thousands of Americans participate in Civil War battle reenactments. Many organizations, magazines, and membership societies are devoted to the study of the Civil War.

Why is the Civil War so fascinating? Part of the answer undoubtedly lies in its staggering number of lives lost and destroyed. The Civil War was America's deadliest war: 620,000 soldiers and unknown numbers of civilians perished in the conflict, a number almost equal to the number of lives lost in the rest of America's wars combined. Behind each casualty lay the tragic irony of countryman killing countryman endemic in all civil wars. Many families served on both sides of the conflict, relative pitted against relative. Many of the key figures in the Union and Confederate armies were fellow West Point graduates, veterans, and friends.

But beyond the sheer carnage and personal tragedy was another important element. The Civil War was about the *meaning* of America. In 1776 the leaders of the American Revolution had sought to create a new nation, based on ideals of political liberty, equality, and self-government expressed in the Declaration of Independence. Eighty-five years later both sides of the Civil War would claim to be fighting for the same ideals as their revolutionary forebears. The theme of fighting for America's revolutionary ideals was expressed not only by the leaders of the Civil War— for example, President Abraham Lincoln and his Confederate counterpart,

Jefferson Davis—but also by the soldiers who fought the war. In his book *What They Fought For*, historian James M. McPherson examines the writings of soldiers from both sides of the Civil War, and argues that many were conscious of their revolutionary heritage. Henry Orr, an enlisted soldier in a Texas cavalry regiment, wrote to his sister comparing the Confederate rebellion with the revolution against Great Britain that established *"Liberty* and freedom in this western world," and declared himself to be fighting for the "Holy Cause of Liberty and Independence" once again. Sullivan Ballou, a major in a Rhode Island regiment, wrote to his wife shortly before he was killed at the First Battle of Bull Run (Manassas):

> I know . . . how great a debt we owe to those who went before us through the blood and sufferings of the Revolution. And I am willing, —perfectly willing—to lay down all my joys in this life, to help maintain this Government, and to pay that debt.

Both the Union and the Confederacy claimed to be fighting for the same revolutionary ideals, but they differed greatly in their definition of these ideals.

Disagreement over the "meaning" of the American Revolution was not a new development in 1861. Americans have argued about the country's ideals of freedom at least since its revolutionary founding. The creation and ratification of the Constitution, the rise of political factions and parties, the debate over whether America should emphasize industry or agriculture in its economic development, and the expansion of territory westward—all have been marked by conflict over the proper function of American government and the practical ramifications of American ideals of freedom. However, for its first eight decades the American political system had enjoyed resounding success in peacefully settling American debates and in reaching compromises on key issues.

An important element of the American system—dating back to 1796, when John Adams defeated Thomas Jefferson in the election to succeed George Washington as president—was the willingness of losers to accept the results of the system, and to work from within the system to change it (Jefferson went on to defeat Adams in the 1800 presidential election). However, when Abraham Lincoln won the presidency in 1860, leaders of several Southern states, led by South Carolina, refused to accept the result and immediately made plans to withdraw from the Union. Why did they react so antithetically to American tradition? Americans have often disagreed bitterly, but only once have those disagreements brought states to secession; only once were they resolved only by total and bitter war.

Historians have long debated the causes of the Civil War, but most agree that two were key. One was the issue of secession itself—whether states had the right to end their status as a part of the United States of America. Many Southerners claimed that the nation was formed by a compact between sovereign states, who had the same right to secede from the Union as the original colonies had when they broke off from Great Britain in 1776. Northerners tended to emphasize the fact that the colonies had acted in *union* to win independence from Great Britain and establish a new republican government. In an era of monarchies and autocracies, republican government of the people was an experiment doomed to failure if states could secede at will, argued Abraham Lincoln. Many agreed, including Connecticut soldier Robert Goodyear, who wrote in a letter to his wife:

> [If] traitors be allowed to overthrow and break asunder ties most sacred—costing our forefathers long years of blood and toil, . . . all the hope and confidence of the world in the capacity of men for self government will be lost . . . and perhaps be followed by a long night of tyranny.

The issue that compelled the Southern states to secede—the second key cause of the war—was slavery. The use of captured Africans and their descendants for slave labor had been abolished in the North, but it remained the foundation for the plantation economy of the Southern states. Slavery dominated public discussion and discourse in the years prior to the Civil War, and was completely abolished following it.

Since the Civil War, some schools of historical thought have deemphasized the issue of slavery as a cause of the war. McPherson writes in *A Reader's Companion to American History:*

> The progressive historians emphasized the widening economic gulf between the North and South. Cultural and social historians stressed the contrast between the civilizations and the values of the two regions. But revisionist historians denied the existence of any fundamental economic or social conflicts. They pointed instead to self-serving politicians who created and then exploited the false issue of slavery's expansion into new territories to whip up sectional passions and get themselves elected to office.

But McPherson goes on to criticize these alternative explanations.

> Few historians today subscribe to either the progressive or the revisionist interpretation in unalloyed form. To be sure, conflicts of interest occurred between the agricultural South and the industrializing North. But issues like tariffs, banks, and land grants divided parties and interest groups more than they did North and South. . . . The Civil War was not fought over the issue of tariffs or of industrialization or of land grants. Nor was it a consequence of false issues invented by demagogues. It was fought over profound, intractable problems that Americans on both sides believed went to the heart of their society and its future. . . .
> What lay at the root of this separation? Slavery. It was the sole in-

16

stitution not shared by North and South. The peculiar institution *defined* the South. "On the subject of slavery," declared the *Charleston Mercury* in 1858, "the North and South . . . are not only two Peoples, but they are rival, hostile Peoples."

In examining why the South seceded after Lincoln's election, it is helpful to review how the issue of slavery had shaped events in prior decades. Slaveholders had been prominent in American life for most of the nation's history. They were instrumental in drafting the founding documents of the American republic—the Declaration of Independence and the Constitution. A few Northerners, such as Benjamin Franklin, were opposed to slavery, but the institution was generally accepted, if not praised, by the nation's founders. Many shared the views of Thomas Jefferson, author of the Declaration of Independence and slaveowner, who wrote that it was a "necessary evil," and expected or hoped the institution would eventually die a natural death.

Five years after Jefferson's death in 1826, the Virginia state legislature was debating what to do in response to the slave rebellion led by Nat Turner, in which 57 whites were killed. The legislature considered proposals to abandon the institution of slavery—the path that had been chosen by Virginia's Northern neighbors—but rejected the idea. The resolution of the debate cemented slavery's entrenchment in the South. Leading Southern statesmen such as South Carolinian John C. Calhoun began to assert that slavery, far from being a "necessary evil," was instead a "positive good" for slave and owner alike.

At about the same time an abolitionist movement, which sought the elimination of slavery in all the states, was growing in the North. Abolitionists were never a majority in the North prior to the Civil War, but they did fashion a strong and influential moral/political movement that was seen as a serious threat by the Southern states, many of which banned all abolitionist speaking and publishing. But despite the rise of abolitionism in the North and the seeming permanence of slavery in the South, war between the two sections might have been avoided but for one complication—the question of whether slavery should be allowed in the western territories of the expanding nation.

The Mexican War brought this question to the forefront of American politics. The 1846-1848 conflict was largely instigated by a Southern-born president, James K. Polk; the American army that fought Mexico was led by two Southern-born generals, Zachary Taylor and Winfield Scott; and Southerners filled two-thirds of the army's ranks. The war netted the United States hundreds of thousands of acres in what is now the American Southwest—land that Southerners expected and Northerners feared would become slave states. That question became the focus of an intense national de-

17

bate when an obscure Pennsylvania congressman, David Wilmot, introduced a resolution in August 1846 calling for the banning of slavery in all territory that might be acquired in the Mexican War.

The Wilmot Proviso was passed in the House and defeated in the Senate several times over the next few years, in votes that were doubly revealing: They marked the first time in American history that sectional differences had outweighed party differences on a critical national issue (Northern Democrats and Whigs voted for the Wilmot Proviso, Southern Whigs and Democrats voted against), and the votes illustrated the critical role of the Senate in preserving the South's interests. The United States in 1848 had a balance of 15 free and 15 slave states; thus Southern senators could block all measures threatening slavery despite the fact that the Northern states had by far the greater population, and thus the greater representation in the House of Representatives. Much of the debate over admitting new states to the Union pivoted on preserving this balance between slave and free states.

Southerners insisted on the expansion of slavery into the territories, fearing that otherwise the political clout of the North, with its growing population, would soon eclipse the South and pose a danger to its way of life. They were especially concerned about the growth of the antislavery movement, a development illustrated by succeeding presidential elections. In 1840 the Liberty Party was founded by abolitionists in New York. Its candidate, James Birney, won 7,000 votes in 1840 and 62,000 votes in 1844. By 1848 it had been replaced by the Free-Soil Party, which featured a more moderate agenda of limiting the expansion of slavery in the territories. Its 1848 and 1852 candidates, Martin Van Buren and Stephen P. Hale, received 291,000 and 156,000 votes respectively. The Free-Soil Party disbanded in 1854, and most of its members joined disenchanted Whigs and Democrats to form the new Republican Party, again opposing the spread of slavery in the territories. Its first presidential candidate, John C. Frémont, received 1.3 million popular votes and 114 out of 296 electoral votes. All of Frémont's electoral votes and virtually all of his popular votes came from the North.

Southerners grew increasingly disturbed at the growing strength of a sectional party that was unsympathetic to slavery. These fears crested in 1860 with the election of Abraham Lincoln, a Republican who won most of the Northern states and none of the Southern ones. Historian Don E. Fehrenbacher writes in *The Civil War: An Illustrated History* that Southerners felt especially threatened because they and their Northern proslavery allies had long enjoyed preeminence in Washington.

> For many southerners, the prospect of a Republican administration summoned up visions of a world in which slaveholding would be officially stigmatized as morally wrong, in which

slaves would be encouraged to rise up against their masters, and in which national policy would move inexorably toward emancipation and racial equality. But to understand fully the reaction of the South to Lincoln's election, one must take into account not only the antislavery complexion of Republicanism but also the proslavery character of the Federal government before 1861. For nearly three quarters of a century, southern slaveholders, along with northerners deferential to the slaveholding interest, had predominated in the presidency, the executive departments, the foreign service, the Supreme Court, the higher military echelons, and the Federal bureaucracy. Cabinet posts and other important positions were frequently entrusted to proslavery militants like John C. Calhoun, but no antislavery leader was appointed to high Federal office before Lincoln became President. . . . The presence of slavery in the national capital testified to its official respectability. In 1857, the Chief Justice of the United States [Roger Taney in the *Dred Scott* case] awarded slavery a privileged status under the Constitution when he declared that the Federal government had no power to regulate the institution but did have "the power coupled with the duty of guarding and protecting the owner in his rights." When the secession crisis arose, James Buchanan, the Pennsylvania Democrat in the White House, blamed it entirely on "the incessant and violent agitation of the slavery question throughout the North." Is it any wonder that most southerners viewed the election of Lincoln as a revolutionary break with the past?

Slavery and secession, therefore, were the two major and festering issues that ultimately plunged the nation into the Civil War. Of course, other questions divided the American people, as illustrated in this volume of viewpoints. Divisions existed between and within the North and the South as to the necessity and desirability of war, strategy and tactics, the growth of national government, the future of blacks in America, and other important issues. But the central issues of the Civil War remained slavery and secession— issues that went to the core of America's identity as a nation of freedom. The Civil War, at great cost, emphatically settled these questions that had been debated since the American Revolution. The right of secession was never seriously pursued after the defeat of the Confederacy. The Emancipation Proclamation and the Thirteenth Amendment to the Constitution freed the nation's four million slaves. Left unresolved was the future of those slaves—and the future meaning of freedom and equality in America.

John C. Chalberg
Consulting Editor

CHAPTER 1

The Roots of Division

Chapter Preface

For the first eight decades of its existence, the United States was able to peacefully resolve or patch over its internal differences over slavery. During this time slavery evolved from a largely national institution into a regional one limited to the South, and opinions on slavery grew polarized and intense. Many historians attribute the Civil War to the breakdown of a peaceful national consensus on slavery. The viewpoints in the following chapter cover the 1850s, a pivotal time when America's leaders struggled to prevent the country from being divided over slavery. America was rapidly expanding westward, and the question facing these leaders was the place of slavery within this growing nation.

During the 1850s two linchpins of the national consensus on slavery came under attack. One was the 1820 Missouri Compromise, which drew a geographical line parallel to Missouri's southern border through territory acquired by the 1803 Louisiana Purchase. This line was to divide future slave states from future free states, keeping a balance between the two. With the enormous acquisition of territory from Mexico following the 1846-48 Mexican War, some people proposed that the Missouri Compromise line be extended to the Pacific Ocean. This suggestion was opposed by two groups: Northerners who wanted slavery banned altogether in the new territories, and slavery partisans of the South who fervently argued that they had a right to bring their "property" into all the jointly acquired land (some even sought expansion into Cuba, Mexico, and Central America as a way to increase the number of slaveholding states). In the face of such dual opposition, a geographical division such as that of the Missouri Compromise became impossible to pass in Congress.

The other linchpin of national unity threatened by slavery was the Constitution itself. The 1787 document that established the national government contained several key provisions protecting slavery. One important clause in Article IV read:

> No person held to service or labor in one state, under the laws thereof, escaping into another, shall, in consequence of any law or regulation therein, be discharged from such service or labor, but shall be delivered up on claim of the party to whom such service or labor may be due.

This provision, which received relatively little notice when the Constitution was ratified, was meant to ensure that slaveowners could reclaim slaves who had escaped to other states. The Fugitive Slave Act passed by Congress in 1793 authorized slaveowners and their agents to recover runaway slaves who had escaped across state lines. By the 1840s, all of the Northern states had abolished slavery, and many came to resent this constitutional clause that seemed to condone the institution. Many states and towns sought to thwart it by passing "personal liberty" laws banning the use of state facilities and officials to capture runaway slaves, and in other ways making it more difficult for owners to capture escaped slaves and send them back to the South. Southerners were quick to attack these laws as unconstitutional and unfair schemes designed by the North to oppress the South. Congress, as part of the Compromise of 1850, passed a new Fugitive Slave Act, which made it a federal crime to refuse to apprehend and return runaway slaves. But many Northern states continued to pass laws intended to protect escaped slaves, leading to Southern calls for greater federal enforcement of the new Fugitive Slave Act.

As the following viewpoints demonstrate, not all Northerners were abolitionists, and not all Southerners were advocates of slavery. However, the issue of slavery was clearly becoming a national conflict between the Northern and Southern regions. In 1850 and again in 1861, the United States teetered on the brink of division and war as Southerners voiced calls for secession. In 1850 politicians were able to compromise and preserve the peace. In 1861 efforts at compromise failed, and the nation went to war.

VIEWPOINT 1

"The South asks for justice, simple justice, and less she ought not to take."

Southern States May Be Forced to Leave the Union

John C. Calhoun (1782-1850)

To examine the reasons for the Southern secession that led to the Civil War, one may arguably need look no further than John C. Calhoun's last speech before the United States Senate, presented on March 4, 1850. Calhoun, who at various times in his long political career was vice president, secretary of war, secretary of state, and United States senator, was recognized as the preeminent defender of the South and its institutions, including slavery. The South Carolinian formed with Henry Clay and Daniel Webster the "great triumvirate" of U.S. senators who, often in agreement but more often in conflict with one another, dominated American political life from 1815 to 1850.

Calhoun's speech was part of an illustrious congressional debate over a series of legislative measures introduced by Clay on January 29, 1850, that aimed to ease sectional tensions over slavery. The immediate crisis began when the residents of California (territory recently won from Mexico) petitioned Congress to enter the Union as a "free" state in which slavery was forbidden. But the admission of California as a free state (which would give free states a 16–15 majority over slave states) was unacceptable to many Southerners. Mississippi called for a convention of Southern leaders to meet the following June in Nashville, Tennessee, to discuss the possibility of seceding from the Union.

Henry Clay's proposals included letting California into the

John C. Calhoun, speech before the U.S. Senate, March 4, 1850.

Union as a free state; admitting the territories of New Mexico and Utah on the basis of popular sovereignty (allowing local residents to decide whether to legalize slavery); and, to satisfy Southern demands, establishing a stricter federal law for the return of runaway slaves while removing from Congress any role in regulating the slave trade between Southern states. Clay, long noted as an advocate both of the Union and of compromise, argued before Congress on February 6 that his proposals were necessary to preserve the Union, and warned that "the dissolution of the Union and war are identical and inseparable." Calhoun's views on the situation facing the nation and his opposition to Clay's compromise were presented on March 4, 1850. Having worked for weeks on his speech, he was too ill to deliver it, and instead sat by as Senator James M. Mason of Virginia read his words.

Calhoun's speech begins with the question "How can the Union be preserved?" and goes on to summarize his views on the history and the political situation of the United States. He argues that the "equilibrium" between Northern and Southern interests that existed at the time of the nation's birth has been destroyed by the increasing population and power of the Northern states. This development, he asserts, was helped by federal government policies concerning tariffs and western territories that favored the North. Calhoun notes that the "cords" binding the nation are fraying, and argues that nothing less than a permanent halt to antislavery "agitation," the opening of all western territories to slaveowners, and amending the Constitution to restore the South's previous power in national affairs (in essence, giving the Southern states veto power over any attempt to abolish slavery) will allow the South to remain with honor in the Union.

Calhoun died less than one month later. His last appearance at the Senate was on March 7, to hear Daniel Webster's rebuttal to his arguments and support of Clay's compromise measures. Calhoun's warnings notwithstanding, the Compromise of 1850 was passed after his death; it is credited with preventing war for another few years. Calhoun's analysis, however, proved in many ways prophetic.

I have, Senators, believed from the first that the agitation of the subject of slavery would, if not prevented by some timely and effective measure, end in disunion. Entertaining this opinion, I have, on all proper occasions, endeavored to call the attention of both the two great parties which divide the country to adopt some measure to prevent so great a disaster, but without success. The agitation has been permitted to proceed, with almost no attempt to resist it, until it has reached a point when it can no longer be disguised or denied that the Union is in danger. You have thus had forced upon you the greatest and gravest question that can ever come under your consideration—How can the Union be preserved?

To give a satisfactory answer to this mighty question, it is indispensable to have an accurate and thorough knowledge of the nature and the character of the cause by which the Union is endangered. Without such knowledge it is impossible to pronounce, with any certainty, by what measure it can be saved; just as it would be impossible for a physician to pronounce, in the case of some dangerous disease, with any certainty, by what remedy the patient could be saved, without similar knowledge of the nature and character of the cause which produced it. The first question, then, presented for consideration, in the investigation I propose to make, in order to obtain such knowledge, is—What is it that has endangered the Union?

Southern Discontent

To this question there can be but one answer,—that the immediate cause is the almost universal discontent which pervades all the States composing the Southern section of the Union. This widely-extended discontent is not of recent origin. It commenced with the agitation of the slavery question, and has been increasing ever since. The next question, going one step further back, is—What has caused this widely diffused and almost universal discontent?

It is a great mistake to suppose, as is by some, that it originated with demagogues, who excited the discontent with the intention of aiding their personal advancement, or with the disappointed ambition of certain politicians, who resorted to it as the means of retrieving their fortunes. On the contrary, all the great political influences of the section were arrayed against excitement, and exerted to the utmost to keep the people quiet. The great mass of the people of the South were divided, as in the other section, into Whigs and Democrats. The leaders and the presses of both parties in the South were very solicitous to prevent excitement and to preserve quiet; because it was seen that the effects of the former would necessarily tend to weaken, if not destroy, the political ties which united them with their respective parties in the other section. Those who know the strength of party ties will readily appreciate the immense force which this cause exerted against agitation, and in favor of preserving quiet. But, great as it was, it was not sufficient to prevent the wide-spread discontent which now pervades the section. No; some cause, far deeper and more powerful than the one supposed, must exist, to account for discontent so wide and deep. The question then recurs—What is the cause of this discontent? It will be found in the belief of the people of the Southern States, as prevalent as the discontent itself, that they cannot remain, as things now are, consistently with honor and safety, in the Union. The next question to be considered is—What has caused this belief?

One of the causes is, undoubtedly, to be traced to the long-continued agitation of the slave question on the part of the North, and the many aggressions which they have made on the rights of the South during the time. I will not enumerate them at present, as it will be done hereafter in its proper place.

There is another lying back of it—with which this is intimately connected—that may be regarded as the great and primary cause. This is to be found in the fact that the equilibrium between the two sections, in the Government as it stood when the constitution was ratified and the Government put in action, has been destroyed. At that time there was nearly a perfect equilibrium between the two, which afforded ample means to each to protect itself against the aggression of the other; but, as it now stands, one section has the exclusive power of controlling the Government, which leaves the other without any adequate means of protecting itself against its encroachment and oppression. To place this subject distinctly before you, I have, Senators, prepared a brief statistical statement, showing the relative weight of the two sections in the Government under the first census of 1790 and the last census of 1840.

Changing Populations

According to the former, the population of the United States, including Vermont, Kentucky, and Tennessee, which then were in their incipient condition of becoming States, but were not actually admitted, amounted to 3,929,827. Of this number the Northern States had 1,997,899, and the Southern 1,952,072, making a difference of only 45,827 in favor of the former States. The number of States, including Vermont, Kentucky, and Tennessee, were sixteen; of which eight, including Vermont, belonged to the Northern section, and eight, including Kentucky and Tennessee, to the Southern—making an equal division of the States between the two sections under the first census. There was a small preponderance in the House of Representatives, and in the electoral college, in favor of the Northern, owing to the fact that, according to the provisions of the constitution, in estimating federal numbers five slaves count but three; but it was too small to affect sensibly the perfect equilibrium which, with that exception, existed at the time. Such was the equality of the two sections when the States composing them agreed to enter into a Federal Union. Since then

26

the equilibrium between them has been greatly disturbed.

According to the last census the aggregate population of the United States amounted to 17,063,357, of which the Northern section contained 9,728,920, and the Southern 7,334,437, making a difference, in round numbers, of 2,400,000. The number of States had increased from sixteen to twenty-six, making an addition of ten States. In the mean time the position of Delaware had become doubtful as to which section she properly belonged. Considering her as neutral, the Northern States will have thirteen and the Southern States twelve, making a difference in the Senate of two Senators in favor of the former. According to the apportionment under the census of 1840, there were two hundred and twenty-three members of the House of Representatives, of which the Northern States had one hundred and thirty-five, and the Southern States (considering Delaware as neutral) eighty-seven, making a difference in favor of the former in the House of Representatives of forty-eight. The difference in the Senate of two members, added to this, gives to the North, in the electoral college, a majority of fifty. Since the census of 1840, four States have been added to the Union—Iowa, Wisconsin, Florida, and Texas. They leave the difference in the Senate as it stood when the census was taken; but add two to the side of the North in the House, making the present majority in the House in its favor fifty, and in the electoral college fifty-two.

The result of the whole is to give the Northern section a predominance in every department of the Government, and thereby concentrate in it the two elements which constitute the Federal Government,—majority of States, and a majority of their population, estimated in federal numbers. Whatever section concentrates the two in itself possesses the control of the entire Government.

But we are just at the close of the sixth decade, and the commencement of the seventh. The census is to be taken this year, which must add greatly to the decided preponderance of the North in the House of Representatives and in the electoral college. The prospect is, also, that a great increase will be added to its present preponderance in the Senate, during the period of the decade, by the addition of new States. Two territories, Oregon and Minnesota, are already in progress, and strenuous efforts are making to bring in three additional States from the territory recently conquered from Mexico; which, if successful, will add three other States in a short time to the Northern section, making five States; and increasing the present number of its States from fifteen to twenty, and of its Senators from thirty to forty. On the contrary, there is not a single territory in progress in the Southern section, and no certainty that any additional State will be added to it during the decade. The prospect then is, that the two sections

27

in the Senate, should the efforts now made to exclude the South from the newly acquired territories succeed, will stand, before the end of the decade, twenty Northern States to fourteen Southern (considering Delaware as neutral), and forty Northern Senators to twenty-eight Southern. This great increase of Senators, added to the great increase of members of the House of Representatives and the electoral college on the part of the North, which must take place under the next decade, will effectually and irretrievably destroy the equilibrium which existed when the Government commenced.

John C. Calhoun of South Carolina was the political hero of many Southerners who would later form the Confederacy.

Had this destruction been the operation of time, without the interference of Government, the South would have had no reason to complain; but such was not the fact. It was caused by the legislation of this Government, which was appointed, as the common agent of all, and charged with the protection of the interests and security of all. The legislation by which it has been effected, may be classed under three heads. The first is, that series of acts [including the 1787 Northwest Ordinance, the 1820 Missouri Compromise, and the 1848 admission of Oregon as a free territory] by which the South has been excluded from the common territory belonging to all the States as members of the Federal Union—which have had the effect of extending vastly the portion allotted to the Northern section, and restricting within narrow limits the portion left the South. The next consists in adopting a system of revenue and disbursements, by which an undue proportion of the burden of taxation has been imposed upon the South, and an undue proportion of its proceeds appropriated to the North; and the last is a system of political measures, by which the original character of the Government has been radically changed. . . .

The Changing Government

That the Government claims, and practically maintains the right to decide in the last resort, as to the extent of its powers, will scarcely be denied by any one conversant with the political history of the country. That it also claims the right to resort to force to maintain whatever power it claims, against all opposition, is equally certain. Indeed it is apparent, from what we daily hear, that this has become the prevailing and fixed opinion of a great majority of the community. Now, I ask, what limitation can possibly be placed upon the powers of a government claiming and exercising such rights? And, if none can be, how can the separate governments of the States maintain and protect the powers reserved to them by the constitution—or the people of the several States maintain those which are reserved to them, and among others, the sovereign powers by which they ordained and established, not only their separate State Constitutions and Governments, but also the Constitution and Government of the United States? But, if they have no constitutional means of maintaining them against the right claimed by this Government, it necessarily follows, that they hold them at its pleasure and discretion, and that all the powers of the system are in reality concentrated in it. It also follows, that the character of the Government has been changed in consequence, from a federal republic, as it originally came from the hands of its framers, into a great national consolidated democracy. It has indeed, at present, all the characteristics of the latter, and not one of the former, although it still retains its outward form.

The result of the whole of these causes combined is—that the North has acquired a decided ascendancy over every department of this Government, and through it a control over all the powers of the system. A single section governed by the will of the numerical majority, has now, in fact, the control of the Government and the entire powers of the system. What was once a constitutional federal republic, is now converted, in reality, into one as absolute as that of the Autocrat of Russia, and as despotic in its tendency as any absolute government that ever existed.

As, then, the North has the absolute control over the Government, it is manifest, that on all questions between it and the South, where there is a diversity of interests, the interest of the latter will be sacrificed to the former, however oppressive the effects may be; as the South possesses no means by which it can resist, through the action of the Government. But if there was no question of vital importance to the South, in reference to which there was a diversity of views between the two sections, this state of things might be endured, without the hazard of destruction to the South. But such is not the fact. There is a question of vital importance to the Southern section, in reference to which the views and feelings of the two sections are as opposite and hostile as they can possibly be.

The Two Races

I refer to the relation between the two races in the Southern section, which constitutes a vital portion of her social organization. Every portion of the North entertains views and feelings more or less hostile to it. Those most opposed and hostile, regard it as a sin, and consider themselves under the most sacred obligation to use every effort to destroy it. Indeed, to the extent that they conceive they have power, they regard themselves as implicated in the sin, and responsible for not suppressing it by the use of all and every means. Those less opposed and hostile, regard it as a crime—an offence against humanity, as they call it; and, although not so fanatical, feel themselves bound to use all efforts to effect the same object; while those who are least opposed and hostile, regard it as a blot and a stain on the character of what they call the Nation, and feel themselves accordingly bound to give it no countenance or support. On the contrary, the Southern section regards the relation as one which cannot be destroyed without subjecting the two races to the greatest calamity, and the section to poverty, desolation, and wretchedness; and accordingly they feel bound, by every consideration of interest and safety, to defend it.

This hostile feeling on the part of the North towards the social organization of the South long lay dormant, but it only required some cause to act on those who felt most intensely that they were responsible for its continuance, to call it into action. The increasing power of this Government, and of the control of the Northern section over all its departments, furnished the cause. It was this which made an impression on the minds of many, that there was little or no restraint to prevent the Government from doing whatever it might choose to do. This was sufficient of itself to put the most fanatical portion of the North in action, for the purpose of destroying the existing relation between the two races in the South.

The first organized movement towards it commenced in 1835. Then, for the first time, societies were organized, presses established, lecturers sent forth to excite the people of the North, and incendiary publications scattered over the whole South, through the mail. The South was thoroughly aroused. Meetings were held every where, and resolutions adopted, calling upon the North to apply a remedy to arrest the threatened evil, and pledging themselves to adopt measures for their own protection, if it was not arrested. At the meeting of Congress, petitions poured in from the North, calling upon Congress to abolish slavery in the District of Columbia, and to prohibit, what they called, the internal slave trade between the States—announcing at the same time, that their ultimate object was to abolish slavery, not only in the District, but in the States and throughout the Union. At this period, the number engaged in the agitation was small, and possessed little or no personal influence. . . .

A True Compromise

Jefferson Davis, senator from Mississippi and later president of the Confederacy, was one of the Southerners who spoke out against Henry Clay's compromise proposals presented January 29, 1850. In this passage he argues that the only acceptable compromise would be to extend the boundary established by the 1820 Missouri Compromise west to the Pacific Ocean, thus guaranteeing that most of the territory won by the United States in the recent Mexican-American War would eventually become slave states.

But, Sir, we are called upon to receive this as a measure of compromise! As a measure in which we of the minority are to receive something. A measure of compromise! I look upon it as but a modest mode of taking that, the claim to which has been more boldly asserted by others; and, that I may be understood upon this question, and that my position may go forth to the country in the same columns that convey the sentiments of the Senator from Kentucky [Clay], I here assert, that never will I take less than the Missouri Compromise line extending to the Pacific Ocean, with the specific recognition of the right to hold Slaves in the territory below that line; and that, before such territories are admitted into the Union as States, slaves may be taken there from any of the United States, at the option of the owners. I can never consent to give additional power to a majority to commit further aggressions upon the minority in this Union; and I will never consent to any proposition which will have such a tendency, without a full guarantee or counteracting measure is connected with it.

[Yet] the party succeeded in their first movements, in gaining what they proposed—a position in Congress, from which agitation could be extended over the whole Union. This was the commencement of the agitation, which has ever since continued, and which, as is now acknowledged, has endangered the Union itself.

As for myself, I believed at that early period, if the party who got up the petitions should succeed in getting Congress to take jurisdiction, that agitation would follow, and that it would in the end, if not arrested, destroy the Union. I then so expressed myself in debate, and called upon both parties to take grounds against assuming jurisdiction; but in vain. Had my voice been heeded, and had Congress refused to take jurisdiction, by the united votes of all parties, the agitation which followed would have been prevented, and the fanatical zeal that gives impulse to the agitation, and which has brought us to our present perilous condition, would have become extinguished, from the want of fuel to feed the flame. *That* was the time for the North to have shown her devotion to the Union; but, unfortunately, both of the great parties of that section were so intent on obtaining or retaining party ascendancy, that all other considerations were overlooked or forgotten.

What has since followed are but natural consequences. With the success of their first movement, this small fanatical party began to acquire strength; and with that, to become an object of courtship to both the great parties. The necessary consequence was, a further increase of power, and a gradual tainting of the opinions of both of the other parties with their doctrines, until the infection has extended over both; and the great mass of the population of the North, who, whatever may be their opinion of the original abolition party, which still preserves its distinctive organization, hardly ever fail, when it comes to acting, to co-operate in carrying out their measures. . . .

Such is a brief history of the agitation, as far as it has yet advanced. Now I ask, Senators, what is there to prevent its further progress, until it fulfills the ultimate end proposed, unless some decisive measure should be adopted to prevent it? Has any one of the causes, which has added to its increase from its original small and contemptible beginning until it has attained its present magnitude, diminished in force? Is the original cause of the movement —that slavery is a sin, and ought to be suppressed—weaker now than at the commencement? Or is the abolition party less numerous or influential, or have they less influence with, or control over the two great parties of the North in elections? Or has the South greater means of influencing or controlling the movements of this Government now, than it had when the agitation commenced? To all these questions but one answer can be given: No—no—no. The very reverse is true. Instead of being weaker, all the elements in favor of agitation are stronger now than they were in 1835, when it first commenced, while all the elements of influence on the part of the South are weaker. Unless something decisive is done, I again ask, what is to stop this agitation, before the great and final object at which it aims—the abolition of slavery in the States—is consummated? Is it, then, not certain, that if something is not done to arrest it, the South will be forced to choose between abolition and secession? Indeed, as events are now moving, it will not require the South to secede, in order to dissolve the Union. Agitation will of itself effect it, of which its past history furnishes abundant proof—as I shall next proceed to show.

It is a great mistake to suppose that disunion can be effected by a single blow. The cords which bound these States together in one common Union, are far too numerous and powerful for that. Disunion must be the work of time. It is only through a long process, and successively, that the cords can be snapped, until the whole fabric falls asunder. Already the agitation of the slavery question has snapped some of the most important, and has greatly weakened all the others, as I shall proceed to show.

The cords that bind the States together are not only many, but various in character. Some are spiritual or ecclesiastical; some political; others social. Some appertain to the benefit conferred by the Union, and others to the feeling of duty and obligation.

The strongest of those of a spiritual and ecclesiastical nature, consisted in the unity of the great religious denominations, all of which originally embraced the whole Union. . . . The ties which held each denomination together formed a strong cord to hold the whole Union together; but, powerful as they were, they have not been able to resist the explosive effect of slavery agitation.

The strongest cord, of a political character, consists of the many and powerful ties that have held together the two great parties which have, with some modifications, existed from the beginning of the Government. They both extended to every portion of the Union, and strongly contributed to hold all its parts together. But this powerful cord has fared no better than the spiritual. It resisted, for a long time, the explosive tendency of the agitation, but has finally snapped under its force—if not entirely, in a great measure. Nor is there one of the remaining cords which has not been greatly weakened. To this extent the Union has already been destroyed by agitation, in the only way it can be, by sundering and weakening the cords which bind it together.

If the agitation goes on, the same force, acting with increased intensity, as has been shown, will finally snap every cord, when nothing will be left to hold the States together except force. But, surely, that can, with no propriety of language, be called a Union, when the only means by which the weaker is held connected with the stronger portion is *force*. It may, indeed, keep them connected; but the connection will partake much more of the character of subjugation, on the part of the weaker to the stronger, than the union of free, independent, and sovereign States, in one confederation, as they stood in the early stages of the Government, and which only is worthy of the sacred name of Union.

Having now, Senators, explained what it is that endangers the Union, and traced it to its cause, and explained its nature and character, the question again recurs—How can the Union be saved? To this I answer, there is but one way by which it can be —and that is—by adopting such measures as will satisfy the States belonging to the Southern section, that they can remain in the Union consistently with their honor and their safety. There is, again, only one way by which this can be effected, and that is— by removing the causes by which this belief has been produced. Do *this*, and discontent will cease—harmony and kind feelings between the sections be restored—and every apprehension of danger to the Union removed. The question, then, is—How can this be done? But, before I undertake to answer this question, I propose to show by what the Union cannot be saved.

It cannot, then, be saved by eulogies on the Union, however splendid or numerous. The cry of "Union, Union—the glorious Union!" can no more prevent disunion than the cry of "Health, health—glorious health!" on the part of the physician, can save a patient lying dangerously ill. So long as the Union, instead of being regarded as a protector, is regarded in the opposite character, by not much less than a majority of the States, it will be in vain to attempt to conciliate them by pronouncing eulogies on it. . . .

Nor can the Union be saved by invoking the name of the illustrious Southerner [George Washington] whose mortal remains repose on the western bank of the Potomac. He was one of us—a slaveholder and a planter. We have studied his history, and find nothing in it to justify submission to wrong. On the contrary, his great fame rests on the solid foundation, that, while he was careful to avoid doing wrong to others, he was prompt and decided in repelling wrong. I trust that, in this respect, we profited by his example.

Nor can we find any thing in his history to deter us from seceding from the Union, should it fail to fulfill the objects for which it was instituted, by being permanently and hopelessly converted into the means of oppressing instead of protecting us. On the contrary, we find much in his example to encourage us, should we be forced to the extremity of deciding between submission and disunion. . . .

Nor can the plan proposed by the distinguished Senator from Kentucky [Henry Clay], nor that of the administration save the Union. . . .

Having now shown what cannot save the Union, I return to the question with which I commenced, How can the Union be saved? There is but one way by which it can with any certainty; and that is, by a full and final settlement, on the principle of justice, of all the questions at issue between the two sections. The South asks for justice, simple justice, and less she ought not to take. She has no compromise to offer, but the constitution; and no concession or surrender to make. She has already surrendered so much that she has little left to surrender. Such a settlement would go to the root of the evil, and remove all cause of discontent, by satisfying the South, she could remain honorably and safely in the Union, and thereby restore the harmony and fraternal feelings between the sections, which existed anterior to the Missouri agitation. Nothing else can, with any certainty, finally and for ever settle the questions at issue, terminate agitation, and save the Union.

But can this be done? Yes, easily; not by the weaker party, for it can of itself do nothing—not even protect itself—but by the stronger. The North has only to will it to accomplish it—to do justice by conceding to the South an equal right in the acquired territory, and to do her duty by causing the stipulations relative to fugitive slaves to be faithfully fulfilled—to cease the agitation of the slave question, and to provide for the insertion of a provision in the constitution, by an amendment, which will restore to the South, in substance, the power she possessed of protecting herself, before the equilibrium between the sections was destroyed by the action of this Government. There will be no difficulty in devising such a provision—one that will protect the South, and which, at the same time, will improve and strengthen the Government, instead of impairing and weakening it.

But will the North agree to this? It is for her to answer the question. But, I will say, she cannot refuse, if she has half the love of the Union which she professes to have, or without justly exposing herself to the charge that her love of power and aggrandizement is far greater than her love of the Union. At all events, the responsibility of saving the Union rests on the North, and not on the South. The South cannot save it by any act of hers, and the North may save it without any sacrifice whatever, unless to do justice, and to perform her duties under the constitution, should be regarded by her as a sacrifice.

It is time, Senators, that there should be an open and manly avowal on all sides, as to what is intended to be done. If the question is not now settled, it is uncertain whether it ever can hereafter be; and we, as the representatives of the States of this Union, regarded as governments, should come to a distinct understanding as to our respective views, in order to ascertain whether the great questions at issue can be settled or not. If you, who represent the stronger portion, cannot agree to settle them on the broad principle of justice and duty, say so; and let the States we both represent agree to separate and part in peace. If you are unwilling we should part in peace, tell us so, and we shall know what to do, when you reduce the question to submission or resistance. If you remain silent, you will compel us to infer by your acts what you intend. In that case, California will become the test question. If you admit her, under all the difficulties that oppose her admission, you compel us to infer that you intend to exclude us from the whole of the acquired territories, with the intention of destroying, irretrievably, the equilibrium between the two sections. We would be blind not to perceive in that case, that your real objects are power and aggrandizement, and infatuated not to act accordingly.

I have now, Senators, done my duty in expressing my opinions fully, freely, and candidly, on this solemn occasion. In doing so, I have been governed by the motives which have governed me in all the stages of the agitation of the slavery question since its commencement. I have exerted myself, during the whole period, to arrest it, with the intention of saving the Union, if it could be done; and if it could not, to save the section where it has pleased Providence to cast my lot, and which I sincerely believe has justice and the constitution on its side. Having faithfully done my duty to the best of my ability, both to the Union and my section, throughout this agitation, I shall have the consolation, let what will come, that I am free from all responsibility.

Viewpoint 2

"Secession! Peaceable secession! Sir, your eyes and mine are never destined to see that miracle."

The Union Must Be Preserved

Daniel Webster (1782-1852)

Daniel Webster of Massachusetts, Henry Clay of Kentucky, and John C. Calhoun of South Carolina, all noted for their oratorical and legislative skills, were the "great triumvirate" of U.S. senators whose achievements and disagreements dominated American political life for most of the first half of the nineteenth century. Like Clay and Calhoun, Webster capped his long political career by playing a major role in the debate on and passing of the Compromise of 1850, a series of legislative measures aimed at preventing the nation's rupturing over slavery.

Although early in his political career Webster was an advocate of states' rights, he later became a noted supporter of the Union and a strong national government. In 1830 when South Carolina, led by Calhoun, declared that states had the right to "nullify" federal laws within their borders, Webster responded in a famous speech arguing that the Constitution had created an inviolable Union of states, closing with the words "Liberty and Union, now and forever, one and inseparable!"

Webster's belief in the importance of preserving the Union led him to support the compromise package of legislation proposed by Clay in January 1850. Clay's proposals included admitting California to the Union as a free state (one that banned slavery), which Southerners objected to because it left states that permitted slavery in a 15–16 minority. Clay also proposed to admit New Mexico and Utah territories without deciding their status on slavery (allowing the people who lived there to choose), compensat-

Daniel Webster, speech before the U.S. Senate, March 7, 1850.

ing Texas for relinquishing its claims to New Mexican territory, and strengthening national laws to make it easier for slave owners to recover slaves who had escaped to Northern states.

Daniel Webster's famous speech on March 7, 1850, was partially in response to Calhoun's speech given three days earlier, and partially addressed to Northern opponents of slavery. Webster, previously a supporter of federal laws banning slavery in western territories, says that such territorial restrictions are unnecessary in this case since slavery is not viable in the western territories under discussion. He also criticizes the Northern states for failing to capture and return escaped slaves to their owners. He concludes his pleas for compromise from both Northerners and Southerners by arguing that the Union must be preserved at all costs, and that peaceable secession is impossible.

Webster's call for compromise was not only opposed by Southern partisans such as Calhoun, but also by his former Northern supporters, who were unwilling to grant any concessions on the issue of slavery. Although Clay's proposals were eventually passed (the Compromise of 1850), Webster's political career was effectively destroyed by accusations of betrayal to the antislavery cause. Webster died in 1852, the last of the "great triumvirate" to pass from the American scene.

Mr. President,—I wish to speak to-day, not as a Massachusetts man, nor as a Northern man, but as an American, and a member of the Senate of the United States. It is fortunate that there is a Senate of the United States; a body not yet moved from its propriety, not lost to a just sense of its own dignity and its own high responsibilities, and a body to which the country looks, with confidence, for wise, moderate, patriotic, and healing counsels. It is not to be denied that we live in the midst of strong agitations, and are surrounded by very considerable dangers to our institutions and government. The imprisoned winds are let loose. The East, the North, and the stormy South combine to throw the whole sea into commotion, to toss its billows to the skies, and disclose its profoundest depths. I do not affect to regard myself, Mr. President, as holding, or as fit to hold, the helm in this combat with the political elements; but I have a duty to perform, and I mean to perform it with fidelity, not without a sense of existing dangers, but not without hope. I have a part to act, not for my own security or safety, for I am looking out for no fragment upon which to float away from the wreck, if wreck there must be, but for the good of the whole, and the preservation of all; and there is that which will keep me to my duty during this struggle, whether the sun and the stars shall appear, or shall not appear for many days. I speak to-day for the preservation of the Union. "Hear me for my cause." I speak to-day, out of a solicitous and anxious heart, for the restoration to the country of that quiet and that harmony which make the blessings of this Union so rich, and so dear to us all. These are the topics that I propose to myself to discuss; these are the motives, and the sole motives, that influence me in the wish to communicate my opinions to the Senate and the country; and if I can do any thing, however little, for the promotion of these ends, I shall have accomplished all that I expect. . . .

The Question of Slavery

It is obvious that the question which has so long harassed the country, and at some times very seriously alarmed the minds of wise and good men, has come upon us for a fresh discussion; the question of slavery in these United States. . . .

Now, sir, upon the general nature and influence of slavery there exists a wide difference of opinion between the northern portion of this country and the southern. It is said on the one side, that, although not the subject of any injunction or direct prohibition in the New Testament, slavery is a wrong; that it is founded merely in the right of the strongest; and that it is an oppression, like unjust wars, like all those conflicts by which a powerful nation subjects a weaker to its will; and that, in its nature, whatever may be said of it in the modifications which have taken place, it is not according to the meek spirit of the Gospel. It is not "kindly affectioned"; it does not "seek another's, and not its own"; it does not "let the oppressed go free." These are sentiments that are cherished, and of late with greatly augmented force, among the people of the Northern States. They have taken hold of the religious sentiment of that part of the country, as they have, more or less, taken hold of the religious feelings of a considerable portion of mankind. The South, upon the other side, having been accustomed to this relation between the two races all their lives, from their birth, having been taught, in general, to treat the subjects of this bondage with care and kindness, and I believe, in general, feeling great kindness for them, have not taken the view of the subject which I have mentioned. There are thousands of religious men, with consciences as tender as any of their brethren at the North, who do not see the unlawfulness of slavery; and there are more thousands, perhaps, that, whatsoever they may think of it in its origin, and as a matter depending upon natural right, yet take things as they are, and, finding slavery to be an established relation of the society in which they live, can see no way in which, let their opinions on the abstract question be what they may, it is in the power of the present generation to relieve themselves from this relation. And candor obliges me to say, that I believe they are just as conscientious, many of them, and the religious people, all of them, as they are at the North who hold different opinions. . . .

Daniel Webster's endorsement of the Compromise of 1850 was harshly criticized by abolitionists in the North.

But we must view things as they are. Slavery does exist in the United States. It did exist in the States before the adoption of this Constitution, and at that time. Let us, therefore, consider for a moment what was the state of sentiment, North and South, in regard to slavery, at the time this Constitution was adopted. A remarkable change has taken place since; but what did the wise and great men of all parts of the country think of slavery then? In what estimation did they hold it at the time when this Constitution was adopted? It will be found, sir, if we will carry ourselves by historical research back to that day, and ascertain men's opinions by authentic records still existing among us, that there was then no diversity of opinion between the North and South upon the subject of slavery. It will be found that both parts of the country held it equally an evil, a moral and political evil. It will not be found that, either at the North or at the South, there was much, though there was some, invective against slavery as inhuman and cruel. The great ground of objection to it was political; that it weakened the social fabric; that, taking the place of free labor, society became less strong and labor less productive; and therefore we find from all the eminent men of the time the clearest expression of their opinion that slavery is an evil. . . .

The Nation's Founders

Then, sir, when this Constitution was framed, this was the light in which the Federal Convention viewed it. That body reflected the judgment and sentiments of the great men of the South. . . . They thought that slavery could not be continued in the country if the importation of slaves were made to cease, and therefore they provided that, after a certain period, the importation might be prevented by the act of the new government. The period of twenty years was proposed by some gentleman from the North, I think, and many members of the Convention from the South opposed it as being too long. . . .

Now, at the very time when the Convention in Philadelphia was framing this Constitution, the Congress in New York was framing the Ordinance of 1787, for the organization and government of the territory northwest of the Ohio. They passed that Ordinance on the 13th of July, 1787, at New York, the very month, perhaps the very day, on which these questions about the importation of slaves and the character of slavery were debated in the Convention at Philadelphia. So far as we can now learn, there was a perfect concurrence of opinion between these two bodies; and it resulted in this Ordinance of 1787, excluding slavery from all the territory over which the Congress of the United States had jurisdiction, and that was all the territory northwest of the Ohio. . . .

Mr. President, three things are quite clear as historical truths. One is, that there was an expectation that, on the ceasing of the importation of slaves from Africa, slavery would begin to run out here. That was hoped and expected. Another is, that, as far as there was any power in Congress to prevent the spread of slavery in the United States, that power was executed in the most absolute manner, and to the fullest extent. An honorable member [John C. Calhoun], whose health does not allow him to be here to-day—

(A SENATOR. *He is here.*)

I am very happy to hear that he is; may he long be here, and in the enjoyment of health to serve his country! The honorable member said, the other day, that he considered this Ordinance as the first in the series of measures calculated to enfeeble the South, and deprive them of their just participation in the benefits and privileges of this government. He says, very properly, that it was enacted under the old Confederation, and before this Constitu-

41

tion went into effect; but my present purpose is only to say, Mr. President, that it was established with the entire and unanimous concurrence of the whole South. Why, there it stands! The vote of every State in the Union was unanimous in favor of the Ordinance, with the exception of a single individual vote, and that individual vote was given by a Northern man. This Ordinance prohibiting slavery for ever northwest of the Ohio has the hand and seal of every Southern member in Congress. It was therefore no aggression of the North on the South. The other and third clear historical truth is, that the Convention meant to leave slavery in the States as they found it, entirely under the authority and control of the States themselves.

This was the state of things, sir, and this the state of opinion, under which those very important matters were arranged, and those three important things done; that is, the establishment of the Constitution of the United States with a recognition of slavery as it existed in the States; the establishment of the Ordinance for the government of the Northwestern Territory, prohibiting, to the full extent of all territory owned by the United States, the introduction of slavery into that territory, while leaving to the States all power over slavery in their own limits; and creating a power, in the new government, to put an end to the importation of slaves, after a limited period. There was entire coincidence and concurrence of sentiment between the North and the South, upon all these questions, at the period of the adoption of the Constitution. But opinions, sir, have changed, greatly changed; changed North and changed South. Slavery is not regarded in the South now as it was then. . . .

Slavery and Cotton

What, then, have been the causes which have created so new a feeling in favor of slavery in the South, which have changed the whole nomenclature of the South on that subject, so that, from being thought and described in the terms I have mentioned and will not repeat, it has now become an institution, a cherished institution, in that quarter; no evil, no scourge, but a great religious, social, and moral blessing, as I think I have heard it latterly spoken of? I suppose this, sir, is owing to the rapid growth and sudden extension of the *cotton* plantations of the South. So far as any motive consistent with honor, justice, and general judgment could act, it was the *cotton* interest that gave a new desire to promote slavery, to spread it, and to use its labor. I again say that this change was produced by causes which must always produce like effects. The whole interest of the South became connected, more or less, with the extension of slavery. . . .

The age of cotton became the golden age of our Southern brethren. It gratified their desire for improvement and accumulation, at the same time that it excited it. The desire grew by what it fed upon, and there soon came to be an eagerness for other territory, a new area or new areas for the cultivation of the cotton crop; and measures leading to this result were brought about rapidly, one after another, under the lead of Southern men at the head of the government, they having a majority in both branches of Congress to accomplish their ends. The honorable member from South Carolina observed that there has been a majority all along in favor of the North. If that be true, sir, the North has acted either very liberally and kindly, or very weakly; for they never exercised that majority efficiently five times in the history of the government, when a division or trial of strength arose. Never. Whether they were out-generalled, or whether it was owing to other causes, I shall not stop to consider; but no man acquainted with the history of the Union can deny that the general lead in the politics of the country, for three fourths of the period that has elapsed since the adoption of the Constitution, has been a Southern lead.

In 1802, in pursuit of the idea of opening a new cotton region, the United States obtained a cession from Georgia of the whole of her western territory, now embracing the rich and growing States of Alabama and Mississippi. In 1803 Louisiana was purchased from France, out of which the States of Louisiana, Arkansas, and Missouri have been framed, as slave-holding States. In 1819 the cession of Florida was made, bringing in another region adapted to cultivation by slaves. Sir, the honorable member from South Carolina thought he saw in certain operations of the government, such as the manner of collecting the revenue, and the tendency of measures calculated to promote emigration into the country, what accounts for the more rapid growth of the North than the South. He ascribes that more rapid growth, not to the operation of time, but to the system of government and administration established under this Constitution. That is a matter of opinion. To a certain extent it may be true; but it does seem to me that, if any operation of the government can be shown in any degree to have promoted the population, and growth, and wealth of the North, it is much more sure that there are sundry important and distinct operations of the government, about which no man can doubt, tending to promote, and which absolutely have promoted, the increase of the slave interest and the slave territory of the South. It was not time that brought in Louisiana; it was the act of men. It was not time that brought in Florida; it was the act of men. And lastly, sir, to complete those acts of legislation which have contributed so much to enlarge the area of the institution of slavery, Texas, great and vast and illimitable Texas, was added to the Union as a slave State in 1845. . . .

Now, as to California and New Mexico, I hold slavery to be excluded from those territories by a law even superior to that which admits and sanctions it in Texas. I mean the law of nature, of physical geography, the law of the formation of the earth. That law settles for ever, with a strength beyond all terms of human enactment, that slavery cannot exist in California or New Mexico. Understand me, sir; I mean slavery as we regard it; the slavery of the colored race as it exists in the Southern States. . . . It is as impossible that African slavery, as we see it among us, should find its way, or be introduced, into California and New Mexico, as any other natural impossibility. California and New Mexico are Asiatic in their formation and scenery. They are composed of vast ridges of mountains, of great height, with broken ridges and deep valleys. The sides of these mountains are entirely barren; their tops capped by perennial snow. There may be in California, now made free by its constitution, and no doubt there are, some tracts of valuable land. But it is not so in New Mexico. Pray, what is the evidence which every gentleman must have obtained on this subject, from information sought by himself or communicated by others? I have inquired and read all I could find, in order to acquire information on this important subject. What is there in New Mexico that could, by any possibility, induce any body to go there with slaves? There are some narrow strips of tillable land on the borders of the rivers; but the rivers themselves dry up before midsummer is gone. All that the people can do in that region is to raise some little articles, some little wheat for their *tortillas*, and that by irrigation. And who expects to see a hundred black men cultivating tobacco, corn, cotton, rice, or any thing else, on lands in New Mexico, made fertile only by irrigation?

I look upon it, therefore, as a fixed fact, to use the current expression of the day, that both California and New Mexico are destined to be free, so far as they are settled at all, which I believe, in regard to New Mexico, will be but partially for a great length of time; free by the arrangement of things ordained by the Power above us. I have therefore to say, in this respect also, that this country is fixed for freedom, to as many persons as shall ever live in it, by a less repealable law than that which attaches to the right of holding slaves in Texas; and I will say further, that, if a resolution or a bill were now before us, to provide a territorial government for New Mexico, I would not vote to put any prohibition into it whatever. Such a prohibition would be idle, as it respects any effect it would have upon the territory; and I would not take pains uselessly to reaffirm an ordinance of nature, nor to reënact the will of God. I would put in no Wilmot Proviso for the mere purpose of a taunt or a reproach. I would put into it no evidence of the votes of superior power, exercised for no purpose but to wound the pride, whether a just and a rational pride, or an irrational pride, of the citizens of the Southern States. I have no such object, no such purpose. . . .

I repeat, therefore, sir, and, as I do not propose to address the Senate often on this subject, I repeat it because I wish it to be distinctly understood, that, for the reasons stated, if a proposition were now here to establish a government for New Mexico, and it was moved to insert a provision for a prohibition of slavery, I would not vote for it. . . .

Stay in the Union

Kentucky senator Henry Clay, an owner of slaves and an advocate of union, concluded his January 29, 1850, speech before the U.S. Senate with a passionate appeal against secession.

I am directly opposed to any purpose of secession, of separation. I am for staying within the Union, and defying any portion of this Union to expel or drive me out of the Union. I am for staying within the Union and fighting for my rights—if necessary, with the sword—within the bounds and under the safeguard of the Union. I am for vindicating these rights; but not by being driven out of the Union rashly and unceremoniously by any portion of this confederacy. Here I am within it, and here I mean to stand and die—as far as my individual purposes or wishes can go—within it to protect myself, and to defy all power upon earth to expel me or drive me from the situation in which I am placed. Will there not be more safety in fighting within the Union than without it? . . .

I think that the Constitution of the thirteen states was made not merely for the generation which then existed but for posterity, undefined, unlimited, permanent, and perpetual; for their posterity; and for every subsequent state which might come into the Union, binding themselves by that indissoluble bond. . . . The dissolution of the Union and war are identical and inseparable; they are convertible terms.

Sir, wherever there is a substantive good to be done, wherever there is a foot of land to be prevented from becoming slave territory, I am ready to assert the principle of the exclusion of slavery. I am pledged to it from the year 1837; I have been pledged to it again and again; and I will perform those pledges; but I will not do a thing unnecessarily that wounds the feelings of others, or that does discredit to my own understanding.

Now, Mr. President, I have established, so far as I proposed to do so, the proposition with which I set out, and upon which I intend to stand or fall; and that is, that the whole territory within the former United States, or in the newly acquired Mexican provinces, has a fixed and settled character, now fixed and settled by law which cannot be repealed; in the case of Texas without a violation of public faith, and by no human power in regard to California or New Mexico; that, therefore, under one or other of these laws, every foot of land in the States or in the Territories has already received a fixed and decided character.

Fugitive Slaves

Mr. President, in the excited times in which we live, there is found to exist a state of crimination and recrimination between the North and South. There are lists of grievances produced by each; and those grievances, real or supposed, alienate the minds of one portion of the country from the other, exasperate the feelings, and subdue the sense of fraternal affection, patriotic love, and mutual regard. I shall bestow a little attention, sir, upon these various grievances existing on the one side and on the other. I begin with complaints of the South. I will not answer, further than I have, the general statements of the honorable Senator from South Carolina [Calhoun], that the North has prospered at the expense of the South in consequence of the manner of administering this government, in the collecting of its revenues, and so forth. These are disputed topics, and I have no inclination to enter into them. But I will allude to other complaints of the South, and especially to one which has in my opinion just foundation; and that is, that there has been found at the North, among individuals and among legislators, a disinclination to perform fully their constitutional duties in regard to the return of persons bound to service who have escaped into the free States. In that respect, the South, in my judgment, is right, and the North is wrong. Every member of every Northern legislature is bound by oath, like every other officer in the country, to support the Constitution of the United States; and the article of the Constitution which says to these States that they shall deliver up fugitives from service is as binding in honor and conscience as any other article. . . . What right have they, in their legislative capacity or any other capacity, to endeavor to get round this Constitution, or to embarrass the free exercise of the rights secured by the Constitution to the persons whose slaves escape from them? None at all; none at all. Neither in the forum of conscience, nor before the face of the Constitution, are they, in my opinion, justified in such an attempt. . . .

I repeat, therefore, sir, that here is a well-founded ground of complaint against the North, which ought to be removed, which it is now in the power of the different departments of this government to remove; which calls for the enactment of proper laws authorizing the judicature of this government, in the several States, to do all that is necessary for the recapture of fugitive slaves and for their restoration to those who claim them. Wherever I go, and whenever I speak on the subject, and when I speak here I desire to speak to the whole North, I say that the South has been injured in this respect, and has a right to complain; and the North has been too careless of what I think the Constitution peremptorily and emphatically enjoins upon her as a duty. . . .

Criticizing Abolitionists

Then, sir, there are the Abolition societies, of which I am unwilling to speak, but in regard to which I have very clear notions and opinions. I do not think them useful. I think their operations for the last twenty years have produced nothing good or valuable. At the same time, I believe thousands of their members to be honest and good men, perfectly well-meaning men. They have excited feelings; they think they must do something for the cause of liberty; and, in their sphere of action, they do not see what else they can do than to contribute to an Abolition press, or an Abolition society, or to pay an Abolition lecturer. I do not mean to impute gross motives even to the leaders of these societies, but I am not blind to the consequences of their proceedings. I cannot but see what mischiefs their interference with the South has produced. And is it not plain to every man? . . .

It is said, I do not know how true it may be, that they sent incendiary publications into the slave States; at any rate, they attempted to arouse, and did arouse, a very strong feeling; in other words, they created great agitation in the North against Southern slavery. Well, what was the result? The bonds of the slaves were bound more firmly than before, their rivets were more strongly fastened. Public opinion, which in Virginia had begun to be exhibited against slavery, and was opening out for the discussion of the question, drew back and shut itself up in its castle. . . . We all know the fact, and we all know the cause; and every thing that these agitating people have done has been, not to enlarge, but to restrain, not to set free, but to bind faster, the slave population of the South. . . .

Now, sir, so far as any of these grievances have their foundation in matters of law, they can be redressed, and ought to be redressed; and so far as they have their foundation in matters of opinion, in sentiment, in mutual crimination and recrimination, all that we can do is to endeavor to allay the agitation, and cultivate a better feeling and more fraternal sentiments between the South and the North.

Secession Without War Is Impossible

Mr. President, I should much prefer to have heard from every member on this floor declarations of opinion that this Union could never be dissolved, than the declaration of opinion by any body, that, in any case, under the pressure of any circumstances, such a dissolution was possible. I hear with distress and anguish the word "secession," especially when it falls from the lips of those who are patriotic, and known to the country, and known all over the world, for their political services. Secession! Peaceable secession! Sir, your eyes and mine are never destined to see that miracle. The dismemberment of this vast country without convulsion! The breaking up of the fountains of the great deep without ruffling the surface! Who is so foolish, I beg every body's pardon, as to expect to see any such thing? Sir, he who sees these States, now revolving in harmony around a common centre, and expects to see them quit their places and fly off without convulsion, may look the next hour to see the heavenly bodies rush from their spheres, and jostle against each other in the realms of space, without causing the wreck of the universe. There can be no such thing as a peaceable secession. Peaceable secession is an utter impossibility. Is the great Constitution under which we live, covering this whole country, is it to be thawed and melted away by secession, as the snows on the mountain melt under the influence of a vernal sun, disappear almost unobserved, and run off? No, sir! No, sir! I will not state what might produce the disruption of the Union; but, sir, I see as plainly as I see the sun in heaven what that disruption itself must produce; I see that it must produce war, and such a war as I will not describe, *in its twofold character.*

Peaceable secession! Peaceable secession! The concurrent agreement of all the members of this great republic to separate! A voluntary separation, with alimony on one side and on the other. Why, what would be the result? Where is the line to be drawn? What States are to secede? What is to remain American? What am I to be? An American no longer? Am I to become a sectional man, a local man, a separatist, with no country in common with the gentlemen who sit around me here, or who fill the other house of Congress? Heaven forbid! Where is the flag of the republic to remain? Where is the eagle still to tower? or is he to cower, and shrink, and fall to the ground? Why, sir, our ancestors, our fathers and our grandfathers, those of them that are yet living amongst us with prolonged lives, would rebuke and reproach us; and our children and our grandchildren would cry out shame upon us, if we of this generation should dishonor these ensigns of the power of the government and the harmony of that union which is every day felt among us with so much joy and gratitude. What is to become of the army? What is to become of the navy? What is to become of the public lands? How is each of the thirty States to defend itself? I know, although the idea has not been stated distinctly, there is to be, or it is supposed possible that there will be, a Southern Confederacy. I do not mean, when I allude to this statement, that any one seriously contemplates such a state of things. I do not mean to say that it is true, but I have heard it suggested elsewhere, that the idea has been entertained, that, after the dissolution of this Union, a Southern Confederacy might be formed. I am sorry, sir, that it has ever been thought of, talked of, or dreamed of, in the wildest flights of human imagination. But the idea, so far as it exists, must be of a separation, assigning the slave States to one side and the free States to the other. Sir, I may express myself too strongly, perhaps, but there are impossibilities in the natural as well as in the physical world, and I hold the idea of a separation of these States, those that are free to form one government, and those that are slave-holding to form another, as such an impossibility. We could not separate the States by any such line, if we were to draw it. We could not sit down here to-day and draw a line of separation that would satisfy any five men in the country. There are natural causes that would keep and tie us together, and there are social and domestic relations which we could not break if we would, and which we should not if we could. . . .

And now, Mr. President, instead of speaking of the possibility or utility of secession, instead of dwelling in those caverns of darkness, instead of groping with those ideas so full of all that is horrid and horrible, let us come out into the light of day; let us enjoy the fresh air of Liberty and Union; let us cherish those hopes which belong to us; let us devote ourselves to those great objects that are fit for our consideration and our action; let us raise our conceptions to the magnitude and the importance of the duties that devolve upon us; let our comprehension be as broad as the country for which we act, our aspirations as high as its certain destiny; let us not be pigmies in a case that calls for men. Never did there devolve on any generation of men higher trusts than now devolve upon us, for the preservation of this Constitution and the harmony and peace of all who are destined to live under it. Let us make our generation one of the strongest and brightest links in that golden chain which is destined, I fondly believe, to grapple the people of all the States to this Constitution for ages to come.

"We . . . have submitted to oppression and wrong incalculably greater than ever England inflicted . . . on her colonies."

Seceding from the Union Will Help the South

Edmund Ruffin (1794-1865)

Despite the attempt of Congress to resolve the national dispute over slavery by passing the Compromise of 1850, the nation still faced sectional divisions over the issue. In 1854 the Kansas-Nebraska Act organized the territories of Kansas and Nebraska on the principle of "popular sovereignty"—the local residents would decide whether to legalize slavery. This development was bitterly attacked by many Northerners because it repealed the boundary between slave and free territory created by Congress in 1820 in the Missouri Compromise, thus opening up more territory to possible slavery. "Bleeding Kansas" became the focus of national attention as settlers clashed violently in efforts to determine whether the territory would become a slave or free state.

The controversy had dramatic national political repercussions. The Democratic party was increasingly divided between Northern and Southern factions. The Whig party disappeared altogether. Many Northern Democrats and Whigs joined to form the new Republican party, dedicated to excluding slavery from the western territories. In 1856 their presidential candidate, John Frémont, won in eleven of the sixteen free states and finished a strong second to Democratic candidate James Buchanan.

A growing number of Southerners, noting the increasing population and political power of the North, began to believe that the best solution for the Southern states wishing to ensure the preservation of slavery was to secede from the United States altogether.

Excerpted from Edmund Ruffin's series of articles titled "Consequences of the Abolition Agitation" that appeared in the June, September, October, November, and December 1857 *De Bow's Review.*

One such person was Edmund Ruffin, an agriculturist and planter. The following consists of excerpts from a series of articles he wrote for the Southern journal *De Bow's Review*. Ruffin examines the results of the 1856 election, and argues that a person could capture the presidency without winning a single Southern state. A loss of control of the federal government, he contends, can result in the abolition of slavery, which Ruffin argues is integral to the Southern way of life. The best course of action for slave states, he concludes, is to withdraw from the United States. Such action, he argues, would expose abolitionism as a political ploy used by Northern politicians to gain power. Secession would not necessarily result in war, Ruffin asserts, and independence from the North would enable the South to develop its industry and economy.

Ruffin's dreams of an independent South were temporarily realized when the Confederacy was formed in 1861. As a member of the Confederate Palmetto Guard volunteers, he is credited with firing the first shot of the Civil War against Fort Sumter in South Carolina on April 12, 1861. He committed suicide in 1865 after the Confederacy's defeat.

The present contest between the Northern and Southern states, in regard to Negro slavery, has been growing in violence for a long time. . . .

But it has been only since the (falsely so-called) compromise enactments of 1850 that Abolition has been hastening toward its object with gigantic strides; and also that the South has been partially roused from its sleep of fancied security. Unfortunate it has been that this sleep had not been effectually shaken off thirty years sooner, and every means then used for defense that was abundantly possessed by the South at that time. If, when the Missouri Compromise was submitted to, the proposed restrictions had been resisted by the South at all hazards, there would have been no further trouble about slavery. And if the fanaticism (or, more truly, the unholy grasping for political power) of the North had then been so unyielding as to permit a separation of the United States, the Southern portion would now have double of their present wealth and power—and the Northern states would not have attained half of their present greatness and wealth, which have been built upon the tribute exacted from the South by legislative policy. But no separation would have been produced.

If, at the time of the Missouri Compromise, the Northern members and states had been firmly resisted, they would have drawn back, and the spirit of political Abolition would have been crushed in the bud. The sincere Abolitionists, who are actuated by what they deem moral and religious considerations, are but the simple and deluded tools of the hypocrites and knaves who are using them to further their own objects of personal ambition and political power.

Consequences of an Abolitionist President

Without looking even as far as twenty years into the future of the effects of the Northern crusade against Southern slavery, let us see what might have been the speedy consequences if the contingency had occurred, which was so near occurring, of an Abolitionist being elected President—he being the candidate of the Northern states only, and on the Abolition question and principle. It is true that a more conciliatory policy would probably have been adopted at first, because the victorious party would not have risked driving their conquered opponents to desperate and revolutionary measures of resistance. But it is fair to suppose that a party so fanatical, greedy, and unscrupulous would have used every means to reach its object that could be used safely and successfully. . . .

If elected, it would have been supported by a majority of the people of the states and of the House of Representatives. It would not have required much time or management (by corruption or other influences) for the President to have also at his command a majority of the Senate—representing states that were already his supporters. Then, the President, with a majority of both houses of Congress, might adopt . . . the following, to weaken and destroy the institution of slavery:

The first and greatest measure is already openly avowed by the Abolitionists and the majority of every Northern state as their designed policy and plan of action hereafter. This is to admit into the Union no new territories as slaveholding states. This alone, even if nothing else is done, will soon increase the nonslaveholding states to three-fourths of the whole, so that the Constitution can be changed and slavery abolished. . . .

Will the Southern states wait for the completion of these surely coming results, or will they take the warning so plainly to be read in their enemies' acts and avowals and save themselves from the impending ruin? The fast-growing strength of the Abolition Party and the signal success of that party in the next presidential election may cause every Southerner to regret that its candidate was not elected in the recent contest, when the South was relatively stronger for defense than it will ever be hereafter.

In such a contingency as we have just now barely escaped, the election of a President by Abolition and sectional votes, there will remain no chance for the slaveholding states to preserve their property and their political rights, unless by another declaration of independence of, and separation from a despotic party, whose wrongful and oppressive acts have already far exceeded, and threaten to exceed much more in future, all the acts of actual and prospective oppression of our mother country, against which our free and patriotic fathers revolted—preferring a struggle for freedom, with all the certain disasters and incalculable dangers of a war with a nation of tenfold their power, to submission to unjust oppression.

Virginia secessionist Edmund Ruffin. Ironically, given that he wrote in 1857 that a seceding South "would desire peace and avoid war, unless necessary for defense," he is credited with later firing the first shot on Fort Sumter in April 1861, launching the Civil War.

We, the sons of those fathers, eulogize and glorify their act of separation from the previous glorious and happy union of these colonies with their mother country. Their act of separation and disunion we deem a noble and patriotic devotion to freedom, worthy of all praise. We, the children of those fathers, in maudlin love of and devotion to a union with those who were formerly deemed our brethren but now are our most malignant and dangerous enemies, have submitted to oppression and wrong incalculably greater than ever England inflicted, or thought of inflicting on her colonies. And, still, many of the South continue to recommend patience and endurance and submission to every wrong and evil rather than the evil of disunion!

Would Secession Lead to War?

If Frémont had been elected, the consequences would have been so manifestly and highly dangerous to the rights and the safety of the slaveholding states that they would scarcely have waited to be completely shackled, and powerless for defense, before they would have seceded or separated from the victorious and hostile states of the present Confederacy. It is proposed here to inquire what would have been the results of such separation, and especially to consider the question of the danger of war, which it is so generally believed would necessarily ensue between the separated communities, and the results of any war.

If the necessity was manifest to the people of the South, there would be no obstacle to their deliberate action and no probability of opposition by the Northern states, nor by the then remaining fragment of shadow of the federal government of the previous Confederacy. The legislatures of the offended states would call conventions, and these conventions would declare their separation and independence, and, by subsequent acts, make a new confederation. If all the fifteen slaveholding states united in this action, they would be far stronger, at home and for repelling invasion, than would be the Northern states as invaders. Even if but five or six adjacent Southern states alone seceded, no remaining power of the federal government, or of all the Northern states, could conquer or coerce the seceders.

But, contrary as is the opinion to that which generally prevails, I maintain that such act of secession would offer no inducement or occasion for war; and that there would be no war, as the immediate or direct result of secession or separation.

The malignant hostility of feeling that is even now entertained by the Abolition Party, and perhaps by a majority of the Northern people, toward those of the South is not here overlooked or underrated. If they could, by merely willing it, they would ruin us, even while united with them under one government—and still more readily if we were separated. If the mere wish of Abolitionists could effect the destruction of our system of Negro slavery, even by the destruction of the entire white population of the South, I would fear that consummation would not be a remote event.

But *to will* and *to do* are very different things. And even Northern fanaticism (to say nothing of Northern self-interest and avarice) would be glad to forgo these gratifications if they were to be purchased only at the cost, to the North, of hundreds of millions of dollars and hundreds of thousands of lives. Even if admit-

54

ting what is so arrogantly and falsely claimed by the North, that it could conquer and desolate the South, any such victory would be scarcely less ruinous to the conquerors than the conquered.

But there would be no such war and no movement toward it, because war could not subserve or advance any interest of the North. It is unnecessary to maintain the like proposition in regard to the South inasmuch as it is universally admitted. No one, of either side, has ever asserted or supposed that the South would assail or make war upon the North in consequence of their separation. Whether this peaceful disposition is ascribed to a greater sense of justice, or to the weakness, or the timidity of the Southern people, all concur in the belief that the South would desire peace and would avoid war, unless necessary for defense. Then, passing by this contingency, deemed impossible by all parties, we have only to examine the supposed inducements for offensive war and attack by the North on the South.

"But," it is urged by many among ourselves, "even if the North refrained from making war, still it would retain the direction of the federal government, and exercise its rights and remaining power—and also hold possession of the seat of government, the Army and Navy, the fortifications, and the public lands. How could the public property be divided peaceably? And, without resorting to war to enforce our right to a fair share, would not all be necessarily lost to the South?" I answer that, even if admitting all these premises, still there would be no need and no advantage for the South to seek justice through war—and no benefit to the North would be gained by withholding our just dues, either by war or in peace.

Nations, in modern days, do not often go to war and never in advance of negotiation, to recover debts or to settle pecuniary accounts and obligations. There are other means, in many cases, to induce, and even constrain, nations to render justice; and, luckily, in our case, the means available for the South would be of the most cogent influence. . . .

As to the public lands, vast as is their extent and enormous their value, the South has already been virtually deprived of them. No Southerner can safely remove with his slaves to any new territory. They were thus unjustly and illegally shut out from the rich fields and richer mines of California by the action of the North and the federal government. The conquest of Mexico was achieved by men and money supplied (as of all other contributions) in much the larger proportion by the Southern states. By their much larger expenditure of both blood and treasure, California and New Mexico were acquired. Yet the people of the South, as slaveholders, were excluded from the territory; and Southern men have had no access to or benefit from the rich mines and lands of California, that were not as open to, and equally enjoyed by, the semi-barbarians of China and the Sandwich Islands, the former convicts of Australia, and the needy and desperate outcasts, invited by these benefits, from every foreign land. . . .

Secession and Abolitionism

When the separation of the present Union has been consummated, there will no longer remain to Northern men any political object or gain for which to agitate the slavery or Abolition questions. . . . It would then be seen that the Abolition question had been agitated only for political effect and benefit to the prime agitators; and when such agitation could no longer serve their interest, the alleged sin and horrors of slavery in the Southern Confederacy would be as little noticed by Abolitionists as has been always the case in regard to Cuba and Brazil.

Certainly the condition of the slaves in those countries was far more wretched and more strongly calling for the sympathy of philanthropists than in these Southern states. Moreover, the illegal African slave trade, of the most cruel and murderous character (and with many of the slave vessels fitted out in Northern cities and by Northern capital), continued to add to the number of slaves and, by such additions, to increase the sufferings of all. These worst evils and sufferings incident to the worst condition of African slavery and the forbidden slave trade certainly were, and are, as much worthy of the attention of moral reformers and philanthropic Abolitionists as the more humane treatment and comfortable condition of slaves in these Southern states. Yet scarcely have the Northern Abolitionists noticed the horrors of Cuban or Brazilian slavery, while all their denunciations and hostility have been reserved for the milder slavery in the Southern states. This, if alone, ought to have shown, in advance, how false and hypocritical has been the pretense of this Abolition Party being influenced by considerations of humanity or benevolence— by morality or religion.

Separation of political connection will be the certain end of all actual and injurious Abolition agitation. The newspapers of the North, after separation, and public speakers, both lay and clerical, may continue to denounce the iniquity of slavery and the atrocious acts of slaveholders. So are we denounced and abused in Canadian papers and speeches, and in British newspapers and reviews. But, as in these latter cases, there has never been sufficient inducement for attempting more active or practical interference with our rights and property, so neither will there be with the people of the Northern states when no political gain can be made or sought by aid of such interference. Then the Abolition agitation by politicians will die for want of object and aliment;

56

and the deluded people of the North will then recover their lost sanity on this subject.

When this change shall have occurred and the now prevailing delusion is at an end, the people of the new Northwestern states, who are especially connected with the South in bonds of trade by the Mississippi and who have no such ties with New England, will see their error in following the fanatical course of the latter to the end of separation from the Southern states, their natural allies and best customers. It will be found by them a source of great inconvenience and loss to have no trade with the Southern states, or a taxed trade in time of peace, though the passage of the Mississippi to the ocean or to foreign ports would be still open to their vessels and freights. And if the North should force war on the South, then, of course, the navigation of the Lower Mississippi will be no longer open to the use of any portion of the hostile country.

This would be ruinous to the Northwestern states. And on this ground, even without the anticipated difficulty growing out of the contest for the public lands, these Northwestern states, on the upper waters of the Mississippi, would soon secede from the Northeastern and Atlantic states and make a separate community, and also would make a separate peace—if not seek to be reunited to the Southern states. This abandonment by this vast and fertile region would leave the Northeastern states in a much more weak and hopeless condition than previously.

And as early, or perhaps earlier, there will be another secession from the first Northern Confederacy, by California, Oregon, Utah, and all the other territory of the present United States lying on the Pacific slope. This separation will take place as soon as the residents of the Pacific states and territories shall deem the measure more beneficial to their interest than to enjoy the bounties and have the protection of the present federal government, and the consummation will only be hastened and hurried by the previous separation of the slaveholding from the nonslaveholding states. And even under the present state of things, if such a separation were to take place, and if the parties would maintain perfect free trade with each other after their separation (as while under one government), it would be no evil to the other portion of the present Union, and especially to the Southern states, if all the Pacific territory would at once declare its independence and secede from the United States. . . .

While such elements of division, if not of strife, would operate to separate the nonslaveholding states into at least three portions, the slaveholding states would have common interests and unity of opinion and principles as to matters of general policy. United in a confederacy, they would possess enough of territory, population, and wealth for an independent community—strong enough for defense in arms against any single power whatever—and of more than double the absolute strength of all the thirteen colonies when they revolted from and defied in arms their mother country, then one of the most powerful nations of the world.

But a guarantee of safe defense, and almost of immunity from war, would be found in the important fact that this Southern Confederacy would supply nearly all the cotton for the factories and the consumption of both Europe and America. The only nations of both hemispheres that could be dreaded as foes would incur far more injury from being shut out by war from the needed supply of our cotton than would be compensated by any possible amount of military success.

Advancing the South's Economy

The revenue and resources of the Southern states, heretofore contributed mainly to aid Northern interests, foster Northern industry and trade, and increase Northern wealth and power, would thenceforward be retained and used to sustain and build up our own commerce and cities and general prosperity. In twenty-five or thirty years our population and wealth will be doubled, and the value of our products and their demand by the commercial world will be increased in still greater proportion. There will probably be no community of more vigorous and healthy growth, or with better prospects of stable prosperity. With the aid of our own annual profits of industry and capital, and the encouragement that the new condition and demands of the Southern states will create, manufactures and navigation and commerce will increase rapidly, even if the growth was stimulated and maintained by Southern resources only.

But in advance of this natural and slower growth, these branches of industry, and the men to carry them on, and the capital to sustain them, will be transplanted to any amount that may be desired and permitted from the Northern to the Southern states, as soon as they shall have become separate political communities. Plenty of manufacturing capital, and also of capitalists and laborers, and plenty of ships and sailors, will come to obtain the benefits of an establishment in the South. There would be nothing more wanting for this speedy and extensive transferrence of capital, industry, and also of (at least) professed allegiance than the sure and simple operation of greatly reduced employment and profits in the Northern states, and the great increase of both in the independent and flourishing Southern Confederacy—then just beginning to use its own funds and resources to build up and sustain their own cities, manufactures, and navigation.

VIEWPOINT 4

"Nothing short of the complete abolition of slavery can save the South from falling into the vortex of utter ruin."

Abolishing Slavery Will Help the South

Hinton R. Helper (1829-1907)

While the majority of white Southerners did not own slaves, they generally accepted the political leadership of those who did and supported the institution of slavery. One noteworthy exception was Hinton R. Helper, a writer born in North Carolina. The following viewpoint is taken from his highly controversial book *The Impending Crisis of the South: How to Meet It*, first published in 1857. In the book Helper states that the South as a region is falling socially and economically behind the North. He argues that the root cause of the problems facing the South is not unfair actions and rule by the Northern states, but the institution of slavery. A racist who believed in "Anglo-American" supremacy, Helper attacks slavery on economic and practical rather than moral grounds, trying to appeal to the "white victims" of slavery. Similar arguments appealing to poor whites were also used by Northern antislavery leaders.

Helper's book, largely because of the Southern origins of its author, was bitterly attacked by Southern leaders while eagerly promoted by such abolitionists as *New York Tribune* editor Horace Greeley. In 1860 the book was reprinted with funding by the Republican party—an endorsement that convinced many Southern leaders to support secession from the Union following Republican victory in the 1860 presidential election.

Excerpted from *The Impending Crisis of the South: How to Meet It* by Hinton R. Helper, 1857.

It is not our intention to enter into an elaborate ethnographical essay, to establish peculiarities of difference, mental, moral, and physical, in the great family of man. Neither is it our design to launch into a philosophical disquisition on the laws and principles of light and darkness, with a view of educing any additional evidence of the fact, that as a general rule, the rays of the sun are more fructifying and congenial than the shades of night. Nor yet is it our purpose, by writing a formal treatise on ethics, to draw a broad line of distinction between right and wrong, to point out the propriety of morality and its advantages over immorality, nor to waste time in pressing a universally admitted truism—that virtue is preferable to vice. Self-evident truths require no argumentative demonstration.

What we mean to do is simply this: to take a survey of the relative position and importance of the several states of this confederacy, from the adoption of the national compact; and when, of two sections of the country starting under the same auspices, and with equal natural advantages, we find the one rising to a degree of almost unexampled power and eminence, and the other sinking into a state of comparative imbecility and obscurity, it is our determination to trace out the causes which have led to the elevation of the former, and the depression of the latter, and to use our most earnest and honest endeavors to utterly extirpate whatever opposes the progress and prosperity of any portion of the union.

This survey we have already made; we have also instituted an impartial comparison between the cardinal sections of the country, north, south, east, and west; and as a true hearted southerner, whose ancestors have resided in North Carolina between one and two hundred years, and as one who would rather have his native clime excel than be excelled, we feel constrained to confess that we are deeply abashed and chagrined at the disclosures of the comparison thus instituted. At the time of the adoption of the Constitution, in 1789, we commenced an even race with the North. All things considered, if either the North or the South had the advantage, it was the latter. In proof of this, let us introduce a few statistics, beginning with the states of

New York and Virginia.

In 1790, when the first census was taken, New York contained 340,120 inhabitants; at the same time the population of Virginia was 748,308, being more than twice the number of New York. Just sixty years afterward, as we learn from the census of 1850, New York had a population of 3,097,394; while that of Virginia was only 1,421,661, being less than half the number of New York! In 1791, the exports of New York amounted to $2,505,465; the exports of Virginia amounted to $3,130,865. In 1852, the exports of New York amounted to $87,484,456; the exports of Virginia, during the same year, amounted to only $2,724,657. In 1790, the imports of New York and Virginia were about equal; in 1853, the imports of New York amounted to the enormous sum of $178,270,999; while those of Virginia, for the same period, amounted to the pitiful sum of only $399,004. In 1850, the products of manufactures, mining and the mechanic arts in New York amounted to $237,597,249; those of Virginia amounted to only $29,705,387. At the taking of the last census, the value of real and personal property in Virginia, including negroes, was $391,646,438; that of New York, exclusive of any monetary valuation of human beings, was $1,080,309,216.

In August, 1856, the real and personal estate assessed in the City of New-York amounted in valuation to $511,740,491, showing that New-York City alone is worth far more than the whole State of Virginia. . . .

The cash value of all the farms, farming implements and machinery in Virginia, in 1850, was $223,423,315; the value of the same in New-York, in the same year, was $576,631,568. In about the same ratio does the value of the agricultural products and live stock of New-York exceed the value of the agricultural products and live stock of Virginia. But we will pursue this humiliating comparison no further. With feelings mingled with indignation and disgust, we turn from the picture, and will now pay our respects to

Massachusetts and North Carolina.

In 1790, Massachusetts contained 378,717 inhabitants; in the same year North Carolina contained 393,751; in 1850, the population of Massachusetts was 994,514, all freemen; while that of North Carolina was only 869,039, of whom 288,548 were slaves. Massachusetts has an area of only 7,800 square miles; the area of North Carolina is 50,704 square miles, which, though less than Virginia, is considerably larger than the State of New-York. Massachusetts and North Carolina each have a harbor, Boston and Beaufort, which harbors, with the States that back them, are, by nature, possessed of about equal capacities and advantages for commercial and manufacturing enterprise. Boston has grown to be the second commercial city in the Union; her ships, freighted with the useful and unique inventions and manufactures of her ingenious artisans and mechanics, and bearing upon their stalwart arms the majestic flag of our country, glide triumphantly through the winds and over the waves of every ocean. She has done, and is now doing, great honor to herself, her State and the nation, and her name and fame are spoken with reverence in the remotest regions of the earth.

How is it with Beaufort, in North Carolina, whose harbor is said to be the safest and most commodious anywhere to be found on the Atlantic coast south of the harbor of New-York, and but little inferior to that? Has anybody every heard of her? Do the masts of her ships ever cast a shadow on foreign waters? Upon what distant or benighted shore have her merchants and mariners ever hoisted our national ensign, or spread the arts of civilization and peaceful industry? What changes worthy of note have taken place in the physical features of her superficies since "the evening and the morning were the third day?" But we will make no further attempt to draw a comparison between the populous, wealthy, and renowned city of Boston and the obscure, despicable little village of Beaufort, which, notwithstanding "the placid bosom of its deep and well-protected harbor," has no place in the annals or records of the country, and has scarcely ever been heard of fifty miles from home.

In 1853, the exports of Massachusetts amounted to $16,895,304, and her imports to $41,367,956; during the same time, and indeed during all the time, from the period of the formation of the government up to the year 1853, inclusive, the exports and imports of North Carolina were so utterly insignificant that we are ashamed to record them. In 1850, the products of manufactures, mining and the mechanic arts in Massachusetts, amounted to $151,137,145; those of North Carolina, to only $9,111,245. In 1856, the products of these industrial pursuits in Massachusetts had increased to something over $288,000,000, a sum more than twice the value of the entire cotton crop of all the Southern States! . . . In 1850, there were in Massachusetts 1,861 native white and free colored persons over twenty years of age who could not read and write; in the same year, the same class of persons in North Carolina numbered 80,083; while her 288,548 slaves were, by legislative enactments, kept in a state of absolute ignorance and unconditional subordination.

Hoping, however, and believing, that a large majority of the most respectable and patriotic citizens of North Carolina have resolved, or will soon resolve, with unyielding purpose, to cast aside the great obstacle that impedes their progress, and bring into action a new policy which will lead them from poverty and ignorance to wealth and intellectual greatness, and which will shield them not only from the rebukes of their own consciences, but also from the just reproaches of the civilized world, we will, for the present, in deference to their feelings, forbear the further enumeration of these degrading disparities, and turn our attention to

Pennsylvania and South Carolina.

An old gentleman, now residing in Charleston, told us, but a few months since, that he had a distinct recollection of the time when Charleston imported foreign fabrics for the Philadelphia trade, and when, on a certain occasion, his mother went into a store on Market-street to select a silk dress for herself, the merchant, unable to please her fancy, persuaded her to postpone the selection for a few days, or until the arrival of a new stock of superb styles and fashions which he had recently purchased in the metropolis of South Carolina. This was all very proper. Charleston had a spacious harbor, a central position, and a mild climate; and from priority of settlement and business connections, to say nothing of other advantages, she enjoyed greater facilities for commercial transactions than Philadelphia. She had a right to get custom wherever she could find it, and in securing so valuable a customer as the Quaker City, she exhibited no small degree of laudable enterprise. But why did she not maintain her supremacy? If the answer to this query is not already in the reader's mind, it will suggest itself before he peruses the whole of this work. For the present, suffice it to say, that the cause of her shameful insignificance and decline is essentially the same that has thrown every other Southern city and State in the rear of progress, and rendered them tributary, in a commercial and manufacturing point of view, almost entirely tributary, to the more sagacious and enterprising States and cities of the North.

A most unfortunate day was that for the Palmetto State, and indeed for the whole South, when the course of trade was changed, and she found herself the retailer of foreign and domestic goods, imported and vended by wholesale merchants at the North. Philadelphia ladies no longer look to the South for late fashions, and fine silks and satins; no Quaker dame now wears drab apparel of Charleston importation. Like all other *niggervilles* in our disreputable part of the confederacy, the commercial emporium of South Carolina is sick and impoverished; her silver cord has been loosed; her golden bowl has been broken; and her unhappy people, without proper or profitable employment, poor in pocket, and few in number, go mourning or loafing about the streets. Her annual importations are actually less now than they were a century ago, when South Carolina was the second commercial province on the continent, Virginia being the first.

In 1760, as we learn from Mr. Benton's "Thirty Years' View," the foreign imports into Charleston were $2,662,000; in 1855, they amounted to only $1,750,000! In 1854, the imports into Philadelphia, which, in foreign trade, ranks at present but fourth among the commercial cities of the union, were $21,963,021. In 1850, the products of manufactures, mining, and the mechanic arts, in Pennsylvania, amounted to $155,044,910; the products of the same in South Carolina, amounted to only $7,063,513. . . .

The incontrovertible facts we have thus far presented are, we think, amply sufficient, both in number and magnitude, to bring conviction to the mind of every candid reader, that there is something wrong, socially, politically and morally wrong, in the policy under which the South has so long loitered and languished. Else, how is it that the North, under the operations of a policy directly the opposite of ours, has surpassed us in almost everything great and good, and left us standing before the world, an object of merited reprehension and derision?

By 1861 nearly four million blacks lived in slavery in the United States, including these slaves working on a plantation in South Carolina.

For one, we are heartily ashamed of the inexcusable weakness, inertia and dilapidation everywhere so manifest throughout our native section; but the blame properly attaches itself to an usurping minority of the people, and we are determined that it shall rest where it belongs. More on this subject, however, after a brief but general survey of the inequalities and disparities that exist between those two grand divisions of the country, which, without reference to the situation that any part of their territory bears to the cardinal points, are every day becoming more familiarly known by the appropriate appellation of

The Free and the Slave States.

It is a fact well known to every intelligent Southerner that we are compelled to go to the North for almost every article of utility and adornment, from matches, shoepegs and paintings up to cotton-mills, steamships and statuary; that we have no foreign trade, no princely merchants, nor respectable artists; that, in comparison with the free states, we contribute nothing to the literature, polite arts and inventions of the age. . . .

All the world sees, or ought to see, that in a commercial, mechanical, manufactural, financial, and literary point of view, we are as helpless as babes; that, in comparison with the Free States, our agricultural resources have been greatly exaggerated, misunderstood and mismanaged; and that, instead of cultivating among ourselves a wise policy of mutual assistance and co-operation with respect to individuals, and of self-reliance with respect to the South at large, instead of giving countenance and encouragement to the industrial enterprises projected in our midst, and instead of building up, aggrandizing and beautifying our own States, cities and towns, we have been spending our substance at the North, and are daily augmenting and strengthening the very power which now has us so completely under its thumb.

It thus appears, in view of the preceding statistical facts and arguments, that the South, at one time the superior of the North in almost all the ennobling pursuits and conditions of life, has fallen far behind her competitor, and now ranks more as the dependency of a mother country than as the equal confederate of free and independent States. Following the order of our task, the next duty that devolves upon us is to trace out the causes which have conspired to bring about this important change, and to place on record the reasons, as we understand them,

Why the North Has Surpassed the South.

And now that we have come to the very heart and soul of our subject, we feel no disposition to mince matters, but mean to speak plainly, and to the point, without any equivocation, mental reservation, or secret evasion whatever. The son of a venerated parent, who, while he lived, was a considerate and merciful slaveholder, a native of the South, born and bred in North Carolina, of a family whose home has been in the valley of the Yadkin [River] for nearly a century and a half, a Southerner by instinct and by all the influences of thought, habits, and kindred, and with the desire and fixed purpose to reside permanently within the limits of the South, and with the expectation of dying there also—we feel that we have the right to express our opinion, however humble or unimportant it may be, on any and every question that affects the public good; and, so help us God, "sink or swim, live or die, survive or perish," we are determined to exercise that right with manly firmness, and without fear, favor or affection.

And now to the point. In our opinion, an opinion which has been formed from data obtained by assiduous researches, and comparisons, from laborious investigation, logical reasoning, and earnest reflection, the causes which have impeded the progress and prosperity of the South, which have dwindled our commerce, and other similar pursuits, into the most contemptible insignificance; sunk a large majority of our people in galling poverty and ignorance, rendered a small minority conceited and tyrannical, and driven the rest away from their homes; entailed upon us a humiliating dependence on the Free States; disgraced us in the recesses of our own souls, and brought us under reproach in the eyes of all civilized and enlightened nations—may all be traced to one common source, and there find solution in the most hateful and horrible word, that was ever incorporated into the vocabulary of human economy—*Slavery!*

Reared amidst the institution of slavery, believing it to be wrong both in principle and in practice, and having seen and felt its evil influences upon individuals, communities and states, we deem it a duty, no less than a privilege, to enter our protest against it, and to use our most strenuous efforts to overturn and abolish it! Then we are an abolitionist? Yes! not merely a freesoiler, but an abolitionist, in the fullest sense of the term. We are not only in favor of keeping slavery out of the territories [the freesoilers' position], but, carrying our opposition to the institution a step further, we here unhesitatingly declare ourself in favor of its immediate and unconditional abolition, in every state in this confederacy, where it now exists! Patriotism makes us a freesoiler; state pride makes us an emancipationist; a profound sense of duty to the South makes us an abolitionist; a reasonable degree of fellow feeling for the negro, makes us a colonizationist. With the free state men in Kansas and Nebraska, we sympathize with all our heart. We love the whole country, the great family of states and territories, one and inseparable, and would have the word Liberty engraved as an appropriate and truthful motto, on the escutcheon of every member of the confederacy. We love freedom, we hate slavery, and rather than give up the one or submit to the other, we will forfeit the pound of flesh nearest our heart. Is this sufficiently explicit and categorical? . . .

The first and most sacred duty of every Southerner, who has the honor and the interest of his country at heart, is to declare himself an unqualified and uncompromising abolitionist. No conditional or half-way declaration will avail; no mere threatening demonstration will succeed. With those who desire to be instrumental in bringing about the triumph of liberty over slavery, there should be neither evasion, vacillation, nor equivocation. We should listen to no modifying terms or compromises that may be proposed by the proprietors of the unprofitable and ungodly institution. Nothing short of the complete abolition of slavery can save the South from falling into the vortex of utter ruin. Too long have we yielded a submissive obedience to the tyrannical domination of an inflated oligarchy; too long have we tolerated their arrogance and self-conceit; too long have we submitted to their unjust and savage exactions. Let us now wrest from them the sceptre of power, establish liberty and equal rights throughout the land, and henceforth and forever guard our legislative halls from the pollutions and usurpations of pro-slavery demagogues. . . .

With regard to the unnational and demoralizing institution of slavery, we believe the majority of Northern people are too scrupulous. They seem to think that it is enough for them to be mere freesoilers, to keep in check the diffusive element of slavery, and to prevent it from crossing over the bounds within which it is now regulated by municipal law. Remiss in their *national* duties, as we contend, they make no positive attack upon the institution in the Southern States. Only a short while since, one of their ablest journals—the *North American and United States Gazette*, published in Philadelphia—made use of the following language:—

> With slavery in the States, we make no pretence of having anything politically to do. For better or for worse, the system belongs solely to the people of those States; and is separated by an impassable gulf of State sovereignty from any legal intervention of ours. We cannot vote it down any more than we can vote down the institution of caste in Hindostan, or abolish polygamy in the Sultan's dominions. Thus, precluded from all political action in reference to it, prevented from touching one stone of the edifice, not the slightest responsibility attaches to us as citizens for its continued existence. But on the question of extending slavery over the free Territories of the United States, it is our right, it is our imperative duty to think, to feel, to speak and to vote. We cannot interfere to cover the shadows of slavery with the sunshine of freedom, but we can interfere to prevent the sunshine of freedom from being eclipsed by the shadows of slavery. We can interpose to stay the progress of that institution, which aims to drive free labor from its own heritage. Kansas should be divided up into countless homes for the ownership of men who have a right to the fruit of their own labors. Free labor would make it bud and blossom like the rose; would cover it with beauty, and draw from it boundless wealth; would throng it with population; would make States, nations, empires out of it, prosperous, powerful, intelligent and free, illustrating on a wide theatre the beneficent ends of Providence in the formation of our government, to advance and elevate the millions of our race, and, like the heart in the body, from its central position, sending out on every side, far and near, the vital influences of freedom and civilization. May that region, therefore, be secured to free labor.

Now we fully and heartily indorse every line of the latter part of this extract; but, with all due deference to our sage cotemporary, we do most emphatically dissent from the sentiments embodied in the first part. Pray, permit us to ask—have the people of the North no interest in the United States as a *nation*, and do they not see that slavery is a great injury and disgrace to the *whole country*? Did they not, in "the days that tried men's souls," strike as hard blows to secure the independence of Georgia as they did in defending the liberties of Massachusetts, and is it not notoriously true that the Toryism of South Carolina prolonged the [Revolutionary] war two years at least? Is it not, moreover, equally true that the oligarchs of South Carolina have been unmitigated pests and bores to the General Government ever since it was organized, and that the free and conscientious people of the North are virtually excluded from her soil, in consequence of slavery? It is a well-known and incontestible fact, that the Northern States furnished about two-thirds of all the American troops engaged in the Revolutionary War; and, though they were neither more nor less brave or patriotic than their fellow-soldiers of the South, yet, inasmuch as the independence of our country was mainly secured by virtue of their numerical strength, we think they ought to consider it not only their right but their *duty* to make a firm and decisive effort to save the States which they fought to free, from falling under the yoke of a worse tyranny than that which overshadowed them under the reign of King George the Third. Freemen of the North! we earnestly entreat you to think of these things. Hitherto, as mere freesoilers, you have approached but half-way to the line of your duty; now, for your own sakes and for ours, and for the purpose of perpetuating this glorious Republic, which your fathers and our fathers founded in septennial streams of blood, we ask you, in all seriousness, to organize yourselves as *one man* under the banners of Liberty, and to aid us in *exterminating* slavery, which is the only thing that militates against our complete aggrandizement as a nation.

In this extraordinary crisis of affairs, no man can be a true patriot without first becoming an abolitionist. (A freesoiler is only a tadpole in an advanced state of transformation; an abolitionist is the full and perfectly developed frog.) . . .

An Ultimatum for Slaveholders

But, Sirs, knights of bludgeons, chevaliers of bowie-knives and pistols, and lords of the lash, we are unwilling to allow you to swindle the slaves out of all the rights and claims to which, as human beings, they are most sacredly entitled. Not alone for ourself as an individual, but for others also—particularly for five or six millions of Southern non-slaveholding whites, whom your iniquitous statism has debarred from almost all the mental and material comforts of life—do we speak, when we say, you *must* emancipate your slaves, and pay each and every one of them at least sixty dollars cash in hand. By doing this, you will be restoring to them their natural rights, and remunerating them at the rate of less than twenty-six cents per annum for the long and cheerless period of their servitude, from the 20th of August, 1620, when, on James River, in Virginia, they became the unhappy slaves of heartless masters. Moreover, by doing this you will be performing but a simple act of justice to the non-slaveholding whites, upon whom the institution of slavery has weighed scarcely less heavily than upon the negroes themselves. You will also be applying a saving balm to your own outraged hearts and consciences, and your children—yourselves in fact—freed from the accursed stain of slavery, will become respectable, useful, and honorable members of society.

And now, Sirs, we have thus laid down our ultimatum. What are you going to do about it? Something dreadful, as a matter of course! Perhaps you will dissolve the Union *again*. Do it, if you dare! Our motto, and we would have you to understand it, is *the abolition of slavery, and the perpetuation of the American Union*. If, by any means, you do succeed in your treasonable attempts to take the South out of the Union to-day, we will bring her back to-morrow—if she goes away with you, she will return without you.

Do not mistake the meaning of the last clause of the last sentence; we could elucidate it so thoroughly that no intelligent person could fail to comprehend it; but, for reasons which may hereafter appear, we forego the task.

Henceforth there are other interests to be consulted in the South, aside from the interests of negroes and slaveholders. A profound sense of duty incites us to make the greatest possible efforts for the abolition of slavery; an equally profound sense of duty calls for a continuation of those efforts until the very last foe to freedom shall have been utterly vanquished. To the summons of the righteous monitor within, we shall endeavor to prove faithful; no opportunity for inflicting a mortal wound in the side of slavery shall be permitted to pass us unimproved. Thus, terror-engenderers of the South, have we fully and frankly defined our position; we have no modifications to propose, no compromises to offer, nothing to retract. Frown, Sirs, fret, foam, prepare your weapons, threat, strike, shoot, stab, bring on civil war, dissolve the Union, nay, annihilate the solar system if you will—do all this, more, less, better, worse, anything—do what you will, Sirs, you can neither foil nor intimidate us; our purpose is as firmly fixed as the eternal pillars of Heaven; we have determined to abolish slavery, and, so help us God, abolish it we will! Take this to bed with you to-night, Sirs, and think about it, dream over it, and let us know how you feel to-morrow morning.

VIEWPOINT 5

"This Union was established on the right of each state to do as it pleased on the question of slavery and every other question."

Popular Sovereignty Should Settle the Slavery Question

Stephen A. Douglas (1813-1861)

Stephen A. Douglas, U.S. senator from Illinois, was one of America's leading national political figures of the 1850s. Today he is best remembered for his political rivalry with Abraham Lincoln.

Elected to the United States Senate in 1846, Douglas played major roles in passing the Compromise of 1850 and the Kansas-Nebraska Act of 1854—both attempts by Congress to resolve the issue of legalizing slavery in America's western territories. Douglas's sponsorship of these laws, especially the Kansas-Nebraska Act, positioned him as the champion of "popular sovereignty"— the idea that territorial settlers would at some point make their own decision whether to legalize slavery.

By 1858 the doctrine of popular sovereignty was under attack from several quarters. For four years the territory of Kansas had been beset by violent confrontations between proslavery and abolitionist settlers who sought to influence the territory's decision on slavery. The Supreme Court had ruled in 1857 in the *Dred Scott* case that Congress lacked the authority to exclude slavery from the territories—a decision that many people argued made slavery legal in all territories regardless of the desires of their inhabitants. Eventually, the controversy over slavery and popular sovereignty helped give birth to a new political party. The Republican Party

From *Political Debates Between Hon. Abraham Lincoln and Hon. Stephen A. Douglas, in the Celebrated Campaign of 1858*, published by Follett, Foster & Co., 1860, for the Ohio Republican State Central Committee.

was formed to oppose the spread of slavery into the territories; it fielded as its candidate for Douglas's Senate seat in 1858 a relatively unknown lawyer named Abraham Lincoln.

Lincoln and Douglas held a series of seven celebrated debates on the future of slavery and of America. The following viewpoint is from Douglas's opening speech at the last debate, which was held in Alton, Illinois, on October 15, 1858. In the speech Douglas reviews what he regards as the basic issues of the debate, and makes his case for popular sovereignty as the true democratic and constitutional alternative to civil war. Douglas won the senatorial race, but two years later was defeated by Lincoln in the 1860 election for president.

––––––––––––––––

It is now nearly four months since the canvass between Mr. Lincoln and myself commenced. On the sixteenth of June the Republican Convention assembled at Springfield and nominated Mr. Lincoln as their candidate for the United States Senate, and he, on that occasion, delivered a speech in which he laid down what he understood to be the Republican creed and the platform on which he proposed to stand during the contest.

The principal points in that speech of Mr. Lincoln's were: First, that this government could not endure permanently divided into free and slave states, as our fathers made it; that they must all become free or all become slave; all become one thing or all become the other, otherwise this Union could not continue to exist. I give you his opinions almost in the identical language he used. His second proposition was a crusade against the Supreme Court of the United States because of the Dred Scott decision; urging as an especial reason for his opposition to that decision that it deprived the Negroes of the rights and benefits of that clause in the Constitution of the United States which guarantees to the citizens of each state all the rights, privileges, and immunities of the citizens of the several states.

On the tenth of July I returned home and delivered a speech to the people of Chicago. . . . In that speech I joined issue with Mr. Lincoln on the points which he had presented. Thus there was an issue clear and distinct made up between us on these two propositions laid down in the speech of Mr. Lincoln at Springfield and controverted by me in my reply to him at Chicago.

On the next day, the eleventh of July, Mr. Lincoln replied to me at Chicago, explaining at some length, and reaffirming the positions which he had taken in his Springfield speech. In that Chicago speech he even went further than he had before and ut-

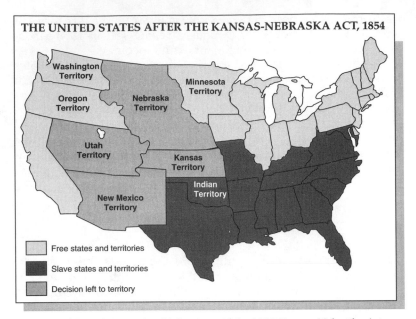

THE UNITED STATES AFTER THE KANSAS-NEBRASKA ACT, 1854

Free states and territories

Slave states and territories

Decision left to territory

Stephen A. Douglas was the chief sponsor of the 1854 Kansas-Nebraska Act, which made the establishment of slavery possible in the Kansas and Nebraska territories if the local settlers wanted it. Northerners criticized the act as a Congressional abdication of any role in banning slavery in the territories.

tered sentiments in regard to the Negro being on an equality with the white man. . . . He insisted, in that speech, that the Declaration of Independence included the Negro in the clause, asserting that all men were created equal, and went so far as to say that if one man was allowed to take the position that it did not include the Negro, others might take the position that it did not include other men. He said that all these distinctions between this man and that man, this race and the other race, must be discarded, and we must all stand by the Declaration of Independence, declaring that all men were created equal.

Lincoln's Three Errors

The issue thus being made up between Mr. Lincoln and myself on three points, we went before the people of the state. . . . In my speeches I confined myself closely to those three positions which he had taken, controverting his proposition that this Union could not exist as our fathers made it, divided into free and slave states, controverting his proposition of a crusade against the Supreme Court because of the Dred Scott decision, and controverting his proposition that the Declaration of Independence included and meant the Negroes as well as the white men when it declared all men to be created equal. . . . I took up Mr. Lincoln's three propositions in my several speeches, analyzed them, and pointed out what I believed to be the radical errors contained in them. First, in regard to his doctrine that this government was in violation of the law of God, which says that a house divided against itself cannot stand, I repudiated it as a slander upon the immortal framers of our Constitution. I then said, I have often repeated, and now again assert, that in my opinion our government can endure forever, divided into free and slave states as our fathers made it—each state having the right to prohibit, abolish, or sustain slavery, just as it pleases. This government was made upon the great basis of the sovereignty of the states, the right of each state to regulate its own domestic institutions to suit itself, and that right was conferred with the understanding and expectation that, inasmuch as each locality had separate interests, each locality must have different and distinct local and domestic institutions, corresponding to its wants and interests. Our fathers knew when they made the government that the laws and institutions which were well adapted to the Green Mountains of Vermont were unsuited to the rice plantations of South Carolina. They knew then, as well as we know now, that the laws and institutions which would be well adapted to the beautiful prairies of Illinois would not be suited to the mining regions of California. They knew that in a republic as broad as this, having such a variety of soil, climate, and interest, there must necessarily be a corresponding variety of local laws—the policy and institutions of each state adapted to its condition and wants. For this reason this Union was established on the right of each state to do as it pleased on the question of slavery and every other question; and the various states were not allowed to complain of, much less interfere with, the policy of their neighbors. . . .

You see that if this abolition doctrine of Mr. Lincoln had prevailed when the government was made, it would have established slavery as a permanent institution, in all the states, whether they wanted it or not, and the question for us to determine in Illinois now as one of the free states is whether or not we are willing, having become the majority section, to enforce a doctrine on the minority which we would have resisted with our heart's blood had it been attempted on us when we were in a minority. How has the South lost her power as the majority section in this Union, and how have the free states gained it, except under the operation of that principle which declares the right of the people of each state and each territory to form and regulate their domestic institutions in their own way. It was under that principle that slavery was abolished in New Hampshire, Rhode Island,

73

Connecticut, New York, New Jersey, and Pennsylvania; it was under that principle that one-half of the slaveholding states became free; it was under that principle that the number of free states increased until, from being one out of twelve states, we have grown to be the majority of states of the whole Union, with the power to control the House of Representatives and Senate, and the power, consequently, to elect a President by northern votes without the aid of a southern state. Having obtained this power under the operation of that great principle, are you now prepared to abandon the principle and declare that merely because we have the power you will wage a war against the southern states and their institutions until you force them to abolish slavery everywhere . . . ?

A Time for Compromise

My friends, there never was a time when it was as important for the Democratic party, for all national men, to rally and stand together as it is today. We find all sectional men giving up past differences and continuing the one question of slavery, and, when we find sectional men thus uniting, we should unite to resist them and their treasonable designs. Such was the case in 1850, when [Henry] Clay left the quiet and peace of his home and again entered upon public life to quell agitation and restore peace to a distracted Union. Then we Democrats, with [Lewis] Cass at our head, welcomed Henry Clay, whom the whole nation regarded as having been preserved by God for the times. He became our leader in that great fight [to pass the Compromise of 1850], and we rallied around him the same as the Whigs rallied around "Old Hickory" [Democratic president Andrew Jackson] in 1832 to put down nullification [an attempt by South Carolina to declare federal tariff laws "null and void" within its borders]. Thus you see that whilst Whigs and Democrats fought fearlessly in old times about banks, the tariff, distribution, the specie circular, and the sub-treasury, all united as a band of brothers when the peace, harmony, or integrity of the Union was imperiled. It was so in 1850, when abolitionism had even so far divided this country, North and South, as to endanger the peace of the Union; Whigs and Democrats united in establishing the compromise measures of that year and restoring tranquillity and good feeling. These measures passed on the joint action of the two parties. They rested on the great principle that the people of each state and each territory should be left perfectly free to form and regulate their domestic institutions to suit themselves. You Whigs and we Democrats justified them in that principle. In 1854, when it became necessary to organize the territories of Kansas and Nebraska, I brought forward the bill on the same principle. In the Kansas-Nebraska Bill you find it declared to be the true intent and meaning of the act not to legislate slavery into

74

any state or territory, nor to exclude it therefrom, but to leave the people thereof perfectly free to form and regulate their domestic institutions in their own way. I stand on that same platform in 1858 that I did in 1850, 1854, and 1856. . . .

Popular Sovereignty

Stephen A. Douglas, in the July 9, 1858, address in Chicago that began his reelection campaign, succinctly defines what he means by "popular sovereignty."

I regard the great principle of popular sovereignty as having been vindicated and made triumphant in this land as a permanent rule of public policy in the organization of territories and the admission of new states. Illinois took her position upon this principle many years ago. . . .

The great principle is the right of every community to judge and decide for itself whether a thing is right or wrong, whether it would be good or evil for them to adopt it; and the right of free action, the right of free thought, the right of free judgment, upon the question is dearer to every true American than any other under a free government. . . . It is no answer to this argument to say that slavery is an evil, and hence should not be tolerated.

You must allow the people to decide for themselves whether it is good or an evil.

I say to you that there is but one hope, one safety, for this country, and that is to stand immovably by that principle which declares the right of each state and each territory to decide these questions for themselves. This government was founded on that principle and must be administered in the same sense in which it was founded.

Declaration of Independence for Whites

But the Abolition party really think that under the Declaration of Independence the Negro is equal to the white man and that Negro equality is an inalienable right conferred by the Almighty, and hence that all human laws in violation of it are null and void. With such men it is no use for me to argue. I hold that the signers of the Declaration of Independence had no reference to Negroes at all when they declared all men to be created equal. They did not mean Negro, nor the savage Indians, nor the Fiji Islanders, nor any other barbarous race. They were speaking of white men. They alluded to men of European birth and European descent— to white men and to none others—when they declared that doctrine. I hold that this government was established on the white basis. It was established by white men for the benefit of white men and their posterity forever and should be administered by white men and none others. But it does not follow, by any means, that merely because the Negro is not a citizen, and merely because he is not our equal, that, therefore, he should be a slave. On the contrary, it does follow that we ought to extend to the Negro race, and to all other dependent races all the rights, all the privileges, and all the immunities which they can exercise consistently with the safety of society. Humanity requires that we should give them all these privileges; Christianity commands that we should extend those privileges to them. The question then arises: What are those privileges and what is the nature and extent of them. My answer is that that is a question which each state must answer for itself. We in Illinois have decided it for ourselves. We tried slavery, kept it up for twelve years, and, finding that it was not profitable, we abolished it for that reason, and became a free state. We adopted in its stead the policy that a Negro in this state shall not be a slave and shall not be a citizen. We have a right to adopt that policy. For my part I think it is a wise and sound policy for us. You in Missouri must judge for yourselves whether it is a wise policy for you. If you choose to follow our example, very good; if you reject it, still well, it is your business, not ours. So with Kentucky. Let Kentucky adopt a policy to suit herself. If we do not like it, we will keep away from it, and if she does not like ours let her stay at home, mind her own business and let us alone. If the people of all the states will act on that great principle, and each state mind its own business, attend to its own affairs, take care of its own Negroes, and not meddle with its neighbors, then there will be peace between the North and the South, the East and the West, throughout the whole Union. Why can we not thus have peace? Why should we thus allow a sectional party to agitate this country, to array the North against the South, and convert us into enemies instead of friends, merely that a few ambitious men may ride into power on a sectional hobby?

VIEWPOINT 6

"[Slavery] should, as far as may be, be treated as a wrong, and one of the methods of treating it as a wrong is to make provision that it shall grow no larger."

Slavery Should Not Be Allowed to Spread

Abraham Lincoln (1809-1865)

Abraham Lincoln was president of the United States during the Civil War, and was perhaps the central figure of the conflict. His election as president in 1860 was due in part to the national prominence he gained while campaigning for the U.S. Senate in 1858. Lincoln and his opponent, incumbent Illinois senator Stephen A. Douglas, held a series of seven public debates in which the main issues discussed were slavery and the future of the American nation.

Lincoln, a self-taught lawyer who had served a term in Congress and had established a successful and busy legal practice, opened his senatorial campaign with a famous speech in Springfield, Illinois. Lincoln, quoting Scripture, stated that:

> "A house divided against itself cannot stand." I believe this government cannot endure, permanently, half slave and half free. . . . It will become all one thing, or all the other.

This statement and others by him were attacked by Douglas who accused Lincoln of being a radical, a "Black Republican" who wished to abolish slavery in the Southern states and promote racial equality, and whose policies would lead the nation into war. Lincoln in his debates with Douglas denied all of these charges.

The following viewpoint is taken from Lincoln's last speech in

From *Political Debates Between Hon. Abraham Lincoln and Hon. Stephen A. Douglas, in the Celebrated Campaign of 1858,* published by Follett, Foster & Co., 1860, for the Ohio Republican State Central Committee.

the debates, given in Alton, Illinois, on October 15, 1858. In this speech he disavows any designs of interfering with slavery in the Southern states. He expresses the hope, which he claims was shared by the writers of the U.S. Constitution, that slavery will be forced into "ultimate extinction" if it is not allowed to grow or spread into the western territories.

It is not true that our fathers, as Judge Douglas assumes, made this government part slave and part free. Understand the sense in which he puts it. He assumes that slavery is a rightful thing within itself—was introduced by the framers of the Constitution. The exact truth is that they found the institution existing among us, and they left it as they found it. But, in making the government, they left this institution with many clear marks of disapprobation upon it. They found slavery among them, and they left it among them because of the difficulty—the absolute impossibility—of its immediate removal. And when Judge Douglas asks me why we cannot let it remain part slave and part free, as the fathers of the government made it, he asks a question based upon an assumption which is itself a falsehood; and I turn upon him and ask him the question, when the policy that the fathers of the government had adopted in relation to this element among us was the best policy in the world—the only wise policy—the only policy that we can ever safely continue upon—that will ever give us peace, unless this dangerous element masters us all and becomes a national institution—*I turn upon him and ask him why he could not leave it alone.* I turn and ask him why he was driven to the necessity of introducing a *new policy* in regard to it. . . . I ask, too, of Judge Douglas and his friends why we shall not again place this institution upon the basis on which the fathers left it. I ask you, when he infers that I am in favor of setting the free and slave states at war, when the institution was placed in that attitude by those who made the Constitution, *did they make any war?* If we had no war out of it, when thus placed, wherein is the ground of belief that we shall have war out of it if we return to that policy? Have we had any peace upon this matter springing from any other basis? I maintain that we have not. I have proposed nothing more than a return to the policy of the fathers.

I confess, when I propose a certain measure of policy, it is not enough for me that I do not intend anything evil in the result, but it is incumbent on me to show that it has not a *tendency* to that result. I have met Judge Douglas in that point of view. I have not

78

This photo of Abraham Lincoln was taken in Springfield, Illinois, in 1860, the year he was elected president.

only made the declaration that I do not *mean* to produce a conflict between the states, but I have tried to show by fair reasoning, and I think I have shown to the minds of fair men, that I propose nothing but what has a most peaceful tendency. The quotation that I happened to make in that Springfield speech, that "a house divided against itself cannot stand," and which has proved so offensive to the Judge, was part and parcel of the same thing. He tries to show that variety in the domestic institutions of the different states is necessary and indispensable. I do not dispute it. I have no controversy with Judge Douglas about that. . . .

States and Territories

The Judge alludes very often in the course of his remarks to the exclusive right which the states have to decide the whole thing [slavery] for themselves. I agree with him very readily that the different states have that right. He is but fighting a man of straw when he assumes that I am contending against the right of the states to do as they please about it. Our controversy with him is in regard to the new territories. We agree that when the states come in as states they have the right and the power to do as they please. We have no power as citizens of the free states, or in our federal capacity as members of the federal Union through the general government, to disturb slavery in the states where it exists.

We profess constantly that we have no more inclination than belief in the power of the government to disturb it; yet we are driven constantly to defend ourselves from the assumption that we are warring upon the rights of the *states*. What I insist upon is that the new territories shall be kept free from it while in the territorial condition. Judge Douglas assumes that we have no interest in them, that we have no right whatever to interfere. I think we have some interest. I think that as white men we have.

Do we not wish for an outlet for our surplus population, if I may so express myself? Do we not feel an interest in getting to that outlet with such institutions as we would like to have prevail there? If *you* go to the territory opposed to slavery, and another man comes upon the same ground with his slaves, upon the assumption that the things are equal, it turns out that he has the equal right all his way, and you have no part of it your way. If he goes in and makes it a slave territory and, by consequence, a slave state, is it not time that those who desire to have it a free state were on equal ground?

Let me suggest it in a different way. How many Democrats are there about here who have left slave states and come into the free state of Illinois to get rid of the institution of slavery? I reckon there are a thousand and one. I will ask you, if the policy you are now advocating had prevailed when this country was in a territorial condition, where would you have gone to get rid of it? Where would you have found your free state or territory to go to? And when, hereafter, for any cause, the people in this place shall desire to find new homes, if they wish to be rid of the institution, where will they find the place to go to? . . .

Now irrespective of the moral aspect of this question as to whether there is a right or wrong in enslaving a Negro, I am still in favor of our new territories being in such a condition that white men may find a home—may find some spot where they can better their condition—where they can settle upon new soil and better their condition in life. I am in favor of this not merely (I must say it here as I have elsewhere) for our own people who are born amongst us, but as an outlet for *free white people everywhere*, the world over—in which Hans and Baptiste and Patrick, and all other men from all the world, may find new homes and better their conditions in life.

The Real Issue

I have stated upon former occasions, and I may as well state again, what I understand to be the real issue in this controversy between Judge Douglas and myself. On the point of my wanting to make war between the free and the slave states, there has been no issue between us. So, too, when he assumes that I am in favor of introducing a perfect social and political equality between the white and black races. These are false issues, upon which Judge Douglas has tried to force the controversy. There is no foundation in truth for the charge that I maintain either of these propositions. The real issue in this controversy—the one pressing upon every mind—is the sentiment on the part of one class that looks upon the institution of slavery *as a wrong* and of another class that *does not* look upon it as a wrong. The sentiment that contemplates the institution of slavery in this country as a wrong is the sentiment

---

An Irrepressible Conflict

In a famous speech in Rochester, New York, on October 25, 1858, William H. Seward declared that "an irrepressible conflict" existed between the slave and free states. Then a United States senator and a contender for the Republican presidential nomination, Seward later served as secretary of state under Abraham Lincoln.

Our country is a theater which exhibits in full operation two radically different political systems; the one resting on the basis of servile or slave labor, the other on the basis of voluntary labor of freemen. . . .

Hitherto, the two systems have existed in different states, but side by side within the American Union. This has happened because the Union is a confederation of states. But in another aspect the United States constitute only one nation. Increase of population which is filling the states out to their very borders, together with a new and extended network of railroads and other avenues, and an internal commerce which daily becomes more intimate, is rapidly bringing the states into a higher and more perfect social unity or consolidation. Thus, these antagonistic systems are continually coming into closer contact, and collision results.

Shall I tell you what this collision means? They who think that it is accidental, unnecessary, the work of interested or fanatical agitators and therefore ephemeral, mistake the case altogether. It is an *irrepressible conflict* between opposing and enduring forces, and it means that the United States must and will, sooner or later, become either entirely a slaveholding nation or entirely a free-labor nation. Either the cotton and rice fields of South Carolina and the sugar plantations of Louisiana will ultimately be tilled by free labor, and Charleston and New Orleans become marts for legitimate merchandise alone, or else the rye fields and wheat fields of Massachusetts and New York must again be surrendered by their farmers to slave culture and to the production of slaves, and Boston and New York become once more markets for trade in the bodies and souls of men. It is the failure to apprehend this great truth that induces so many unsuccessful attempts at final compromise between the slave and free states, and it is the existence of this great fact that renders all such pretended compromises, when made, vain and ephemeral.

of the Republican party. It is the sentiment around which all their actions—all their arguments circle—from which all their propositions radiate. They look upon it as being a moral, social, and political wrong; and, while they contemplate it as such, they nevertheless have due regard for its actual existence among us, and the difficulties of getting rid of it in any satisfactory way and to all the constitutional obligations thrown about it. Yet having a due regard for these, they desire a policy in regard to it that looks to its not creating any more danger. They insist that it should, as far as may be, *be treated* as a wrong, and one of the methods of treating it as a wrong is to *make provision that it shall grow no larger.* They also desire a policy that looks to a peaceful end of slavery at some time as being wrong. These are the views they entertain in regard to it as I understand them; and all their sentiments—all their arguments and propositions—are brought within this range. I have said, and I repeat it here, that if there be a man amongst us who does not think that the institution of slavery is wrong in any one of the aspects of which I have spoken, he is misplaced and ought not to be with us. And if there be a man amongst us who is so impatient of it as a wrong as to disregard its actual presence among us and the difficulty of getting rid of it suddenly in a satisfactory way, and to disregard the constitutional obligations thrown about it, that man is misplaced if he is on our platform. We disclaim sympathy with him in practical action. He is not placed properly with us.

On this subject of treating it as a wrong, and limiting its spread, let me say a word. Has anything ever threatened the existence of this Union save and except this very institution of slavery? What is it that we hold most dear amongst us? Our own liberty and prosperity. What has ever threatened our liberty and prosperity save and except this institution of slavery? If this is true, how do you propose to improve the condition of things by enlarging slavery—by spreading it out and making it bigger? You may have a wen or cancer upon your person and not be able to cut it out lest you bleed to death; but surely it is no way to cure it, to engraft it and spread it over your whole body. That is no proper way of treating what you regard a wrong. You see this peaceful way of dealing with it as a wrong—restricting the spread of it, and not allowing it to go into new countries where it has not already existed. That is the peaceful way, the old-fashioned way, the way in which the fathers themselves set us the example.

Is Slavery Wrong?

On the other hand, I have said there is a sentiment which treats it as *not* being wrong. That is the Democratic sentiment of this day. I do not mean to say that every man who stands within that range positively asserts that it is right. That class will include all who positively assert that it is right, and all who like Judge Douglas treat it as indifferent and do not say it is either right or wrong. These two classes of men fall within the general class of those who do not look upon it as a wrong. . . .

The Democratic policy in regard to that institution will not tolerate the merest breath, the slightest hint, of the least degree of wrong about it. Try it by some of Judge Douglas' arguments. He says he "don't care whether it is voted up or voted down" in the territories. I do not care myself in dealing with that expression, whether it is intended to be expressive of his individual sentiments on the subject or only of the national policy he desires to have established. It is alike valuable for my purpose. Any man can say that who does not see anything wrong in slavery, but no man can logically say it who does see a wrong in it; because no man can logically say he does not care whether a wrong is voted up or voted down. He may say he does not care whether an indifferent thing is voted up or down, but he must logically have a choice between a right thing and a wrong thing. He contends that whatever community wants slaves has a right to have them. So they have if it is not a wrong. But if it is a wrong, he cannot say people have a right to do wrong. He says that, upon the score of equality, slaves should be allowed to go in a new territory, like other property. This is strictly logical if there is no difference between it and other property. If it and other property are equal, his argument is entirely logical. But if you insist that one is wrong and the other right, there is no use to institute a comparison between right and wrong. You may turn over everything in the Democratic policy from beginning to end, whether in the shape it takes on the statute book, in the shape it takes in the Dred Scott decision, in the shape it takes in conversation, or the shape it takes in short maxim-like arguments—it everywhere carefully excludes the idea that there is anything wrong in it.

That is the real issue. That is the issue that will continue in this country when these poor tongues of Judge Douglas and myself shall be silent. It is the eternal struggle between these two principles—right and wrong—throughout the world. They are the two principles that have stood face to face from the beginning of time and will ever continue to struggle. The one is the common right of humanity and the other the divine right of kings. It is the same principle in whatever shape it develops itself. It is the same spirit that says, "You work and toil and earn bread, and I'll eat it." No matter in what shape it comes, whether from the mouth of a king who seeks to bestride the people of his own nation and live by the fruit of their labor, or from one race of men as an apology for enslaving another race, it is the same tyrannical principle.

CHAPTER 2

Crisis of Secession

Chapter Preface

On December 20, 1860, South Carolina declared itself independent and separate from the United States of America. It was soon followed by Alabama, Mississippi, Florida, Georgia, Louisiana, and Texas. While leaders in Washington tried to work out formulas for compromise, Americans came to realize that the nation faced the stark choice of letting the states secede or going to war. The viewpoints in this chapter focus on the debates of this critical period.

The secession of South Carolina and the other states was the culmination of longstanding tensions in America, and historians still debate the South's motives for leaving the Union. Most agree that two events are key to understanding the background of secession: John Brown's rebellion, and the election of Abraham Lincoln as president of the United States.

John Brown was a radical abolitionist who moved to Kansas in 1855 and became involved in the conflict between proslavery and antislavery groups in that territory. In 1856 he and a small band of followers killed five proslavery settlers in Pottawatomie Creek. He then moved east and in 1859 formed a plan to lead a slave insurrection in Virginia. With secret financial support from prominent Northern abolitionists, some if not all of whom were aware of his violent past and plans, Brown and eighteen of his followers (including two of his sons and five black men) raided the federal arsenal at Harper's Ferry. Brown hoped to give the captured arms to the escaping slaves he was sure would join his cause; he planned to establish a base of operations for guerrilla warfare against slavery in the Appalachian Mountains of Virginia. The raid was a fiasco. Local slaves did not respond to Brown's call for rebellion, and his forces were quickly defeated by local militia and a detachment of U.S. Army troops commanded by Colonel Robert E. Lee. Brown was captured and his two sons were killed. He was tried and convicted in a Virginia state court on charges of treason.

Brown proved to be a far more effective martyr than revolutionary. He was considered a hero in much of the North for his dignified bearing during his trial, his refusal to preserve his life by pleading insanity, and his last speech before his hanging: "If it is deemed necessary that I should forfeit my life for the furtherance of the ends of justice, and mingle my blood further with the blood of my children and with the blood of millions in this slave country whose rights are disregarded by wicked, cruel, and unjust enactments,—I submit; so let it be done!" Northern praise of Brown's goals, along with evidence of Northern abolitionist support for his plan of insurrection, disturbed Southerners even more than the original raid. Historian Irwin Unger writes in *These United States*:

> Brown's raid raised sectional feelings once again to a fever pitch. . . . To southerners, who lived in constant dread of slave revolt, the raid was traumatic. Hundreds of southern students at northern colleges packed their bags and returned home. Georgians attacked the crew of a Yankee ship at Savannah, and a New Yorker newly installed as president of an Alabama college was forced to flee for his life. To many southerners the message seemed clear: The South was no longer safe in the Union.

The sectional divisions magnified by John Brown's rebellion affected the second major event leading up to secession—the presidential election of 1860. The Democratic Party, which had controlled the White House for 24 of the previous 32 years and which was one of the few genuinely national organizations remaining, finally split along sectional lines when convention delegates were unable to agree on a candidate. Southern delegates, insisting on a platform calling for federal protection of slavery in all western territories and refusing to support the leading candidate, Stephen A. Douglas, left the party and nominated their own candidate, John Breckinridge. The two Democrats were opposed by John Bell of the newly formed Constitutional Union Party, which sought to avoid the slavery issue, and by Abraham Lincoln of the Republican Party.

The Republican Party was also new; it was formed in the 1850s by Northerners who opposed both the extension of slavery into the western territories and what they saw as Southern domination of national politics. Opponents derided them as "Black Republicans" determined to abolish slavery and promote social equality between blacks and whites. The Republicans sought to dispel this image in 1860 by adopting a platform that, while advocating the restriction of slavery in the territories, also endorsed the right of each state to maintain slavery and condemned John Brown's raid as "the gravest of crimes." Despite these efforts at moderation, the Republican Party and its candidate remained anathema in the South, where many people predicted that a Republican victory would result in the destruction of the Union.

Lincoln was elected by winning most of the Northern states; he won none of the Southern ones. Between his election in November 1860 and his inauguration in March 1861, people in the South debated whether to leave the Union, and people in the North debated how to respond. Lincoln, in his inaugural address, declared secession illegal and pledged to preserve the Union. His first major act in fulfilling his pledge was to send provisions to Fort Sumter in Charleston, South Carolina—one of the few federal installations that had not been seized by the seceding states. The Confederacy responded by attacking Fort Sumter on April 12, firing the first shots of the Civil War.

VIEWPOINT 1

"The door of conciliation and compromise is finally closed by our adversaries, and it remains only to us to meet the conflict with the . . . firmness of men worthy of freedom."

Georgia Should Secede

Robert Toombs (1810-1885)

The election of Abraham Lincoln as president in 1860 prompted many people in the South to seriously entertain the possibility of secession from the Union. One of the many debates over the issue occurred in the Georgia state legislature on November 13–14, 1860, over a proposal to call a special convention to consider secession. The state legislators invited Georgia's two leading politicians to debate whether Georgia should secede immediately, or whether it should wait in the hopes that some compromise could be reached (or, failing that, to put the onus for dividing the Union on some overt action by the North).

Speaking for immediate secession was Robert Toombs. Toombs's long political career included service in the state legislature, House of Representatives, and, since 1851, the United States Senate. A former moderate who had worked for the Compromise of 1850, Toombs had ten years later become Georgia's most prominent advocate for leaving the Union. The following viewpoint is excerpted from his address to the Georgia state legislature on November 13, 1860. He argues that "Lincoln and his Abolition horde," having gained control of the executive branch of the federal government, are determined to end slavery in the South. He concludes that immediate resistance is the only logical alternative if the South is to preserve its freedoms (including the freedom to own slaves).

During the Civil War Toombs served the Confederacy as its first

From Document 67 of the supplement to *The Rebellion Record: A Diary of American Events, with Documents, Narratives, Illustrative Incidents, Poetry, etc., etc.,* edited by Frank Moore. New York: G.P. Putnam, 1864.

secretary of state, and later as a brigadier general. Following the Civil War he fled to Europe. He returned to Georgia in 1867 and practiced law the rest of his life without ever applying for pardon or regaining his U.S. citizenship.

I very much regret, in appearing before you at your request, to address you on the present state of the country and the prospect before us, that I can bring you no good tidings. The stern, steady march of events has brought us in conflict with our nonslave-holding confederates upon the fundamental principles of our compact of Union. We have not sought this conflict; we have sought too long to avoid it; our forbearance has been construed into weakness, our magnanimity into fear, until the vindication of our manhood, as well as the defense of our rights, is required at our hands. The door of conciliation and compromise is finally closed by our adversaries, and it remains only to us to meet the conflict with the dignity and firmness of men worthy of freedom.

We need no declaration of independence. Above eighty-four years ago, our fathers won that by the sword from Great Britain, and above seventy years ago, Georgia, with the twelve other confederates, as free, sovereign, and independent states, having perfect governments already in existence, for purposes and objects clearly expressed and with powers clearly defined, erected a common agent for the attainment of these purposes by the exercise of those powers, and called this agent the United States of America.

The basis, the cornerstone of this government, was the perfect equality of the free, sovereign, and independent states which made it. They were unequal in population, wealth, and territorial extent; they had great diversities of interests, pursuits, institutions, and laws; but they had common interests, mainly exterior, which they proposed to protect by this common agent—a constitutional united government—without in any degree subjecting their inequalities and diversities to federal control or action. . . .

We had a large common domain, already added by the several states for the common benefit of all; purchase and war might make large additions to this common domain; hence, the power over existing and future territories, with the stipulation to admit new states, was conferred. . . .

Slavery and the Territories

The South at all times demanded nothing but equality in the common territories, equal enjoyment of them with their property

88

to that extended to Northern citizens and their property—nothing more. They said, we pay our part in all the blood and treasure expended in their acquisition. Give us equality of enjoyment, equal right to expansion—it is as necessary to our prosperity as yours. In 1790 we had less than 800,000 slaves. Under our mild and humane administration of the system, they have increased above 4 million. The country has expanded to meet this growing want; and Florida, Alabama, Mississippi, Louisiana, Texas, Arkansas, Kentucky, Tennessee, and Missouri have received this increasing tide of African labor; before the end of this century, at precisely the same rate of increase, the Africans among us in a subordinate condition will amount to 11 million persons. What shall be done with them?

Culver Pictures, Inc.

Robert Toombs, a strong advocate of secession, served as secretary of state and later as brigadier general for the Confederacy.

We must expand or perish. We are constrained by an inexorable necessity to accept expansion or extermination. Those who tell you that the territorial question is an abstraction, that you can never colonize another territory without the African slave trade are both deaf and blind to the history of the last sixty years. All just reasoning, all past history condemn the fallacy. The North understand it better—they have told us for twenty years that their object was to pen up slavery within its present limits—surround it with a border of free states, and, like the scorpion surrounded with fire, they will make it sting itself to death. One thing at least is certain, that whatever may be the effect of your exclusion from the territories, there is no dispute but that the North mean it, and adopt it as a measure hostile to slavery upon this point. . . .

This conflict, at least, is irrepressible—it is easily understood—we demand the equal right with the North to go into the common territories with all of our property, slaves included, and to be there protected in its peaceable enjoyment by the federal government, until such territories may come into the Union as equal states—then we admit them with or without slavery, as the people themselves may decide for themselves. Will you surrender this principle? The day you do this base, unmanly deed you embrace political degradation and death. . . .

Why Immediate Secession?

I am asked, why do you demand action now? The question is both appropriate and important; it ought to be frankly met. The Abolitionists say you are raising a clamor because you were beaten in the election. The falsity of this statement needs no confirmation. Look to our past history for its refutation. Some excellent citizens and able men in Georgia say the election of any man constitutionally is no cause for a dissolution of the Union. That position is calculated only to mislead and not to enlighten. It is not the issue. I say the election of Lincoln, with all of its surroundings, is sufficient. What is the significance of his election? It is the endorsement, by the nonslaveholding states, of all those acts of aggression upon our rights by all these states, legislatures, governors, judges, and people. He is elected by the perpetrators of these wrongs with the purpose and intent to aid and support them in wrongdoing.

Hitherto, the Constitution has had on its side the federal executive, whose duty it is to execute the laws and Constitution against these malefactors. It has earnestly endeavored to discharge that duty. Relying upon its power and good faith to remedy these wrongs, we have listened to conservative counsels, trusting to time, to the federal executive, and to a returning sense of justice in the North. The executive has been faithful—the federal judiciary have been faithful—the President has appointed sound judges, sound marshals, and other subordinate officers to interpret and to execute the laws. With the best intentions, they have all failed—our property has been stolen, our people murdered; felons and assassins have found sanctuary in the arms of the party which elected Mr. Lincoln. The executive power, the last bulwark of the Constitution to defend us against these enemies of the Constitution, has been swept away, and we now stand without a shield, with bare bosoms presented to our enemies, and we demand at your hands the sword for our defense, and if you will not give it to us, we will take it—take it by the divine right of self-defense, which governments neither give nor can take away.

Therefore, redress for past and present wrongs demands resistance to the rule of Lincoln and his Abolition horde over us; he comes at their head to shield and protect them in the perpetration of these outrages upon us, and, what is more, he comes at their head to aid them in consummating their avowed purposes by the power of the federal government. Their main purpose, as indicated by all their acts of hostility to slavery, is its final and total abolition. His party declare it; their acts prove it. He has declared it; I accept his declaration. The battle of the irrepressible conflict has hitherto been fought on his side alone. We demand service in this war. Surely no one will deny that the election of Lincoln is the endorsement of the policy of those who elected him, and an endorsement of his own opinions.

Lincoln's Party

The opinions of those who elected him are to be found in their solemn acts under oath—in their state governments, endorsed by their constituents. To them I have already referred. They are also to be found in the votes of his supporters in Congress—also endorsed by the party, by their return. Their opinions are to be found in the speeches of [William] Seward, and [Charles] Sumner, and [Elijah] Lovejoy, and their associates and confederates in the two houses of Congress. Since the promotion of Mr. Lincoln's party, all of them speak with one voice, and speak trumpet-tongued their fixed purpose to outlaw $4 billion of our property in the territories, and to put it under the ban of the empire in the states where it exists. They declare their purpose to war against slavery until there shall not be a slave in America, and until the African is elevated to a social and political equality with the white man. Lincoln endorses them and their principles, and in his own speeches declares the conflict irrepressible and enduring, until slavery is everywhere abolished.

Hitherto, they have carried on this warfare by state action, by individual action, by appropriation, by the incendiary's torch and the poisoned bowl. They were compelled to adopt this method because the federal executive and the federal judiciary were against them. They will have possession of the federal executive with its vast power, patronage, prestige of legality, its Army, its Navy, and its revenue on the 4th of March next. Hitherto, it has been on the side of the Constitution and the right; after the 4th of March it will be in the hands of your enemy. Will you let him have it? [*Cries of "No, no. Never."*]

Then strike while it is yet today. Withdraw your sons from the Army, from the Navy, and every department of the federal public service. Keep your own taxes in your own coffers—buy arms with them and throw the bloody spear into this den of incendiaries and assassins, and let God defend the right.

But you are advised to wait, send soft messages to their brethren, to beg them to relent, to give you some assurances of their better fidelity for the future. What more can you get from

Secession, Not Submission

Joseph E. Brown, the governor of Georgia from 1857 to 1865, came out in favor of secession in a public letter written on December 7, 1860. Ironically, Brown later became a strong critic of the Confederacy, arguing that measures taken by its central government threatened states' rights.

The present is a critical time with the people of the South. We all, poor and rich, have a common interest, a common destiny. It is no time to be wrangling about old party strifes. Our common enemy, the Black Republican party, is united and triumphant. Let us all unite. If we cannot all see alike, let us have charity enough towards each other, to admit that all are equally patriotic in their efforts to advance the common cause. My honest convictions are, that we can never again live in peace with the Northern abolitionists, unless we can have new constitutional guarantees, which will secure our equal rights in the Territories, and effectually stop the discussion of the slavery question in Congress, and secure the rendition of fugitive slaves. These guarantees I do not believe the people of the Northern States will ever give, while we remain together in the Union. Their opinion is, that we will always compromise away a portion of our rights, and submit, for the sake of peace. If the Cotton States would all secede from the Union before the inauguration of Mr. Lincoln, this might possibly lead to a Convention of all the States, which might terminate in a reunion with the new constitutional guarantees necessary for our protection. If the Northern States then failed to give these guarantees, there can be no doubt that Virginia, Maryland, North Carolina, Delaware, Kentucky, Missouri, and Tennessee would unite with the Cotton States in a Southern Confederacy and we should form a Republic in which, under the old Constitution of our fathers, our people could live in security and peace. I know that many of our people honestly believe that it would be best to wait for these border slave States to go out with us. If we wait for this, we shall *submit;* for some of those States will not consent to go, and the North will then consent to give us no new guarantees of peace. They will say that we have again blustered and submitted, as we always do.

them under this government? You have the Constitution—you have its exposition by themselves for seventy years—you have their oaths—they have broken all these, and will break them again. They tell you everywhere, loudly and defiantly, you shall have no power, no security until you give up the right of governing yourselves according to your own will—until you submit to theirs. For this is the meaning of Mr. Lincoln's irrepressible conflict—this is his emphatic declaration to all the world. Will you heed it? For myself, like the Athenian ambassador, I will take no security but this, that it shall not be in the power of our enemies to injure my country if they desire it. Nothing but ruin will follow delay. The enemy on the 4th of March will entrench himself behind a quintuple wall of defense. Executive power, judiciary (Mr. Seward has already proclaimed its reformation), Army, Navy, and Treasury. Twenty years of labor and toil and taxes all expended upon preparation would not make up for the advantage your enemies would gain if the rising sun on the 5th of March should find you in the Union. Then strike while it is yet time.

The Constitution

But we are told that secession would destroy the fairest fabric of liberty the world ever saw, and that we are the most prosperous people in the world under it. The arguments of tyranny as well as its acts always reenact themselves. The arguments I now hear in favor of this Northern connection are identical in substance and almost in the same words as those which were used in 1775 and 1776 to sustain the British connection. We won liberty, sovereignty, and independence by the American Revolution—we endeavored to secure and perpetuate these blessings by means of our Constitution. The very men who use these arguments admit that this Constitution, this compact is violated, broken, and trampled under foot by the Abolition Party. Shall we surrender the jewels because their robbers and incendiaries have broken the casket? Is this the way to preserve liberty? I would as lief surrender it back to the British Crown as to the Abolitionists. I will defend it from both. Our purpose is to defend those liberties. What baser fate could befall us or this great experiment of free government than to have written upon its tomb: "Fell by the hands of Abolitionists and the cowardice of its natural defenders." If we quail now, this will be its epitaph.

We are said to be a happy and prosperous people. We have been, because we have hitherto maintained our ancient rights and liberties—we will be until we surrender them. They are in danger; come, freemen, to the rescue. . . .

I can go to England or France, or any other country in Europe with my slave without molestation or violating any law. I can go anywhere except in my own country, whilom [formerly] called "the glorious Union"; here alone am I stigmatized as a felon; here alone am I an outlaw; here alone am I under the ban of the empire; here alone I have neither security nor tranquillity; here alone are organized governments ready to protect the incendiary, the assassin who burns my dwelling or takes my life or those of my wife and children; here alone are hired emissaries paid by brethren to glide through the domestic circle and intrigue insurrection with all of its nameless horrors.

My countrymen, "if you have nature in you, bear it not." Withdraw yourselves from such a confederacy; it is your right to do so—your duty to do so. I know not why the Abolitionists should object to it, unless they want to torture and plunder you. If they resist this great sovereign right, make another war of independence, for that then will be the question; fight its battles over again—reconquer liberty and independence. As for me, I will take any place in the great conflict for rights which you may assign. I will take none in the federal government during Mr. Lincoln's administration.

If you desire a senator after the 4th of March, you must elect one in my place. I have served you in the state and national councils for nearly a quarter of a century without once losing your confidence. I am yet ready for the public service when honor and duty call. I will serve you anywhere where it will not degrade and dishonor my country. Make my name infamous forever, if you will, but save Georgia. I have pointed out your wrongs, your danger, your duty. You have claimed nothing but that rights be respected and that justice be done. Emblazon it on your banner—fight for it, win it, or perish in the effort.

VIEWPOINT 2

"Shall the people of the South secede from the Union in consequence of the election of Mr. Lincoln? . . . I do not think that they ought."

Georgia Should Not Secede

Alexander H. Stephens (1812-1883)

Shortly after Abraham Lincoln was elected president of the United States in November 1860 but before he took office, the Georgia legislature held a debate over whether the state should hold a special convention to consider seceding from the Union. Among the prominent participants in the debate was Alexander H. Stephens, a longtime Georgia statesman who had recently retired from Congress to his private law practice.

The following is taken from Stephens's address to the legislature on November 14, 1860. Stephens spoke after many people, including his close friend Robert Toombs, had called for Georgia's immediate secession from the Union. Stephens argues that the mere election of Lincoln as president is not sufficient cause for secession. He asserts that the South has greatly benefited from both the Union and the Constitution, and urges that Georgia wait and see what actions the North will take before deserting both.

Stephens's moderate address drew the attention of Lincoln, who wrote him a letter pledging not to interfere with slavery in the Southern states. But when Georgia and other states decided to secede, Stephens, like most Southern moderates, accepted the decision. He was elected vice president of the Confederacy under Jefferson Davis. Following the Civil War, he wrote *Constitutional View of the Late War Between the States*, a history of the conflict from a Southern perspective, and was an advocate of reconciliation between North and South.

From Document 147½ of the supplement to *The Rebellion Record: A Diary of American Events, with Documents, Narratives, Illustrative Incidents, Poetry, etc., etc.,* edited by Frank Moore. New York: G.P. Putnam, 1864.

Fellow-Citizens: I appear before you tonight at the request of members of the Legislature and others to speak of matters of the deepest interest that can possibly concern us all of an earthly character. There is nothing—no question or subject connected with this life—that concerns a free people so intimately as that of the Government under which they live. We are now, indeed, surrounded by evils. Never since I entered upon the public stage has the country been so environed with difficulties and dangers that threatened the public peace and the very existence of society as now. I do not now appear before you at my own instance. It is not to gratify desire of my own that I am here. Had I consulted my own ease and pleasure I should not be before you; but, believing that it is the duty of every good citizen to give his counsels and views whenever the country is in danger, as to the best policy to be pursued, I am here. For these reasons, and these only, do I bespeak a calm, patient, and attentive hearing.

My object is not to stir up strife, but to allay it; not to appeal to your passions, but to your reason. Good governments can never be built up or sustained by the impulse of passion. I wish to address myself to your good sense, to your good judgment, and if after hearing you disagree, let us agree to disagree, and part as we met, friends. We all have the same object, the same interest. That people should disagree in republican governments, upon questions of public policy, is natural. That men should disagree upon all matters connected with human investigation, whether relating to science or human conduct, is natural. Hence, in free governments parties will arise. But a free people should express their different opinions with liberality and charity, with no acrimony toward those of their fellows, when honestly and sincerely given. These are my feelings to-night.

Let us, therefore, reason together. It is not my purpose to say aught to wound the feelings of any individual who may be present; and if in the ardency with which I shall express my opinions, I shall say any thing which may be deemed too strong, let it be set down to the zeal with which I advocate my own convictions. There is with me no intention to irritate or offend.

Against Immediate Secession

The first question that presents itself is, shall the people of the South secede from the Union in consequence of the election of Mr. Lincoln to the presidency of the United States? My countrymen, *I tell you frankly, candidly, and earnestly, that I do not think that they ought.* In my judgment, the election of no man, constitutionally chosen to that high office, is sufficient cause for any State to

This cartoon published by Currier & Ives in New York shows the state of Georgia as having second thoughts about joining in the chase after the "Secession Humbug."

separate from the Union. It ought to stand by and aid still in maintaining the constitution of the country. To make a point of resistance to the Government, to withdraw from it because a man has been constitutionally elected, puts us in the wrong. We are pledged to maintain the Constitution. Many of us have sworn to support it. Can we, therefore, for the mere election of a man to the Presidency, and that too in accordance with the prescribed forms of the Constitution, make a point of resistance to the Government without becoming the breakers of that sacred instrument ourselves, withdraw ourselves from it? Would we not be in the wrong? Whatever fate is to befall this country, let it never be laid to the charge of the people of the South, and especially to the people of Georgia, that we were untrue to our national engagements. Let the fault and the wrong rest upon others. If all our hopes are to be blasted, if the Republic is to go down, let us be found to the last moment standing on the deck, with the Constitution of the United States waving over our heads. *(Applause.)* Let the fanatics of the North break the Constitution, if such is their fell purpose. Let the responsibility be upon them. I shall speak presently more of their acts; but let not the South, let us not be the ones to commit the aggression. We went into the election with this people. The result was different from what we wished; but the election

97

has been constitutionally held. Were we to make a point of resistance to the Government and go out of the Union on that account, the record would be made up hereafter against us.

But it is said Mr. Lincoln's policy and principles are against the Constitution, and that if he carries them out it will be destructive of our rights. Let us not anticipate a threatened evil. If he violates the Constitution then will come our time to act. Do not let us break it because, forsooth, he may. If he does, that is the time for us to strike. (*Applause.*) I think it would be injudicious and unwise to do this sooner. I do not anticipate that Mr. Lincoln will do any thing to jeopard our safety or security, whatever may be his spirit to do it; for he is bound by the constitutional checks which are thrown around him, which at this time renders him powerless to do any great mischief. This shows the wisdom of our system. The President of the United States is no emperor, no dictator—he is clothed with no absolute power. He can do nothing unless he is backed by power in Congress. The House of Representatives is largely in the majority against him.

In the Senate he will also be powerless. There will be a majority of four against him. . . . Mr. Lincoln cannot appoint an officer without the consent of the Senate—he cannot form a Cabinet without the same consent. He will be in the condition of George III., (the embodiment of Toryism,) who had to ask the Whigs to appoint his ministers, and was compelled to receive a cabinet utterly opposed to his views; and so Mr. Lincoln will be compelled to ask of the Senate to choose for him a cabinet, if the Democracy of that body choose to put him on such terms. He will be compelled to do this or let the Government stop, if the National Democratic men—for that is their name at the North—the conservative men in the Senate, should so determine. Then, how can Mr. Lincoln obtain a cabinet which would aid him, or allow him to violate the Constitution?

Why then, I say, should we disrupt the ties of this Union when his hands are tied, when he can do nothing against us? I have heard it mooted that no man in the State of Georgia, who is true to her interests, could hold office under Mr. Lincoln. But, I ask, who appoints to office? Not the President alone; the Senate has to concur. No man can be appointed without the consent of the Senate. Should any man then refuse to hold office that was given to him by a Democratic Senate? . . .

My honorable friend who addressed you last night, (Robert Toombs,) and to whom I listened with the profoundest attention, asks if we would submit to Black Republican rule? I say to you and to him, as a Georgian, I never would submit to any Black Republican *aggression* upon our constitutional rights. I will never consent myself, as much as I admire this Union for the glories of the past, or the blessings of the present, as much as it has done for the people of all these States, as much as it has done for civilization, as much as the hopes of the world hang upon it, I would never submit to aggression upon my rights to maintain it longer; and if they cannot be maintained in the Union, standing on the Georgia platform, where I have stood from the time of its adoption, I would be in favor of disrupting every tie which binds the States together.

I will have equality for Georgia and for the citizens of Georgia in this Union, or I will look for new safeguards elsewhere. This is my position. The only question now is, can they be secured in the Union? That is what I am counselling with you to-night about. Can it be secured? In my judgment it may be, but it may not be; but let us do all we can, so that in the future, if the worst come, it may never be said we were negligent in doing our duty to the last.

The Union Is Not a Curse

My countrymen, I am not of those who believe this Union has been a curse up to this time. True men, men of integrity, entertain different views from me on this subject. I do not question their right to do so; I would not impugn their motives in so doing. Nor will I undertake to say that this Government of our fathers is perfect. There is nothing perfect in this world of a human origin. Nothing connected with human nature, from man himself to any of his works. You may select the wisest and best men for your judges, and yet how many defects are there in the administration of justice? You may select the wisest and best men for your legislators, and yet how many defects are apparent in your laws? And it is so in our Government.

But that this Government of our fathers, with all its defects, comes nearer the objects of all good Governments than any other on the face of the earth is my settled conviction. Contrast it now with any on the face of the earth. . . .

Compare, my friends, this Government with that of Spain, Mexico, the South American Republics, Germany, Ireland—are there any sons of that down-trodden nation here tonight?—Prussia, or if you travel further East, to Turkey or China. Where will you go, following the sun in its circuit round our globe, to find a Government that better protects the liberties of its people, and secures to them the blessings we enjoy? . . .

Have we not at the South, as well as the North, grown great, prosperous, and happy under its operation? Has any part of the world ever shown such rapid progress in the development of wealth, and all the material resources of national power and greatness, as the Southern States have under the General Government, notwithstanding all its defects?

Mr. Toombs—In spite of it.

Mr. Stephens—My honorable friend says we have, in spite of the General Government; that without it I suppose he thinks we might have done as well, or perhaps better, than we have done this in spite of it. That may be, and it may not be; but the great fact that we have grown great and powerful under the Government as it exists, there is no conjecture or speculation about that; . . . whether all this is in spite of the Government—whether we of the South would have been better off without the Government— is, to say the least, problematical. On the one side we can only put the fact against speculation and conjecture on the other. But even as a question of speculation I differ with my distinguished friend.

What we would have lost in border wars without the Union, or what we have gained simply by the peace it has secured, no estimate can be made of. Our foreign trade, which is the foundation of all our prosperity, has the protection of the navy, which drove the pirates from the waters near our coast, where they had been buccaneering for centuries before, and might have been still had it not been for the American Navy. . . . Now that the coast is clear, that our commerce flows freely outwardly, we cannot well estimate how it would have been under other circumstances. The influence of the Government on us is like that of the atmosphere around us. Its benefits are so silent and unseen that they are seldom thought of or appreciated.

We seldom think of the single element of oxygen in the air we breathe, and yet let this simple, unseen, and unfelt agent be withdrawn, this life-giving element be taken away from this all-pervading fluid around us, and what instant and appalling changes would take place in all organic creation. . . .

Recalling the Compromise of 1850

There are defects in our Government, errors in administration, and shortcomings of many kinds, but in spite of these defects and errors, Georgia has grown to be a great State. Let us pause here a moment. In 1850 there was a great crisis, but not so fearful as this, for of all I have ever passed through, this is the most perilous, and requires to be met with the greatest calmness and deliberation.

There were many amongst us in 1850 zealous to go at once out of the Union, to disrupt every tie that binds us together. Now do you believe, had that policy been carried out at that time, we would have been the same great people that we are to-day? It may be that we would, but have you any assurance of that fact? Would you have made the same advancement, improvement, and progress in all that constitutes material wealth and prosperity that we have? . . .

I think not. Well, then, let us be careful now before we attempt any rash experiment of this sort. I know that there are friends whose patriotism I do not intend to question, who think this Union a curse, and that we would be better off without it. I do not so think; if we can bring about a correction of these evils which threaten—and I am not without hope that this may yet be done—this appeal to go out, with all the provisions for good that accompany it, I look upon as a great and I fear a fatal temptation. . . .

If any view that I may present, in your judgment, be inconsistent

---

Seeking Solutions Within the Union

Benjamin H. Hill, a Georgia legislator who after the Civil War became a United States senator, was usually a strong political opponent of Alexander H. Stephens. However, speaking to the Georgia legislature on November 15, 1860, one day after Stephens's plea against secession, Hill sided with his former rival in arguing that Georgia should seek to resolve its differences with the Union peaceably before resorting to secession and possible war.

But suppose our secession be not peaceable. In what conditions are we for war? No navy, no forts, no arsenals, no arms but bird guns for low trees. Yet a scattered people, with nothing dividing us from our enemy but an imaginary line, and a long sea and gulf coast extending from the Potomac to Galveston Bay, if all should secede. In what condition are we to meet the thousand ills that would beset us, and every one of which can be avoided by taking time. . . . Secession is no holiday work.

While we are seeking to redress our wrongs in the Union, we can go forward, making all necessary preparations to go out if it should become necessary. We can have a government system perfect, and prepared, ready for the emergency, when the necessity for separation shall come.

If we fail to get redress in the Union, that very failure will unite the people of our State. The only real ground of difference now is: some of us think we can get redress in the Union, and others think we cannot. Let those of us who still have faith make that effort which has never been made, and if we fail, then we are ready to join you. If you will not help us make that effort, at least do not try to prevent [it]. Let us have a fair trial. Keep cool and keep still. If we cannot save our equality, and rights, and honor in the Union, we shall join you and save them out of it. . . .

Now, my secession friends, I have all confidence in your zeal and patriotism, but simply let us take time and get ready. Let us work for the best, and prepare for the worst. Until an experiment is made, I shall always believe that the Constitution has strength enough to conquer all its enemies—even the Northern fanatic. If it proves to have not that strength, I will not trust it another hour.

with the best interests of Georgia, I ask you, as patriots, not to regard it. After hearing me and others whom you have advised with, act in the premises according to your own conviction of duty as patriots. I speak now particularly to the members of the Legislature present. There are, as I have said, great dangers ahead. Great dangers may come from the election I have spoken of. If the policy of Mr. Lincoln and his Republican associates shall be carried out, or attempted to be carried out, no man in Georgia will be more willing or ready than myself to defend our rights, interest, and honor at every hazard, and to the last extremity. *(Applause.)*

What is this policy? It is in the first place to exclude us by an act of Congress from the Territories with our slave property. He is for using the power of the General Government against the extension of our institutions. Our position on this point is and ought to be, at all hazards, for perfect equality between all the States, and the citizens of all the States, in the Territories, under the Constitution of the United States. If Congress should exercise its power against this, then I am for standing where Georgia planted herself in 1850. These were plain propositions which were then laid down in her celebrated platform as sufficient for the disruption of the Union if the occasion should ever come: on these Georgia has declared that she will go out of the Union; and for these she would be justified by the nations of the earth in so doing.

I say the same; I said it then; I say it now, if Mr. Lincoln's policy should be carried out. I have told you that I do not think his bare election sufficient cause: but if his policy should be carried out in violation of any of the principles set forth in the Georgia Platform, that would be such an act of aggression which ought to be met as therein provided for. If his policy shall be carried out in repealing or modifying the Fugitive Slave law so as to weaken its efficacy, Georgia has declared that she will in the last resort disrupt the ties of the Union, and I say so too. . . .

The People Are Sovereign

Now, then, my recommendation to you would be this: In view of all these questions of difficulty, let a convention of the people of Georgia be called, to which they may be all referred. Let the sovereignty of the people speak. Some think that the election of Mr. Lincoln is cause sufficient to dissolve the Union. Some think those other grievances are sufficient to dissolve the same, and that the Legislature has the power thus to act, and ought thus to act. I have no hesitancy in saying that the Legislature is not the proper body to sever our Federal relations, if that necessity should arise. An honorable and distinguished gentleman, the other night, (Mr. T.R.R. Cobb,) advised you to take this course— not to wait to hear from the cross-roads and groceries. I say to you, you have no

102

power so to act. You must refer this question to the people and you must wait to hear from the men at the cross-roads and even the groceries; for the people in this country, whether at the cross-roads or the groceries, whether in cottages or palaces, are all equal, and they are the sovereigns in this country. Sovereignty is not in the legislature. We, the people, are the sovereigns. I am one of them and have a right to be heard, and so has any other citizen of the State. You legislators, I speak it respectfully, are but our servants. You are the servants of the people, and not their masters. Power resides with the people in this country. . . .

Should Georgia determine to go out of the Union, I speak for one, though my views might not agree with them, whatever the result may be, I shall bow to the will of her people. Their cause is my cause, and their destiny is my destiny; and I trust this will be the ultimate course of all. The greatest curse that can befall a free people is civil war.

But, as I said, let us call a convention of the people; let all these matters be submitted to it, and when the will of a majority of the people has thus been expressed, the whole State will present one unanimous voice in favor of whatever may be demanded; for I believe in the power of the people to govern themselves when wisdom prevails and passion is silent.

Look at what has already been done by them for their advancement in all that ennobles man. There is nothing like it in the history of the world. Look abroad from one extent of the country to the other, contemplate our greatness. We are now among the first nations of the earth. Shall it be said, then, that our institutions, founded upon principles of self-government, are a failure?

Thus far it is a noble example, worthy of imitation. The gentleman, Mr. Cobb, the other night said it had proven a failure. A failure in what? In growth? Look at our expanse in national power. Look at our population and increase in all that makes a people great. A failure? Why we are the admiration of the civilized world, and present the brightest hopes of mankind.

Some of our public men have failed in their aspirations; that is true, and from that comes a great part of our troubles. *(Prolonged applause.)*

No, there is no failure of this Government yet. We have made great advancement under the Constitution, and I cannot but hope that we shall advance higher still. Let us be true to our cause.

Now, when this convention assembles, if it shall be called, as I hope it may, I would say in my judgment, without dictation, for I am conferring with you freely and frankly, and it is thus that I give my views, I should take into consideration all those questions which distract the public mind; should view all the grounds of secession so far as the election of Mr. Lincoln is concerned, and I have no doubt they would say that the constitutional election of no man is a sufficient cause to break up the Union, but that the State should wait until he at least does some unconstitutional act. . . .

I am for exhausting all that patriotism can demand before taking the last step. I would invite, therefore, South Carolina to a conference. I would ask the same of all the other Southern States, so that if the evil has got beyond our control, which God, in his mercy, grant may not be the case, let us not be divided among ourselves—*(cheers)*—but, if possible, secure the united coöperation of all the Southern States; and then, in the face of the civilized world, we may justify our action; and, with the wrong all on the other side, we can appeal to the God of battles to aid us in our cause. *(Loud applause.)* But let us not do any thing in which any portion of our people may charge us with rash or hasty action. It is certainly a matter of great importance to tear this Government asunder. You were not sent here for that purpose. I would wish the whole South to be united if this is to be done; and I believe if we pursue the policy which I have indicated, this can be effected.

In this way our sister Southern States can be induced to act with us, and I have but little doubt that the States of New York and Pennsylvania and Ohio, and the other Western States, will compel their Legislatures to recede from their hostile attitudes if the others do not. Then with these we would go on without New England if she chose to stay out.

A voice in the assembly—We will kick them out.

Mr. Stephens—I would not kick them out. But if they chose to stay out they might. I think moreover that these Northern States being principally engaged in manufactures, would find that they had as much interest in the Union under the Constitution as we, and that they would return to their constitutional duty—this would be my hope. If they should not, and if the Middle States and Western States do not join us, we should at least have an undivided South. I am, as you clearly perceive, for maintaining the Union as it is, if possible. I will exhaust every means thus to maintain it with an equality in it. . . .

If all this fails, we shall at least have the satisfaction of knowing that we have done our duty and all that patriotism could require.

VIEWPOINT 3

"If disunion must come, let it come without war."

The Northern States Should Let the Southern States Secede

Albany Atlas and Argus and
William Lloyd Garrison (1805-1879)

The crisis of secession set off by Abraham Lincoln's 1860 election as president created stark choices for all Americans. On December 20, 1860, South Carolina became the first state to officially declare secession, and other states soon followed. Lame-duck president James Buchanan pronounced secession illegal, but did not take any steps to use force to prevent it. While the Southern states considered secession, people of the Northern states disagreed over what their response should be. Should they let the Southern states secede in peace? Or should they attempt to prevent their secession by force, risking war? The concept of "peaceable secession"—letting the Southern states go to avoid war—was widely discussed in the North in the months after Lincoln's election. What follows are two views supporting this idea—by people who, ironically, probably disagreed on most other issues.

Part I of the following viewpoint is an editorial published by the *Atlas and Argus*, an Albany, New York, newspaper edited by Calvert Comstock and William Cassidy. The newspaper had supported Stephen A. Douglas for president, warning that a Republican victory would provoke the Southern states to secede from the United States. In a January 12, 1861, editorial, reprinted here, the editors assert that the United States faces the choice of "peaceable separation

Editorial in the January 12, 1861, Albany, New York, *Atlas and Argus* by Calvert Comstock and William Cassidy. William Lloyd Garrison, cited in *William Lloyd Garrison* by Wendell Phillips Garrison and Francis Jackson Garrison, vol. 4. New York: Houghton Mifflin, 1894.

or civil war" and supports the former, arguing that war would cause national desolation but not be able to restore the Union.

Part II of the viewpoint is by William Lloyd Garrison, one of the nation's most prominent abolitionists. As editor of the *Liberator* newspaper from 1831 to 1865, he wrote hundreds of editorials and articles calling for the immediate abolition of slavery. In an article written for the *Liberator* in January 1861, Garrison argues that while the federal government has the full legal and constitutional authority to forcibly quell secession, the better course would be to accept the dissolution of the Union and to create a Northern confederacy free of any taint of slavery.

I

The sectional doctrines of the Republican party have—as thinking men have foreseen—at last brought us to the verge of civil war. Indeed, war has already commenced. Four States have formally separated from the Confederacy [Union] and declared themselves independent of the Federal Union and are in the attitude of supporting their position by arms. The Republican leaders adhere to their partisan and sectional dogmas and utterly refuse to do anything to arrest this impending danger and restore peace to the country. The present Congress will do nothing and before its term expires on the 4th of March, thirteen or fourteen of the slave States will have established a separate government, which they will sustain at the hazard of fortune and life. We shall be confronted with the stern issue of peaceable, voluntary separation, or of civil war. We shall be compelled to bid a sad farewell to the brethren with whom we have so long dwelt in liberty and happiness and divide with them the inheritance of our fathers—or to undertake, by all the terrors and horrors of war, to compel them to continue in union with us. We must separate from them peaceably, and each seek happiness and prosperity in our own way—or we must conquer them and hold them as subjugated provinces. Fellow citizens, of all parties and of whatever past views, which course do you prefer? Shall it be peaceable separation or civil war?

If such be the issue—and none can now deny it—before choosing war, it will be well to reflect whether it will effect the desired object of preserving the Union of these States? With thirteen or fourteen States banded together and fighting with as much pertinacity, as our fathers of the Thirteen Colonies, for what *they* deem their rights and liberties, the war must be a deadly and protracted one. We do not doubt that the superior numbers and resources of the Northern States might prevail. We might defeat them in battle, overrun their country, and capture and sack and burn their cities, and carry terror and desolation, by fire and sword, over their several States. We might ruin the commerce and industry of the country, North and South, sweep the whole land with the besom of war, and cause the nation to resound with the groans of widows and orphans; all this we might do, and through it all, possibly [illegible] st of the triumph of the Federal arms, and to see [illegible] ipes wave over every battle field and every smoki[illegible]

But [illegible] ereby be restored? Would the Union be thus prese[illegible] ese conquered States quietly assume their old pla[illegible] federacy? Would they send Representatives to Congr[illegible] rt in the Presidential elections, and perform their funct[illegible] yal members of the Union? Would they be

The Right to Secede

Horace Greeley, influential editor of the New York Tribune, *wrote an editorial on November 9, 1860—two days after Abraham Lincoln's election as president—that defended a state's right to secede from the Union.*

The telegraph informs us that most of the Cotton States are meditating a withdrawal from the Union, because of Lincoln's election. Very well: they have a right to meditate, and meditation is a profitable employment of leisure. We have a chronic, invincible disbelief in Disunion as a remedy for either Northern or Southern grievances. We cannot see any necessary connection between the alleged disease and this ultra-heroic remedy; still, we say, if any one sees fit to meditate Disunion, let him do so unmolested. . . . And now, if the Cotton States consider the value of the Union debatable, we maintain their perfect right to discuss it. Nay: we hold, with Jefferson, to the inalienable right of communities to alter or abolish forms of government that have become oppressive or injurious; and, if the Cotton States shall decide that they can do better out of the Union than in it, we insist on letting them go in peace. The right to secede may be a revolutionary one, but it exists nevertheless; and we do not see how one party can have a right to do what another party has a right to prevent. We must ever resist the asserted right of any State to remain in the Union, and nullify or defy the laws thereof: to withdraw from the Union is quite another matter. And, whenever a considerable section of our Union shall deliberately resolve to go out, we shall resist all coërcive measures designed to keep it in. We hope never to live in a republic, whereof one section is pinned to the residue by bayonets.

anything but conquered States, held in subjection by military restraint? No—peace and concord between these States cannot be reached through the medium of war. The probable result of a long and deadly struggle would be a treaty of peace, agreeing to a division. War is necessarily disunion and division, and we prefer division without war—if it must come. By a peac[e]able separation the enmities of the two sections will not be inflamed beyond all possible hope of reconciliation and reconstruction, but war will be eternal hostility and division. Let the people of this country pause before they draw the sword ... a fratricidal strife.

We say emphatically, let th... be ... the stars and str... e foremost in kindling a flame, w. the city. ...pt in the blood of our kindred. T... would peace th... used and the great danger at this r ...would t... ll take possession of the populace arved? Would the Co... try on to ruin. The press, influential citiz...ess, in the Co... her public men—instead of inflaming this fee...take p... ephemeral popularity by ministering to it, should s... ...ains as l... ...ain it and lead the people of this State to act with moderation. New York should not forget her position, as the most powerful State of the Union and should put forth her influence, in this emergency, in favor of peace, and if she cannot stay the mad torrent of disunion, should hold herself in condition to be able, when the passions of men shall have cooled, to engage in the work of reconstruction and of reuniting States now dissevered, for causes so trivial that time and reflection—if we escape war—may be expected to remove them.

We repeat—if disunion must come, let it come without war. Peaceable separation is a great calamity—but dissolution, with the superadded horrors of internal war, including the ruin of business, the destruction of property, oppressive debt, grinding taxation and sacrifice of millions of lives, is a scourge from which, let us pray, that a merciful Providence may protect us.

If the present Congress, and the political leaders in it, who have brought the country into this danger, have not the patriotism to adopt measures for the restoration of peace, better than plunge the nation into civil war, let them propose Constitutional amendments, which will enable the people to pass upon the question of a voluntary and peaceful separation. Then, at least the hope will remain that the people may in good time discard their fanatical political leaders and apply themselves to the reconstruction and renovation of the Constitution and the Union.

II

Under these circumstances, what is the true course to be pursued by the people of the North? Is it to vindicate the sovereignty by the sword till the treason is quelled and allegiance restored? Constitutionally, the sword may be wielded to this extent, and must be, whether by President Buchanan or President Lincoln, if the Union is to be preserved. The Federal Government must not pretend to be in actual operation, embracing thirty-four States, and then allow the seceding States to trample upon its flag, steal its property, and defy its authority with impunity; for it would then be (as it is at this moment) a mockery and a laughing-stock. Nevertheless, to think of whipping the South (for she will be a unit on the question of slavery) into subjection, and extorting allegiance from millions of people at the cannon's mouth, is utterly chimerical. True, it is in the power of the North to deluge her soil with blood, and inflict upon her the most terrible sufferings; but not to conquer her spirit, or change her determination.

What, then, ought to be done? The people of the North should recognize the fact that THE UNION IS DISSOLVED, and act accordingly. They should see, in the madness of the South, the hand of God, liberating them from "a covenant with death and an agreement with hell," made in a time of terrible peril, and without a conception of its inevitable consequences, and which has corrupted their morals, poisoned their religion, petrified their humanity as towards the millions in bondage, tarnished their character, harassed their peace, burdened them with taxation, shackled their prosperity, and brought them into abject vassalage. . . .

Now, then, let there be a CONVENTION OF THE FREE STATES called to organize an independent government on free and just principles; and let them say to the slave States—"Though you are without excuse for your treasonable conduct, depart in peace! Though you have laid piratical hands upon property not your own, we surrender it all in the spirit of magnanimity! And if nothing but the possession of the Capitol will appease you, take even that, without a struggle! Let the line be drawn between us where free institutions end and slave institutions begin! Organize your own confederacy, if you will, based on violence, tyranny, and blood, and relieve us from all responsibility for your evil course!"

VIEWPOINT 4

"Peaceable separation leads as surely to war as night follows day."

The Northern States Should Not Let the Southern States Secede

Indianapolis Daily Journal and *Peoria Daily Transcript*

By February 1, 1861, seven southern states had seceded from the Union: South Carolina, Mississippi, Florida, Alabama, Georgia, Louisiana, and Texas. All cited interference from the North with their "institutions" as reason for withdrawing from the Union. As tensions mounted and the nation wondered what Abraham Lincoln would do once he took office on March 4, some political leaders and newspaper editorialists argued that the Southern states should be allowed to secede—that war was a worse alternative than "peaceable secession."

The following viewpoint consists of two newspaper editorials that argue that peaceful secession is no longer an option. Part I is from the *Indianapolis Daily Journal*, a newspaper edited by J. M. Tilford that had endorsed Abraham Lincoln in the 1860 presidential election. Ironically, an earlier editorial published on December 22, 1860, had responded to South Carolina's secession from the Union on December 20 by arguing that the country was better off without South Carolina, and that war would be "a thousand times worse evil than the loss of a State, or a dozen States, that hate us." However, in the January 17, 1861, editorial reprinted below, the newspaper argues that the actions of the Southern states, including open defiance of the federal government and the seizure of federal property including Fort Moultrie in South Carolina, leave the rest of the country no honorable alternative other

Editorials in the January 17, 1861, *Indianapolis Daily Journal* and the February 22, 1861, *Peoria (Ill.) Daily Transcript*. Reprinted from *Northern Editorials on Secession*, edited by Howard C. Perkins, ©1942 by the American Historical Association.

than to fight to preserve the Union.

The second part of the viewpoint is an editorial that appeared on February 22, 1861, in the *Peoria Daily Transcript*, an Illinois newspaper that had supported Lincoln in the presidential race. Probably the work of editors Enoch Emery and/or Edward Andrews, the essay considers four alternatives proposed for Northern states facing the secession crisis. The editors argue that peaceable separation is now impossible, and that the North will undoubtedly be victorious if war comes.

I

There was a time before South Carolina had placed herself in open hostility to the Union, when we, and we believe a large majority of the North, would have consented to part with her, if she had consulted the other States, and requested permission to try a peaceful experiment as a separate nation. Her turbulence, and avowed maintenance of doctrines at war with the existence of the nation, made her, at the best, a useless member of the confederacy, and very many would have been glad to give her a chance to test the wisdom of her theories in a solitary existence. So with those States that sympathized with her, and were preparing to follow in her lead. But the case *now* is widely and fearfully changed. These States do not ask, or care to consult their associates, and learn whether it may not be possible to arrange our difficulties so as to move on in harmony as heretofore. They have put it out of our power to *consent* to anything.—They have met us, not with a request for peaceful consultation, but with war. If we concede their demands now it is the surrender of a nation *conquered* by rebel members. If we make no effort to resist the wrong we submit at once to disunion and national degradation. There is no course left, either for honor or patriotism, but to reclaim by the strong hand, if it must be so, all that the seceding States have taken, enforce the laws, and learn the traitors the wisdom of the maxim that it takes two to make a bargain.—All questions of expediency were thrust out of reach by the act which took Fort Moultrie as a hostile fortress, and hauled down the national flag as a sign of the conquest.—They have all been decided without our help. We have had no opportunity to say a word.—The seceding States have raised the issue, argued it to their own satisfaction, and decided it by war. We have been left no alternative but to resist or submit. We deplore this state of things. We had earnestly hoped that the Gulf States would give all shades of sen-

111

timent a fair opportunity of expression in the election of their Conventions, discuss their grievances calmly, request a consultation with the nation, and if they firmly and deliberately refused to abide in the Union as it is, we were willing to let them drop out, still holding our government unchanged over ourselves. In this way it *was* possible to get rid of the rebellious States, by simply diminishing, instead of dissolving the Union, which the London *Times* says is impossible. It is now, but it was not, and need not have been, if the seceding States had been willing to meet the Union fairly and come to an understanding.—Such a course would have been in accordance with the enlightenment of the age, the dictates of Christianity, and the best interests of both sections. But the hope of such an adjustment is all past, at least till the seceding States restore the government property, submit to the laws, and return to their former position of peaceful members of the Union. *There can be no conciliation with them till they do.* The government must be preserved. It is ours as well as theirs, and when they attempt to overturn it by force, we must preserve it by force. A government kicked aside at the will of any State, is nothing. The right of secession would make the government a mere accident, subsisting because thirty or forty members happened to agree in regard to it. We insist that our government is neither an accident or a trifle. It is the best yet devised by the wit of man, and is worth a dozen wars to keep. And we mean to keep it. To allow a State to rebel against it, and give way to the rebellion, is to consent to its destruction. We cannot claim that it exists even for those still remaining in it, when it is set at naught and defied by any other member. It must be whole or it cannot be at all. The people may let a member out of it, but no member can break it down to get out without breaking it to pieces. We are therefore for the most determined measures of resistance to the rebellion in the Gulf States. We insist that the Union shall be preserved till those who made it shall consent to change it. No refractory State or combination of traitors must be permitted to peril it in the pursuit of insane vengeance or impracticable theories. And if their madness leads them to open war let them suffer the doom of traitors.

II

When men get into a difficulty the great question is to get out. The people of the United States are in the midst of a great national difficulty. Let us cast aside the question how we came in it, who is to blame in the matter, and address ourselves to the question how we shall get out. If our dwelling were on fire we would not spend our time running about to ascertain through whose culpability or carelessness it occurred, but we would go at once to work to quell the conflagration.

Several methods have been proposed for the settlement of our national troubles, which we propose now to consider. They are, 1st, Compromise, 2d, Peaceable Separation, 3d, Masterly Inactivity, 4th, Enforcement of the Laws.

The first method, that of compromise in the manner proposed in Congress (amendment to the Constitution of the United States [forbidding Congress from abolishing slavery in the States]) is, in the present condition of the country, wholly out of the question. We need not discuss whether such a course is proper or improper. It is

---

Secession Means War

John Sherman was a public official who represented the state of Ohio in both the House of Representatives and the Senate. He was the brother of William T. Sherman, who was to become one of the Union's leading generals. On December 22, 1860, while in Washington, D.C., as Congress was debating compromise measures that sought to prevent war, he wrote a letter to a group of Philadelphia residents (he later sent a copy to his brother). In this excerpt, Sherman argues that peaceably letting states secede is not a viable option for the country.

It becomes the people of the United States seriously to consider whether the government shall be arrested in the execution of its undisputed powers by the citizens of one or more states, or whether we shall test the power of the government to defend itself against dissolution. Can a separation take place without war? If so, where will be the line? Who shall possess this magnificent capital, with all its evidences of progress and civilization? Shall the mouth of the Mississippi be separated from its sources? Who shall possess the territories? Suppose these difficulties to be overcome; suppose that in peace we should huckster and divide up our nationality, our flag, our history, all the recollections of the past; suppose all these difficulties overcome, how can two rival republics, of the same race of men, divided only by a line or a river for thousands of miles, with all the present difficulties aggravated by separation, avoid forays, disputes, and war? How can we travel our future march of progress in Mexico, or on the high seas, or on the Pacific slope, without collision? It is impossible. To peaceably accomplish such results, we must change the nature of man.

Disunion is war! God knows, I do not threaten it, for I will seek to prevent it in every way possible. I speak but the logic of facts, which we should not conceal from each other. It is either hostilities between the government and the seceding states; or, if separation is yielded peaceably, it is a war of factions—a rivalry of insignificant communities, hating each other, and contemned by the civilized world. If war results, what a war it will be! Contemplate the North and South in hostile array against each other. If these sections do not know each other *now*, they will *then*.

113

sufficient that it is impossible. The Constitution of the United States requires the concurrence of three-fourths of the States to give force and vitality to any amendment. To do this, twenty-six States must concur. Seven have left the Union and will not vote. At least a half dozen of the remaining States will vote down any amendment that may be proposed. The border States will vote them down if they do not concede their demands, and certain Northern States will vote them down if they do. Any compromise not incorporated into the Constitution will not be accepted by the South. Any compromise not incorporated into the Constitution in the manner proposed by that instrument will not be accepted by the North. To incorporate amendments in the manner provided we have shown to be impossible, and that puts an end to the first method.

Separation and War

Peaceable separation is proposed by those who perceive that compromise is impolitic or impossible, and who hope by it to avoid war. But peaceable separation leads as surely to war as night follows day. The United States would not allow Great Britain, France, Russia, nor all Europe combined, to maltreat citizens as our citizens are maltreated daily at the South, without war.—Maritime and border disputes would arise which would plunge us into strife before six months had passed over the heads of the two confederacies. Escape of slaves and attempted recapture and reprisals would bring the people to blows without any action of the two governments. We fought Great Britain in 1812 for one–half the provocation that would be given us. No dread of civil war would stay our hands. The Southern Confederacy would be a foreign nation. We would not have to fight it for once only, but unless we absolutely conquored it, we should have to fight it forever. It would be hostile in interests, hostile in institutions, hostile in everything.

The third method is that of "masterly inactivity," the policy inaugurated by our present imbecile executive [President James Buchanan]. Such a course leads to national debasement, anarchy and ruin. It is a confession that no power exists in the government for the enforcement of the laws, or that we are too cowardly to enforce them. Our revenue would be cut off, for if the South refuse to pay duties the North will refuse likewise. We could not raise money by taxation, for we can no more collect taxes than we can collect revenue.

The fourth method is enforcement of the laws. This is the only method that indicates the least chance of success. People say we have no right to coerce a State. We say a State has no right to contravene the Constitution. The Constitution of the United States, is in certain particulars supreme, and is clothed with full power to

114

enforce those particulars. Every law passed by a State or the people of a State, in contravention of the Constitution is null and void. Any attempt to enforce those pretended laws is without legal sanction, and is as much a crime to be punished as counterfeiting, smuggling, and piracy. The question is,—Is secession right or wrong, lawful or unlawful? If not right and lawful, it ought to be put down. If we attempt to put it down, what are the chances of success? It will be the government against a faction. It will be a nation of seventy years['] growth, fighting for the supremacy of the principles which brought it into being, against a wicked combination to defeat those principles. It will be might and right against weakness and wickedness. It will be the memory of the heroes of the revolution, against the dogmas of [John C.] Calhoun, the thievings of [John B.] Floyd, and perjuries of those who plotted to overturn the Constitution while their oaths to support it were yet warm on their lips. It will be a people with a navy against a people without a navy. It will be a people with the sympathy of the civilized world in its favor, against a people without that sympathy. It will be a people connected by treaties with other governments, against a people cut off from all communication with the rest of mankind. It will be numbers against numbers as four to one, and that one hampered by a servile population ready, it knows not how soon, to rise and cut its throat. It will be wealth ready to be poured into the lap of the Government, against oppressive taxation and forced loans. It will be all the holy traditions[,] treasured songs, brave speeches and glories of the past, the Declaration of Independence, the love of freedom, the hopes of the future, the preservation of free speech and a free press, against the eruption of a plague spot, and the rebellion of a petty oligarchy who would "rather reign in hell than serve in Heaven." Under these circumstances who doubts our success? We have the right and the might, and there is no such word as fail.

VIEWPOINT 5

"The constitutional compact has been deliberately broken and disregarded by the nonslaveholding states; and . . . South Carolina is released from her obligation."

Secession Is Justified

South Carolina Declaration

South Carolina's state legislature was in session when news arrived of Abraham Lincoln's election as president, and legislators immediately called for a special secession convention. On December 20, 1860, by unanimous convention vote, the state became the first to secede from the United States. It presented its reasons for seceding in the form of a declaration, a document parallel in some respects to America's 1776 Declaration of Independence from Great Britain—which this declaration mentions several times.

The legal arguments used in the declaration closely follow those made by former South Carolina senator John C. Calhoun a decade earlier when debating the Compromise of 1850. The secession convention asserts that the United States of America is in fact a confederation of sovereign states, with each state the final arbiter of its own constitutional rights. If other states have violated those rights, or have otherwise failed to fulfill their obligations under the U.S. Constitution, that compact of Union is made null and void, leaving South Carolina and other states free to withdraw from it. The declaration lists South Carolina's grievances against the Northern states, including the failure to enforce fugitive slave laws as called for by the Constitution, antislavery "agitation," and restricting slaveowners' property rights by banning slavery in the western territories. The Northern states, by contravening the Constitution, have thus left South Carolina with no honorable choice but to secede. The convention concludes by declaring that "the Union heretofore existing between this state and the other states of North America is dissolved."

From Document 3 of the supplement to *The Rebellion Record: A Diary of American Events, with Documents, Narratives, Illustrative Incidents, Poetry, etc., etc.*, edited by Frank Moore. New York: G.P. Putnam, 1864.

The people of the state of South Carolina, in convention assembled, on the 2nd day of April, A.D. 1852, declared that the frequent violations of the Constitution of the United States by the federal government, and its encroachments upon the reserved rights of the states, fully justified this state in their withdrawal from the federal Union; but in deference to the opinions and wishes of the other slaveholding states, she forbore at that time to exercise this right. Since that time, these encroachments have continued to increase, and further forbearance ceases to be a virtue.

And, now, the state of South Carolina, having resumed her separate and equal place among nations, deems it due to herself, to the remaining United States of America, and to the nations of the world, that she should declare the immediate causes which have led to this act.

The Right of Self-Government

In the year 1765, that portion of the British empire embracing Great Britain undertook to make laws for the government of that portion composed of the thirteen American colonies. A struggle for the right of self-government ensued, which resulted, on the 4th of July, 1776, in a Declaration, by the colonies, "that they are, and of right ought to be, *free and independent states;* and that, as free and independent states, they have full power to levy war, conclude peace, contract alliances, establish commerce, and to do all other acts and things which independent states may of right do."

They further solemnly declared that whenever any "form of government becomes destructive of the ends for which it was established, it is the right of the people to alter or abolish it, and to institute a new government." Deeming the government of Great Britain to have become destructive of these ends, they declared that the colonies "are absolved from all allegiance to the British Crown, and that all political connection between them and the state of Great Britain is, and ought to be, totally dissolved."

In pursuance of this Declaration of Independence, each of the thirteen states proceeded to exercise its separate sovereignty; adopted for itself a constitution, and appointed officers for the administration of government in all its departments—Legislative, Executive, and Judicial. For purposes of defense, they united their arms and their counsels, and, in 1778, they entered into a league known as the Articles of Confederation, whereby they agreed to entrust the administration of their external relations to a common agent, known as the Congress of the United States, expressly declaring, in the 1st Article, "that each state retains its sovereignty, freedom, and independence, and every power, jurisdiction, and right which is not, by this Confederation, expressly delegated to the United States in Congress assembled."

The Right to Change Governments

Representatives of the seceded states elected Jefferson Davis president of the Confederate States of America in February 1861. On February 18 Davis delivered his inaugural address, in which he reiterated the rights of the states to leave the Union.

Our present condition, achieved in a manner unprecedented in the history of nations, illustrates the American idea that governments rest upon the consent of the governed, and that it is the right of the people to alter or abolish governments whenever they become destructive to the ends for which they were established. The declared compact of the Union from which we have withdrawn was to establish justice, insure domestic tranquillity, provide for the common defense, promote the general welfare, and secure the blessings of liberty to ourselves and our posterity; and when, in the judgment of the sovereign states now composing this Confederacy, it has been perverted from the purposes for which it was ordained, and ceased to answer the ends for which it was established, a peaceful appeal to the ballot box declared that, so far as they are concerned, the government created by that compact should cease to exist.

In this they merely asserted the right which the Declaration of Independence of 1776 defined to be "inalienable." Of the time and occasion of its exercise, they, as sovereigns, were the final judges, each for itself. The impartial, enlightened verdict of mankind will vindicate the rectitude of our conduct; and He who knows the hearts of men will judge of the sincerity with which we labored to preserve the government of our fathers in its spirit.

Under this Confederation, the War of the Revolution was carried on; and on the 3rd of September, 1783, the contest ended, and a definite treaty was signed by Great Britain, in which she acknowledged the independence of the colonies in the following terms:

Article I. His Britannic Majesty acknowledges the said United States, viz.: New Hampshire, Massachusetts Bay, Rhode Island and Providence Plantations, Connecticut, New York, New Jersey, Pennsylvania, Delaware, Maryland, Virginia, North Carolina, South Carolina, and Georgia, to be *free, sovereign, and independent states;* that he treats with them as such; and, for himself, his heirs, and successors, relinquishes all claims to the government, propriety, and territorial rights of the same and every part thereof.

Thus were established the two great principles asserted by the colonies, namely, the right of a state to govern itself; and the right of a people to abolish a government when it becomes destructive of the ends for which it was instituted. And concurrent with the establishment of these principles was the fact that each colony became and was recognized by the mother country as a *free, sovereign, and independent state.*

The Constitution

In 1787, deputies were appointed by the states to revise the Articles of Confederation; and on Sept. 17, 1787, these deputies recommended, for the adoption of the states, the Articles of Union, known as the Constitution of the United States.

The parties to whom this Constitution was submitted were the several sovereign states; they were to agree or disagree, and when nine of them agreed, the compact was to take effect among those concurring; and the general government, as the common agent, was then to be invested with their authority.

If only nine of the thirteen states had concurred, the other four would have remained as they then were—separate, sovereign states, independent of any of the provisions of the Constitution. In fact, two of the states did not accede to the Constitution until long after it had gone into operation among the other eleven; and during that interval, they each exercised the functions of an independent nation.

By this Constitution, certain duties were imposed upon the several states, and the exercise of certain of their powers was restrained, which necessarily impelled their continued existence as sovereign states. But, to remove all doubt, an amendment was added which declared that the powers not delegated to the United States by the Constitution, nor prohibited by it to the states, are reserved to the states respectively, or to the people. On the 23rd of May, 1788, South Carolina, by a convention of her people, passed an ordinance assenting to this Constitution, and afterward altered her own constitution to conform herself to the obligations she had undertaken.

Thus was established, by compact between the states, a government with defined objects and powers, limited to the express words of the grant. This limitation left the whole remaining mass of power subject to the clause reserving it to the states or the people, and rendered unnecessary any specification of reserved rights. We hold that the government thus established is subject to the two great principles asserted in the Declaration of Independence; and we hold further that the mode of its formation subjects it to a third fundamental principle, namely, the law of compact. We maintain that in every compact between two or more parties, the obligation is mutual; that the failure of one of the contracting parties to perform a material part of the agreement en-

119

tirely releases the obligation of the other; and that, where no arbiter is provided, each party is remitted to his own judgment to determine the fact of failure, with all its consequences.

The People Must Choose

James Chesnut Jr., husband of noted Civil War diarist Mary Chesnut, was a United States senator from South Carolina. In a speech on November 5, 1860, recorded by the Charleston Courier, *he speaks out against submission to the "Black Republican President," Abraham Lincoln, and the "Black Republican Congress" (a term he uses despite the fact the Republicans were unable to secure a congressional majority in the 1860 elections).*

But the question now was, Would the South submit to a Black Republican President and a Black Republican Congress, which will claim the right to construe the Constitution of the country and administer the Government in their own hands, not by the law of the instrument itself, nor by that of the fathers of the country, nor by the practices of those who administered seventy years ago, but by rules drawn from their own blind consciences and crazy brains. They call us inferiors, semi-civilized barbarians, and claim the right to possess our lands, and give them to the destitute of the Old World and the profligates of this. They claim the dogmas of the Declaration of Independence as part of the Constitution, and that it is their right and duty to so administer the Government as to give full effect to them. The people now must choose whether they would be governed by enemies, or govern themselves.

In the present case, the fact is established with certainty. We assert that fourteen of the states have deliberately refused for years past to fulfill their constitutional obligations, and we refer to their own statutes for the proof.

The Fugitive Slave Provision

The Constitution of the United States, in its 4th Article, provides as follows: "No person held to service or labor in one state, under the laws thereof, escaping into another shall, in consequence of any law or regulation therein, be discharged from such service or labor, but shall be delivered up, on claim of the party to whom such service or labor may be due."

This stipulation was so material to the compact that without it that compact would not have been made. The greater number of the contracting parties held slaves, and they had previously evinced their estimate of the value of such a stipulation by making it a condition in the ordinance for the government of the territory ceded by Virginia, which obligations, and the laws of the general government, have ceased to effect the objects of the Constitution. The states of Maine, New Hampshire, Vermont, Massachusetts, Connecticut, Rhode Island, New York, Pennsylvania, Illinois, Indiana, Michigan, Wisconsin, and Iowa have enacted laws which either nullify the acts of Congress or render useless any attempt to execute them. In many of these states the fugitive is discharged from the service of labor claimed, and in none of them has the state government complied with the stipulation made in the Constitution.

The state of New Jersey, at an early day, passed a law in conformity with her constitutional obligation; but the current of antislavery feeling has led her more recently to enact laws which render inoperative the remedies provided by her own laws and by the laws of Congress. In the state of New York even the right of transit for a slave has been denied by her tribunals; and the states of Ohio and Iowa have refused to surrender to justice fugitives charged with murder and with inciting servile insurrection in the state of Virginia. Thus the constitutional compact has been deliberately broken and disregarded by the nonslaveholding states; and the consequence follows that South Carolina is released from her obligation.

The ends for which this Constitution was framed are declared by itself to be "to form a more perfect union, to establish justice, insure domestic tranquillity, provide for the common defense, promote the general welfare, and secure the blessings of liberty to ourselves and our posterity." These ends it endeavored to accomplish by a federal government in which each state was recognized as an equal and had separate control over its own institutions. The right of property in slaves was recognized by giving to free persons distinct political rights; by giving them the right to represent, and burdening them with direct taxes for, three-fifths of their slaves; by authorizing the importation of slaves for twenty years; and by stipulating for the rendition of fugitives from labor.

Antislavery Agitation

We affirm that these ends for which this government was instituted have been defeated, and the government itself has been destructive of them by the action of the nonslaveholding states. Those states have assumed the right of deciding upon the propriety of our domestic institutions; and have denied the rights of property established in fifteen of the states and recognized by the Constitution. They have denounced as sinful the institution of slavery; they have permitted the open establishment among them of societies, whose avowed object is to disturb the peace of and eloign the property of the citizens of other states. They have encouraged and assisted thousands of our slaves to leave their homes; and, those who remain, have been incited by emissaries, books, and pictures to servile insurrection.

For twenty-five years this agitation has been steadily increasing, until it has now secured to its aid the power of the common government. Observing the *forms* of the Constitution, a sectional party has found, within that article establishing the Executive Department, the means of subverting the Constitution itself. A geographical line has been drawn across the Union, and all the states north of that line have united in the election of a man to the high office of President of the United States whose opinions and purposes are hostile to slavery. He is to be entrusted with the administration of the common government, because he has declared that "Government cannot endure permanently half slave, half free," and that the public mind must rest in the belief that slavery is in the course of ultimate extinction.

This sectional combination for the subversion of the Constitution has been aided, in some of the states, by elevating to citizenship persons who, by the supreme law of the land, are incapable of becoming citizens; and their votes have been used to inaugurate a new policy, hostile to the South and destructive of its peace and safety.

On the 4th of March next this party will take possession of the government. It has announced that the South shall be excluded from the common territory, that the judicial tribunal shall be made sectional, and that a war must be waged against slavery until it shall cease throughout the United States.

The guarantees of the Constitution will then no longer exist; the equal rights of the states will be lost. The slaveholding states will no longer have the power of self-government or self-protection, and the federal government will have become their enemy.

Sectional interest and animosity will deepen the irritation; and all hope of remedy is rendered vain by the fact that the public opinion at the North has invested a great political error with the sanctions of a more erroneous religious belief.

We, therefore, the people of South Carolina, by our delegates in convention assembled, appealing to the Supreme Judge of the world for the rectitude of our intentions, have solemnly declared that the Union heretofore existing between this state and the other states of North America is dissolved; and that the state of South Carolina has resumed her position among the nations of the world, as [a] separate and independent state, with full power to levy war, conclude peace, contract alliances, establish commerce, and to do all other acts and things which independent states may of right do.

VIEWPOINT 6

"No state, upon its own mere motion, can lawfully get out of the Union."

Secession Is Not Justified

Abraham Lincoln (1809-1865)

In the four months between Abraham Lincoln's election as president on November 6, 1860, and his inauguration on March 4, 1861, momentous events rocked the nation. South Carolina seceded from the Union on December 20, 1860, and was shortly joined by Mississippi, Florida, Alabama, Georgia, Louisiana, and Texas. On February 4, 1861, representatives from these states (except Texas) met in Montgomery, Alabama, to form a new government—the Confederate States of America. They wrote a new constitution and elected Jefferson Davis as president. Southern politicians resigned from Congress, and Southern states seized federal property. Lame-duck U.S. president James Buchanan hesitated to act, arguing that the Constitution gave the states no legal right to secede, but that Congress and the president had no power under the Constitution to prevent them. States in the upper South—Virginia, North Carolina, and Maryland—as well as states farther west, including Kentucky, Missouri, and Tennessee, were deeply divided over whether to join the Confederacy. Various settlement proposals were discussed in Congress and elsewhere. Most foundered on the issue of federal protection of slavery in the western territories, something both sides refused to compromise on.

It was against this backdrop that Lincoln was inaugurated, took the presidential oath "to preserve, protect, and defend the Constitution of the United States," and gave the address reprinted here before a relatively small crowd of 10,000 in Washington, D.C. After writing a first draft in Springfield, Illinois, in January 1861,

Abraham Lincoln, First Inaugural Address. Reprinted from vol. 6 of *A Compilation of the Messages and Papers of the Presidents, 1798-1897*, edited by James D. Richardson. Washington, DC, 1896-1899.

Lincoln had rewritten and reworked the speech many times over. In his address the new president seeks to placate the South by pledging not to interfere with slavery in the Southern states, while promising to enforce fugitive slave laws in the Northern states. But he also refutes the legal arguments found in the secession declarations of South Carolina and other states, arguing that "the union of these states is perpetual" and that ordinances of secession by individual states are meaningless. He pledges, without specifying what measures or force he would use, to enforce the authority of the nation in all the states. He concludes his address with a plea for peace, asserting that "the momentous issue of civil war" is in the hands of those who seek to secede and destroy the Union.

Poet and Lincoln biographer Carl Sandburg wrote that Lincoln's first inaugural address "was the most widely read and closely scrutinized utterance that had ever come from an American President." Reactions to it split largely on sectional lines, with Northerners viewing it as conciliatory, Southerners as an act of war on the Confederacy. Six weeks later, Confederate guns fired on Fort Sumter, and the war came.

Fellow Citizens of the United States:

In compliance with a custom as old as the government itself, I appear before you to address you briefly and to take, in your presence, the oath prescribed by the Constitution of the United States to be taken by the President "before he enters on the execution of his office."

I do not consider it necessary, at present, for me to discuss those matters of administration about which there is no special anxiety or excitement. Apprehension seems to exist among the people of the Southern states that, by the accession of a Republican administration, their property and their peace and personal security are to be endangered. There has never been any reasonable cause for such apprehension. Indeed, the most ample evidence to the contrary has all the while existed and been open to their inspection. It is found in nearly all the published speeches of him who now addresses you.

No Intent to Abolish Slavery

I do but quote from one of those speeches when I declare that "I have no purpose, directly or indirectly, to interfere with the institution of slavery in the states where it exists. I believe I have no lawful right to do so, and I have no inclination to do so." Those who nominated and elected me did so with full knowledge that I had made this and many similar declarations, and had never recanted them. And, more than this, they placed in the platform, for my acceptance, and as a law to themselves and to me, the clear and emphatic resolution which I now read:

> *Resolved*, that the maintenance inviolate of the rights of the states, and especially the right of each state, to order and control its own domestic institutions according to its own judgment exclusively is essential to that balance of power on which the perfection and endurance of our political fabric depend; and we denounce the lawless invasion by armed force of the soil of any state or territory, no matter under what pretext, as among the gravest of crimes.

I now reiterate these sentiments; and in doing so, I only press upon the public attention the most conclusive evidence, of which the case is susceptible, that the property, peace, and security of no section are to be in any way endangered by the now incoming administration. I add, too, that all the protection which, consistently with the Constitution and the laws, can be given will be cheerfully given to all the states when lawfully demanded, for whatever cause—as cheerfully to one section as to another.

There is much controversy about the delivering up of fugitives from service or labor. The clause I now read is as plainly written in the Constitution as any other of its provisions:

> No person held to service or labor in one state, under the laws thereof, escaping into another, shall, in consequence of any law or regulation therein, be discharged from such service or labor, but shall be delivered up on claim of the party to whom such service or labor may be due.

It is scarcely questioned that this provision was intended by those who made it for the reclaiming of what we call fugitive slaves; and the intention of the lawgiver is the law.

All members of Congress swear their support to the whole Constitution—to this provision as much as to any other. To the proposition, then, that slaves whose cases come within the terms of this clause "shall be delivered up," their oaths are unanimous. Now, if they would make the effort in good temper, could they not, with nearly equal unanimity, frame and pass a law by means of which to keep good that unanimous oath?

There is some difference of opinion whether this clause should be enforced by national or by the state authority; but surely that difference is not a very material one. If the slave is to be surrendered, it can be of but little consequence to him or to others by which authority it is done. And should anyone, in any case, be content that his oath shall go unkept on a merely unsubstantial controversy as to *how* it shall be kept?

Again, in any law upon this subject, ought not all the safeguards of liberty known in civilized and humane jurisprudence to be introduced, so that a freeman be not, in any case, surrendered as a slave? And might it not be well, at the same time, to provide by law for the enforcement of that clause in the Constitution which guarantees that "the citizen of each state shall be entitled to all privileges and immunities of citizens in the several states"?

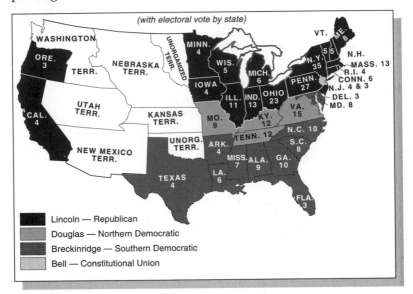

Abraham Lincoln had won the four-way presidential race of 1860 by capturing 39 percent of the vote and winning the electoral votes of all the nonslaveholding states. He received little support in the South, which was mostly carried by John C. Breckinridge (although Breckinridge received fewer popular votes than the combined total of Stephen A. Douglas and John Bell, both strong Unionists). Opponents of Lincoln warned that his election would divide the country, and by the time of his inauguration on March 4, 1861, the states of South Carolina, Mississippi, Florida, Alabama, Georgia, Louisiana, and Texas had seceded and formed the Confederacy.

I take the official oath today with no mental reservations and with no purpose to construe the Constitution or laws by any hypercritical rules. And while I do not choose now to specify particular acts of Congress as proper to be enforced, I do suggest that it will be much safer for all, both in official and private stations, to conform to and abide by all those acts which stand unrepealed than to violate any of them, trusting to find impunity in having them held to be unconstitutional.

It is seventy-two years since the first inauguration of a President under our national Constitution. During that period fifteen different and greatly distinguished citizens have, in succession, administered the executive branch of the government. They have conducted it through many perils, and generally with great success. Yet, with all this scope of precedent, I now enter upon the same task for the brief constitutional term of four years under great and peculiar difficulties.

A disruption of the federal Union, heretofore only menaced, is now formidably attempted.

The Union Is Perpetual

I hold that, in contemplation of universal law and of the Constitution, the Union of these states is perpetual. Perpetuity is implied, if not expressed, in the fundamental law of all national governments. It is safe to assert that no government proper ever had a provision in its organic law for its own termination. Continue to execute all the express provisions of our national Constitution, and the Union will endure forever—it being impossible to destroy it except by some action not provided for in the instrument itself.

Again, if the United States be not a government proper, but an association of states in the nature of contract merely, can it, as a contract, be peaceably unmade by less than all the parties who made it? One party to a contract may violate it—break it, so to speak—but does it not require all to lawfully rescind it? Descending from these general principles, we find the proposition that in legal contemplation, the Union is perpetual, confirmed by the history of the Union itself.

The Union is much older than the Constitution. It was formed, in fact, by the Articles of Association in 1774. It was matured and continued by the Declaration of Independence in 1776. It was further matured, and the faith of all the then thirteen states expressedly plighted and engaged, that it should be perpetual by the Articles of Confederation of 1778. And finally, in 1787, one of the declared objects for ordaining and establishing the Constitution, was *"to form a more perfect Union."*

But if destruction of the Union by one or by a part only of the states be lawfully possible, the Union is *less* perfect than before the Constitution, having lost the vital element of perpetuity.

It follows from these views that no state, upon its own mere motion, can lawfully get out of the Union—that *resolves* and *ordinances* to that effect are legally void; and that acts of violence within any state or states against the authority of the United States are insurrectionary or revolutionary, according to circumstances.

I therefore consider that, in view of the Constitution and the laws, the Union is unbroken; and to the extent of my ability, I shall take care, as the Constitution itself expressly enjoins upon me, that the laws of the Union be faithfully executed in all the states. Doing this I deem to be only a simple duty on my part; and I shall perform it, so far as practicable, unless my rightful masters, the American people, shall withhold the requisite means or in some authoritative manner direct the contrary.

No Need for Violence

I trust this will not be regarded as a menace but only as the declared purpose of the Union that it *will* constitutionally defend and maintain itself. In doing this, there needs to be no bloodshed or violence; and there shall be none unless it be forced upon the national authority.

The power confided to me will be used to hold, occupy, and possess the property and places belonging to the government, and to collect the duties and imposts; but beyond what may be necessary for these objects, there will be no invasion—no using of force against or among the people anywhere.

Where hostility to the United States, in any interior locality, shall be so great and universal as to prevent competent resident citizens from holding the federal offices, there will be no attempt to force obnoxious strangers among the people for that object. While the strict legal right may exist in the government to enforce the exercise of these offices, the attempt to do so would be so irritating, and so nearly impracticable withal, that I deem it best to forego, for the time, the uses of such offices.

The mails, unless repelled, will continue to be furnished in all parts of the Union.

So far as possible, the people everywhere shall have that sense of perfect security which is most favorable to calm thought and reflection.

The course here indicated will be followed unless current events and experience shall show a modification or change to be proper; and in every case and exigency, my best discretion will be exercised, according to circumstances actually existing, and with a view and a hope of a peaceful solution of the national troubles, and the restoration of fraternal sympathies and affections.

That there are persons in one section or another who seek to destroy the Union at all events and are glad of any pretext to do it, I will neither affirm nor deny; but if there be such, I need address no word to them. To those, however, who really love the Union, may I not speak?

Before entering upon so grave a matter as the destruction of our national fabric, with all its benefits, its memories, and its hopes, would it not be wise to ascertain precisely why we do it? Will you hazard so desperate a step while there is any possibility that any portion of the ills you fly from have no real existence? Will you, while the certain ills you fly to are greater than all the real ones you fly from—will you risk the commission of so fearful a mistake?

A Southern Comment on Lincoln's Inaugural Address

In a March 9, 1861, editorial in the North Carolina Standard, *the editors interpret Lincoln's inaugural address to be conciliatory, and criticize those in South Carolina and other states who argue for the destruction of the Union.*

If Mr. Lincoln were mad enough to attempt to subjugate the Southern States, or even if he were disposed to do so—as his Inaugural shows he is not—he has no army at his command. He might spare a thousand troops from the forts and frontiers, but what could these do against the armies of the fifteen slaveholding States? Then he has no money. The Treasury is empty. Then he has no authority for raising troops, even if he had money to pay them with. The "force bill" so-called, was defeated in the House of Representatives. What then? He is powerless. He is not only powerless at present, but the tone of his Inaugural shows that he is alarmed in view of the calamities that impend. Will he be stronger in future? We do not believe he will.—His party is already demoralized, and in addition to this, the great body of the Northern people will never consent to an aggressive war on the South. . . .

We approve portions of [his Inaugural], and we disapprove other portions. *It is not a war message.* It is not, strictly speaking, a Black Republican message; for while he recognizes slavery in the States as perpetual, and as never to be interfered with in any way by the abolitionists, he deliberately refrains from pressing the main principle in his platform, to wit, the exclusion of the South from all the Territories of the Union. It is not unfriendly to the South. It deprecates war, and bloodshed, and it pleads for the Union. That any portion of it will be approved by the Disunionists we have no idea. If it had breathed violence and war—if it had claimed the government for the North exclusively, and had threatened the South with subjugation, the Disunionists would have shouted for joy, as they did in Charleston when they learned that Lincoln was elected, for they would then have been sure of the attainment of their darling purpose, the permanent and final disruption of the Union.

All profess to be content in the Union if all constitutional rights can be maintained. Is it true, then, that any right plainly written in the Constitution has been denied? I think not. Happily, the human mind is so constituted that no party can reach to the audacity of doing this. Think, if you can, of a single instance in which a plainly written provision of the Constitution has ever been denied. If, by the mere force of numbers, a majority should deprive a minority of any clearly written constitutional right, it might, in a moral point of view, justify revolution—certainly would, if such right were a vital one. But such is not our case.

All the vital rights of minorities and of individuals are so plainly assured to them by affirmations and negations, guarantees and prohibitions, in the Constitution that controversies never arise concerning them. But no organic law can ever be framed with a provision specifically applicable to every question which may occur in practical administration. No foresight can anticipate nor any document of reasonable length contain express provisions for all possible questions. Shall fugitives from labor be surrendered by national or by state authority? The Constitution does not expressly say. *May* Congress prohibit slavery in the territories? The Constitution does not expressly say. *Must* Congress protect slavery in the territories? The Constitution does not expressly say.

Secession Is Anarchy

From questions of this class spring all our constitutional controversies, and we divide upon them into majorities and minorities. If the minority will not acquiesce, the majority must, or the government must cease. There is no other alternative; for continuing the government is acquiescence on one side or the other. If a minority, in such case, will secede rather than acquiesce, they make a precedent which in turn will divide and ruin them; for a minority of their own will secede from them whenever a majority refuses to be controlled by such minority.

For instance, why may not any portion of a new confederacy, a year or two hence, arbitrarily secede again, precisely as portions of the present Union now claim to secede from it? All who cherish disunion sentiments are now being educated to the exact temper of doing this. Is there such perfect identity of interests among the states to compose a new Union as to produce harmony only and prevent renewed secession?

Plainly, the central idea of secession is the essence of anarchy. A majority, held in restraint by constitutional checks and limitations, and always changing easily with deliberate changes of popular opinions and sentiments, is the only true sovereign of a free people. Whoever rejects it does of necessity fly to anarchy or to despotism. Unanimity is impossible. The rule of a minority, as a permanent arrangement, is wholly inadmissible; so that, rejecting the majority principle, anarchy or despotism in some form is all that is left.

I do not forget the position assumed by some, that constitutional questions are to be decided by the Supreme Court; nor do I deny that such decisions must be binding in any case upon the parties to a suit as to the object of that suit, while they are also entitled to very high respect and consideration, in all parallel cases, by all other departments of the government. And while it is obviously possible that such decision may be erroneous in any given case, still the evil effect following it, being limited to that particular case, with the chance that it may be overruled and never become a precedent for other cases, can better be borne than could the evils of a different practice.

At the same time, the candid citizen must confess that if the policy of the government, upon vital questions affecting the whole people, is to be irrevocably fixed by decisions of the Supreme Court, the instant they are made, in ordinary litigation between parties in personal actions, the people will have ceased to be their own rulers, having, to that extent, practically resigned their government into the hands of that eminent tribunal.

Nor is there, in this view, any assault upon the Court or the judges. It is a duty from which they may not shrink to decide cases properly brought before them; and it is no fault of theirs if others seek to turn their decisions to political purposes.

One section of our country believes slavery is *right* and ought to be extended, while the other believes it is *wrong* and ought not to be extended. This is the only substantial dispute. The fugitive slave clause of the Constitution and the law for the suppression of the foreign slave trade are each as well enforced, perhaps, as any law can ever be in a community where the moral sense of the people imperfectly supports the law itself. The great body of the people abide by the dry legal obligation in both cases, and a few break over in each. This, I think, cannot be perfectly cured; and it would be worse in both cases *after* the separation of the sections than before. The foreign slave trade, now imperfectly suppressed, would be ultimately revived without restriction in one section; while fugitive slaves, now only partially surrendered, would not be surrendered at all by the other.

We Cannot Separate

Physically speaking, we cannot separate. We cannot remove our respective sections from each other, nor build an impassable wall between them. A husband and wife may be divorced, and go out of the presence and beyond the reach of each other, but the different parts of our country cannot do this. They cannot but remain face to face; and intercourse, either amicable or hostile, must continue between them. Is it possible, then, to make that intercourse more advantageous or more satisfactory *after* separation than *before?* Can aliens make treaties easier than friends can make laws? Can treaties be more faithfully enforced between aliens than laws can among friends? Suppose you go to war, you cannot fight always; and when, after much loss on both sides and no gain on either, you cease fighting, the identical old questions as to terms of intercourse are again upon you.

This country, with its institutions, belongs to the people who inhabit it. Whenever they shall grow weary of the existing government, they can exercise their *constitutional* right of amending it or their *revolutionary* right to dismember or overthrow it. I cannot be ignorant of the fact that many worthy and patriotic citizens are desirous of having the national Constitution amended. While I make no recommendation of amendments, I fully recognize the rightful authority of the people over the whole subject, to be exercised in either of the modes prescribed in the instrument itself; and I should, under existing circumstances, favor rather than oppose a fair opportunity being afforded the people to act upon it.

I will venture to add that, to me, the convention mode seems preferable, in that it allows amendments to originate with the people themselves, instead of only permitting them to take or reject propositions originated by others, not especially chosen for the purpose, and which might not be precisely such as they would wish to either accept or refuse. I understand a proposed amendment to the Constitution—which amendment, however, I have not seen—has passed Congress, to the effect that the federal government shall never interfere with the domestic institutions of the states, including that of persons held to service. To avoid misconstruction of what I have said, I depart from my purpose not to speak of particular amendments so far as to say that, holding such a provision to now be implied constitutional law, I have no objection to its being made express and irrevocable.

The chief magistrate derives all his authority from the people, and they have conferred none upon him to fix terms for their separation of the states. The people themselves can do this also if they choose; but the executive, as such, has nothing to do with it. His duty is to administer the present government, as it came to his hands, and to transmit it, unimpaired by him, to his successor. Why should there not be a patient confidence in the ultimate justice of the people? Is there any better or equal hope in the world? In our present differences, is either party without faith of being in the right?

If the Almighty Ruler of nations, with His eternal truth and justice, be on your side of the North, or on yours of the South, that truth and that justice will surely prevail, by the judgment of this great tribunal, the American people. By the frame of the government under which we live, this same people have wisely given their public servants but little power for mischief; and have, with equal wisdom, provided for the return of that little to their own hands at very short intervals. While the people retain their virtue and vigilance, no administration, by any extreme of wickedness or folly, can very seriously injure the government in the short space of four years.

My countrymen, one and all, think calmly and *well* upon this whole subject. Nothing valuable can be lost by taking time. If there be an object to *hurry* any of you, in hot haste, to a step which you would never take *deliberately*, that object will be frustrated by taking time; but no good object can be frustrated by it.

Such of you as are now dissatisfied still have the old Constitution unimpaired, and, on the sensitive point, the laws of your own framing under it; while the new administration will have no immediate power, if it would, to change either.

If it were admitted that you who are dissatisfied hold the right side in the dispute, there still is no single good reason for precipitate action. Intelligence, patriotism, Christianity, and a firm reliance on Him, who has never yet forsaken this favored land, are still competent to adjust, in the best way, all our present difficulty.

In *your* hands, my dissatisfied fellow countrymen, and not in *mine* is the momentous issue of civil war. The government will not assail *you*. You can have no conflict without being yourselves the aggressors. *You* have no oath registered in heaven to destroy the government, while *I* shall have the most solemn one to "preserve, protect, and defend" it.

Friends, Not Enemies

I am loathe to close. We are not enemies but friends. We must not be enemies. Though passion may have strained, it must not break our bonds of affection.

The mystic chords of memory, stretching from every battlefield and patriot grave to every living heart and hearthstone all over this broad land, will yet swell the chorus of the Union, when again touched, as surely they will be, by the better angels of our nature.

VIEWPOINT 7

"All we ask is to be let alone—that those who never held power over us shall not now attempt our subjugation by arms. This we will, we must resist, to the direst extremity."

War Is Necessary to Preserve the Confederacy

Jefferson Davis (1808-1889)

Jefferson Davis was inaugurated as president of the Confederate States of America on February 18, 1861. A Mississippi plantation owner and U.S. senator who resigned from the Senate after his state seceded from the United States, he was viewed as one of the South's elder statesmen. One of his first acts as president was to send three commissioners to Washington, D.C., to negotiate a peaceful withdrawal from the United States.

Among the items the commissioners sought to negotiate was the return of Fort Sumter, a fort in the harbor at Charleston, South Carolina, which was held by a small federal garrison under Major Robert Anderson. The commissioners received secret (and unauthorized) assurances by Abraham Lincoln's new secretary of state, William H. Seward, that the fort would be evacuated. However, after much deliberation, Lincoln decided instead to send a ship of supplies to the besieged fort. Interpreting this resupply mission as a hostile act, Jefferson Davis and his cabinet decided to attack Fort Sumter.

On April 12, Confederate forces fired on Fort Sumter. On April 13, Anderson surrendered the fort, and formally evacuated it on April 14. The following day Abraham Lincoln issued a proclamation declaring that "combinations too powerful to be suppressed" by ordinary means existed in the seven Confederate states and

Jefferson Davis, speech before the Confederate Congress, April 29, 1861. Reprinted from *The Rebellion Record: A Diary of American Events, with Documents, Narratives, Illustrative Incidents, Poetry, etc., etc.*, vol. 1, edited by Frank Moore. New York: G.P. Putnam, 1861.

called on the remaining states to furnish soldiers to suppress the "insurrection." Four days later he proclaimed a blockade of the Confederate coastline. Lincoln's proclamation stirred four more states to secede: Virginia, Arkansas, Tennessee, and North Carolina.

Davis viewed Lincoln's proclamation as an act of war, and quickly summoned a special session of the Confederate Congress. What follows are excerpts from his April 29 address to that body. Davis reiterates Southern grievances against the North, accuses the Lincoln administration of duplicity in its attempts to provision Fort Sumter, and calls for the Confederate States to unite in war to preserve their independence. The address provides a summary of what many Southerners believed the Civil War was about, and is regarded by many historians as Davis's most accomplished state paper.

The declaration of war made against this Confederacy, by Abraham Lincoln, President of the United States, in his proclamation, issued on the 15th day of the present month, renders it necessary, in my judgment, that you should convene at the earliest practicable moment to devise the measures necessary for the defence of the country.

The occasion is, indeed, an extraordinary one. It justifies me in giving a brief review of the relations heretofore existing between us and the States which now unite in warfare against us, and a succinct statement of the events which have resulted to the end, that mankind may pass intelligent and impartial judgment on our motives and objects.

The Revolution of Sovereign States

During the war waged against Great Britain by her colonies on this continent, a common danger impelled them to a close alliance, and to the formation of a Confederation by the terms of which the colonies, styling themselves States, entered severally into a firm league of friendship with each other for their common defence, the security of their liberties, and their mutual and general welfare, binding themselves to assist each other against all force offered to, or attacks made upon them, or any of them, on account of religion, sovereignty, trade, or any other pretence whatever.

In order to guard against any misconstruction of their compact, the several States made an explicit declaration in a distinct article—that each State retain its sovereignty, freedom and independence, and every power of jurisdiction and right which is not by this said Confederation expressly delegated to the United States in Congress assembled under this contract of alliance.

The war of the Revolution was successfully waged, and resulted in the treaty of peace with Great Britain in 1783, by the terms of which the several States were each by name recognized to be independent.

The articles of confederation contained a clause whereby all alterations were prohibited, unless confirmed by the Legislatures of every State after being agreed to by the Congress; and in obedience to this provision, under the resolution of Congress of the 21st of February, 1787, the several States appointed delegates for the purpose of revising the articles of confederation, and reporting to Congress and the several Legislatures such alterations and provisions therein as shall, when agreed to in Congress, and confirmed by the States, render the Federal Constitution adequate to the exigencies, of the Government and the preservation of the Union.

The Constitution

It was by the delegates chosen by the several States under the resolution just quoted, that the Constitution of the United States was formed in 1787, and submitted to the several States for ratification, as shown by the seventh Article, which is in these words: "The ratification of the conventions of nine States shall be sufficient for the establishment of this Constitution between the States so ratifying the same."

I [emphasize] the singular and marked caution with which the States endeavored in every possible form to exclude the idea that the separate and independent sovereignty of each State was merged into one common government or nation; and the earnest desire they evinced to impress on the Constitution its true character— that of a compact between independent States—the Constitution of 1787, however, admitting the clause already recited from the articles of confederation, which provided in explicit terms that each State reclaimed its sovereignty and independence.

Some alarm was felt in the States, when invited to ratify the Constitution, lest this omission should be construed into an abandonment of their cherished principles, and they refused to be satisfied until amendments were added to the Constitution, placing beyond any pretence of doubt the reservation by the States of their sovereign rights and powers not expressly delegated to the United States by the Constitution.

Strange, indeed, must it appear to the impartial observer, that it is none the less true that all these carefully worded clauses proved unavailing to prevent the rise and growth in the Northern States of a political school which has persistently claimed that the Government set above and over the States, an organization cre-

136

ated by the States, to secure the blessings of liberty and independence against foreign aggression, has been gradually perverted into a machine for their control in their domestic affairs.

The creature has been exalted above its Creator—the principals have been made subordinate to the agent appointed by themselves.

The people of the Southern States, whose almost exclusive occupation was agriculture, early perceived a tendency in the Northern States to render a common government subservient to their own purposes by imposing burthens on commerce as protection to their manufacturing and shipping interests.

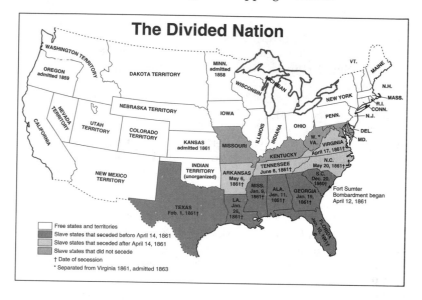

The Divided Nation

Long and angry controversies grew out of these attempts, often successful, to benefit one section of the country at the expense of the other, and the danger of disruption arising from this cause was enhanced by the fact that the Northern population was increasing, by emigration and other causes, more than the population of the South.

By degrees, as the Northern States gained preponderance in the National Congress, self-interest taught their people to yield ready assent to any plausible advocacy of their right as majority to govern the minority. Without control, they learn to listen with impatience to the suggestion of any constitutional impediment to the exercise of their will, and so utterly have the principles of the Constitution been corrupted in the Northern mind that, in the inaugural address delivered by President Lincoln in March last, he asserts a maxim which he plainly deems to be undeniable, that the theory of the Constitution requires, in all cases, that the majority shall govern. And in another memorable instance the same Chief Magistrate did not hesitate to liken the relations between States and the United States to those which exist between the county and the State in which it is situated, and by which it was created.

This is the lamentable and fundamental error in which rests the policy that has culminated in his declaration of war against these Confederate States.

In addition to the long-continued and deep-seated resentment felt by the Southern States at the persistent abuse of the powers they had delegated to the Congress for the purpose of enriching the manufacturing and shipping classes of the North at the expense of the South, there has existed for nearly half a century another subject of discord, involving interests of such transcendent magnitude as at all times to create the apprehension in the minds of many devoted lovers of the Union that its permanence was impossible.

When the several States delegated certain powers to the United States Congress, a large portion of the laboring population were imported into the colonies by the mother country. In twelve out of the fifteen States, negro slavery existed, and the right of property existing in slaves was protected by law; this property was recognized in the Constitution, and provision was made against its loss by the escape of the slave. . . .

Slavery in North and South

The climate and soil of the Northern States soon proved unpropitious to the continuance of slave labor, while the reverse being the case in the South, made unrestricted free intercourse between the two sections unfriendly.

The Northern States consulted their own interests by selling their slaves to the South and prohibiting slavery between their limits. The South were willing purchasers of property suitable to their wants, and paid the price of the acquisition, without harboring a suspicion that their quiet possession was to be disturbed by those who were not only in want of constitutional authority, but by good faith as vendors, from disquieting a title emanating from themselves.

As soon, however, as the Northern States, that prohibited African slavery within their limits, had reached a number sufficient to give their representation a controlling vote in the Congress, a persistent and organized system of hostile measures against the rights of the owners of slaves in the Southern States was inaugurated and gradually extended. A series of measures was devised and prosecuted for the purpose of rendering insecure the tenure of property in slaves.

Fanatical organizations, supplied with money by voluntary

subscriptions, were assiduously engaged in exciting amongst the slaves a spirit of discontent and revolt. Means were furnished for their escape from their owners, and agents secretly employed to entice them to abscond.

The constitutional provision for their rendition to their owners was first evaded, then openly denounced as a violation of conscientious obligation and religious duty. Men were taught that it was a merit to elude, disobey, and violently oppose the execution of the laws enacted to secure the performance of the promise contained in the constitutional compact. Often owners of slaves were mobbed and even murdered in open day solely for applying to a magistrate for the arrest of a fugitive slave.

The dogmas of the voluntary organization soon obtained control of the Legislatures of many of the Northern States, and laws were passed for the punishment, by ruinous fines, and long-continued imprisonment in gaols and penitentiaries, of citizens of the Southern States who should dare ask of the officers of the law for the recovery of their property. Emboldened by success, on the theatre of agitation and aggression, against the clearly expressed constitutional rights of the Congress, Senators and Representatives were sent to the common councils of the nation, whose chief title to this distinction consisted in the display of a spirit of ultra fanaticism, and whose business was not to promote the general welfare, or ensure domestic tranquillity—but to awaken the bitterest hatred against the citizens of sister States by violent denunciations of their institutions.

The transactions of public affairs was impeded by repeated efforts to usurp powers not delegated by the Constitution, for the purpose of impairing the security of property in slaves, and reducing those States which held slaves to a condition of inferiority.

Finally, a great party was organized for the purpose of obtaining the administration of the Government, with the avowed object of using its power for the total exclusion of the slave States from all participation in the benefits of the public domain acquired by all the States in common, whether by conquest or purchase, surrounded them entirely by States in which slavery should be prohibited, thus rendering the property in slaves so insecure as to be comparatively worthless, and thereby annihilating in effect property worth thousands of millions of dollars.

This party, thus organized, succeeded in the month of November last in the election of its candidate for the Presidency of the United States.

In the meantime, under the mild and genial climate of the Southern States, and the increasing care for the well-being and comfort of the laboring classes, dictated alike by interest and humanity, the African slaves had augmented in number from about six hundred thousand, at the date of the adoption of the constitutional compact, to upwards of four millions.

In a moral and social condition they had been elevated from brutal savages into docile, intelligent, and civilized agricultural laborers, and supplied not only with bodily comforts, but with

We Are Prepared for War

The vice president of the Confederacy was Alexander H. Stephens, a Georgian who had previously advocated moderation on the secession question. In a May 23, 1861, speech in Atlanta, Georgia, he proclaims his confidence in the Confederate cause.

The time for speech-making has passed. The people have heard all that can be said. The time for prompt, vigorous, decisive action is upon us, and we must do our duty. . . .

Some think there will be no war; as to that I know not. But whatever others wanted, the object of the Confederate Government is *peace*. Come peace or war, however, it is determined to maintain our position at every hazard and at every cost, and to drive back the myrmidons of Abolitionism. It is to be hoped that Lincoln will perceive his error and cease his warlike preparations. The war is against all the principles on which the Government of the United States is based. . . .

The proclamation declaring our ports in a state of blockade, is in violation of the oath taken by Lincoln when he was inaugurated President of the United States; for he swore to maintain the Constitution of the United States, which declares that "no preference shall be given by any regulation of commerce or revenue to the ports of one State over those of another State;" and he considers us a part of the United States; yet the ports of Boston and New York were open to the world, while Charleston and other Southern ports were declared to be in a state of blockade. How dare he issue such an ukase? How *dare* he, with the oath upon his lips to support the Constitution, trample that instrument in the dust? But he declared, shortly after his inauguration, that he had an "oath registered in high Heaven." By this he means that he has sworn the subjugation of the South to the legions of Abolitiondom. Well, let them come. *We are prepared for them.* . . .

Whether brought to a bloody conflict or not, we are prepared. Our people everywhere are full of enthusiasm, and strong in their determination never to submit to the rule of Lincoln. Fathers, and mothers, and sisters are all ready, and doing all they can in aid of the cause. We are in the right; and justice is upon our side. We must succeed. The same God who guided our fathers in the bloody Revolution, and who made the glory of the late United States, is yet upon the side of right and justice. Relying upon Him who holds the destinies of all nations in His hands, we will go forth to battle, resolved to conquer or die!

careful religious instruction, under the supervision of a superior race. Their labor had been so directed as not only to allow a gradual and marked amelioration of their own condition, but to convert hundreds of thousands of square miles of the wilderness into cultivated lands covered with a prosperous people. Towns and cities had sprung into existence, and it rapidly increased in wealth and population under the social system of the South.

The white population of the Southern slaveholding States had augmented from about 1,250,000, at the date of the adoption of the Constitution, to more than 8,500,000 in 1860, and the productions of the South in cotton, rice, sugar and tobacco, for the full development and continuance of which the labor of African slaves was and is indispensable, had swollen to an amount which formed nearly three-fourths of the export of the whole United States, and had become absolutely necessary to the wants of civilized man.

With interests of such overwhelming magnitude imperiled, the people of the Southern States were driven by the conduct of the North to the adoption of some course of action to avoid the dangers with which they were openly menaced. With this view, the Legislatures of the several States invited the people to select delegates to conventions to be held for the purpose of determining for themselves what measures were best to be adopted to meet so alarming a crisis in their history.

The Rights of States

Here it may be proper to observe that, from a period as early as 1798, there had existed in all of the States of the Union a party almost uninterruptedly in the majority, based upon the creed that each State was, in the last resort, the sole judge as well of its wrongs as of the mode and measures of redress. Indeed, it is obvious that under the law of nations this principle is an axiom as applied to the relations of independent sovereign States, such as those which had united themselves under the constitutional compact. . . .

In the exercise of a right so ancient, so well established, and so necessary for self-preservation, the people of the Confederate States in their conventions determined that the wrongs which they had suffered, and the evils with which they were menaced, required that they should revoke the delegation of powers to the Federal Government which they had ratified in their several conventions. They consequently passed ordinances resuming all their rights as sovereign and independent States, and dissolved their connection with the other States of the Union. Having done this, they proceeded to form a new compact among themselves by new articles of confederation, which have been also ratified by conventions of the several States, with an approach to unanimity far exceeding that of the conventions which adopted the Constitution of 1787. They have organized their new government in all its departments. The functions of the executive, legislative and judicial magistrates are performed in accordance with the will of the people, as displayed not merely in a cheerful acquiescence, but in the enthusiastic support of the government thus established by themselves; and but for the interference of the Government of the United States, this legitimate exercise of a people to self-government has been manifested in every possible form.

Scarce had you assembled in February last, when, prior even to the inauguration of the chief-magistrate you had elected, you expressed your desire for the appointment of commissioners, and for the settlement of all questions of disagreement between the two governments upon principles of right, justice, equity and good faith.

It was my pleasure as well as my duty to cooperate with you in this work of peace. Indeed, in my address to you on taking the oath of office, and before receiving from you the communication of this resolution, I had said that "as a necessity, not as a choice, we have resorted to the remedy of separating, and henceforth our energies must be directed to the conduct of our own affairs, and the perpetuity of the Confederacy which we have formed. If a just perception of mutual interest shall permit us to peaceably pursue our separate political career, my most earnest desire will then have been fulfilled."

It was in furtherance of these accordant views of the congress and the executive, that I made choice of three discreet, able and distinguished citizens, who repaired to Washington. . . . Every effort compatible with self-respect and the dignity of the Confederacy was exhausted before I allowed myself to yield to the conviction that the Government of the United States was determined to attempt the conquest of this people, and that our cherished hopes of peace were unobtainable.

On the arrival of our commissioners in Washington on the 5th of March, they postponed, at the suggestion of a friendly intermediator, doing more than giving informal notice of their arrival. This was done with a view to afford time to the President of the United States, who had just been inaugurated, for the discharge of other pressing official duties in the organization of his administration, before engaging his attention in the object of their mission.

It was not until the 12th of the month that they officially addressed the Secretary of State, informing him of the purpose of their arrival, and stating in the language of their instructions their wish to make to the Government of the United States overtures for the opening of negotiations, assuring the Government of the United States that the president, congress, and people of the Confederate States desired a peaceful solution of these great questions—that it was neither their interest nor their wish to make any demand which is not founded on the strictest principles of justice, nor to do any act to injure their late confederates.

To this communication no formal reply was received until the 8th of April. During the interval, the commissioners had consented to waive all questions of form, with the firm resolve to avoid war if possible. They went so far even as to hold, during that long period, unofficial intercourse through an intermediary, whose high position and character inspired the hope of success, and through whom constant assurances were received from the Government of the United States of its peaceful intentions—of its determination to evacuate Fort Sumter; and further, that no measure would be introduced changing the existing status prejudicial to the Confederate States; that in the event of any change in regard to Fort Pickens, notice would be given to the commissioners.

The crooked path of diplomacy can scarcely furnish an example so wanting in courtesy, in candor and directness, as was the course of the United States Government toward our commissioners in Washington. . . .

It appears that during the whole interval, whilst the commissioners were receiving assurances calculated to inspire hope of the success of their mission, the Secretary of State and the President of the United States had already determined to hold no intercourse with them whatever—to refuse even to listen to any proposals they had to make, and had profited by the delay created by their own assurances, in order to prepare secretly the means for effective hostile operations.

That these assurances were given, has been virtually confessed by the Government of the United States, by its act of sending a messenger to Charleston to give notice of its purpose to use force if opposed in its intention of supplying Fort Sumter.

No more striking proof of the absence of good faith in the confidence of the Government of the United States toward the Confederacy can be required, than is contained in the circumstances which accompanied this notice.

According to the usual course of navigation, the vessels composing the expedition, and designed for the relief of Fort Sumter, might be looked for in Charleston harbor on the 9th of April. Yet our commissioners in Washington were detained under assurances that notice should be given of any military movement. The notice was not addressed to them, but a messenger was sent to Charleston to give notice to the Governor of South Carolina, and the notice was so given at a late hour on the 8th of April, the eve of the very day on which the fleet might be expected to arrive.

That this manœuvre failed in its purpose was not the fault of those who controlled it. A heavy tempest delayed the arrival of the expedition, and gave time to the commander of our forces at Charleston to ask and receive instructions of the government. Even then, under all the provocation incident to the contemptuous refusal to listen to our commissioners, and the treacherous course of the Government of the United States, I was sincerely anxious to avoid the effusion of blood, and directed a proposal to be made to the commander of Fort Sumter, who had avowed himself to be nearly out of provisions, that we would abstain from directing our fire on Fort Sumter if he would promise to not open fire on our forces unless first attacked. This proposal was refused. The conclusion was, that the design of the United States was to place the besieging force at Charleston between the simultaneous fire of the fleet. The fort should, of course, be at once reduced. This order was executed by Gen. Beauregard with skill and success, which were naturally to be expected from the well-known character of that gallant officer; and, although the bombardment lasted some thirty-three hours, our flag did not wave over the battered walls until after the appearance of the hostile fleet off Charleston.

Fortunately not a life was lost on our side, and we were gratified in being prepared. The necessity of an useless effusion of blood by the prudent caution of the officers who commanded the fleet, in abstaining from the evidently futile effort to enter the harbor for the relief of Major Anderson, was spared.

I refer to the report of the Secretary of War, and the papers accompanying it, for further particulars of this brilliant affair.

In this connection I cannot refrain from a well-deserved tribute to the noble State, the eminently soldierly qualities of whose people were conspicuously displayed. The people of Charleston for months had been irritated by the spectacle of a fortress held within their principal harbor as a standing menace against their peace and independence—built in part with their own money—its custody confided with their long consent to an agent who held no power over them other than such as they had themselves delegated for their own benefit, intended to be used by that agent for their own protection against foreign attack. How it was held out with persistent tenacity as a means of offence against them by the very Government which they had established for their own protection, is well known. They had beleaguered it for months, and felt entire confidence in their power to capture it, yet yielded to the requirements of discipline, curbed their impatience, submitted without complaint to the unaccustomed hardships, labors and privations of a protracted siege, and when at length their patience was relieved by the signal for attack, and success had crowned their steady and gallant conduct, even in the very moment of triumph they evinced a chivalrous regard for the feelings of the brave but unfortunate officer who had been compelled to lower his flag.

All manifestations or exultations were checked in his presence. Their commanding general, with their cordial approval and consent of his government, refrained from imposing any terms that would wound the sensibility of the commander of the fort. He was permitted to retire with the honors of war, to salute his flag, to depart freely with all his command, and was escorted to the vessel on which he embarked with the highest marks of respect from those against whom his guns had so recently been directed.

Not only does every event connected with the siege reflect the highest honor on South Carolina, but the forbearance of her people and of this government from making any harangue of a victory obtained under circumstances of such peculiar provocation, attest to the fullest extent the absence of any purpose beyond securing their own tranquillity, and the sincere desire to avoid the calamities of war.

Lincoln's Declaration of War

Scarcely had the President of the United States received intelligence of the failure of the scheme which he had devised for the reinforcement of Fort Sumter, when he issued the declaration of war against this Confederacy, which has prompted me to convoke you. In this extraordinary production, that high functionary affects total ignorance of the existence of an independent government, which, possessing the entire and enthusiastic devotion of its people, is exercising its functions without question over seven sovereign States—over more than five millions of people—and over a territory whose area exceeds five hundred thousand square miles.

He terms sovereign States "combinations too powerful to be suppressed in the ordinary course of judicial proceedings, or by the powers vested in the marshals by law."

He calls for an army of seventy-five thousand men to act as the posse comitatus [a body of men summoned to keep the peace] in aid of the process of the courts of justice in States where no courts exist, whose mandates and decrees are not cheerfully obeyed and respected by a willing people.

He avows that the first service to be assigned to the forces which have been called out will not be to execute the processes of courts, but to capture forts and strongholds situated within the admitted limits of this Confederacy, and garrisoned by its troops, and declares that this effort is intended to maintain the perpetuity of popular government

He concludes by commanding the persons composing the "combinations" aforesaid, to wit: the five millions of inhabitants of these States, to retire peaceably to their respective abodes within twenty days.

Apparently contradictory as are the terms of this singular document, one point was unmistakably evident. The President of the United States calls for an army of 75,000 men, whose first service was to be to capture our forts. It was a plain declaration of war which I was not at liberty to disregard, because of my knowledge that under the Constitution of the United States the President was usurping a power granted exclusively to the Congress.

He is the sole organ of communication between that country and foreign powers. The law of nations did not permit me to question the authority of the Executive of a foreign nation to declare war against this Confederacy. Although I might have refrained from taking active measures for our defence, if the States of the Union had all imitated the action of Virginia, North Carolina, Arkansas, Kentucky, Tennessee and Missouri, by denouncing it as an unconstitutional usurpation of power to which they refuse to respond, I was not at liberty to disregard the fact that many of the States seemed quite content to submit to the exercise of the powers assumed by the President of the United States, and were actively engaged in levying troops for the purpose indicated in the proclamation. Deprived of the aid of Congress, at the moment I was under the necessity of confining my action to a call on the States for volunteers for the common defence, in accordance with the authority you had confided to me before your adjournment.

I deemed it proper further to issue a proclamation, inviting applications from persons disposed to aid in our defence in private armed vessels on the high seas, to the end that preparations might be made for the immediate issue of letters of marque and reprisal [government license authorizing private ships to capture ships of another nation], which you alone, under the Constitution, have the power to grant.

I entertain no doubt that you will concur with me in the opinion, that in the absence of an organized navy, it will be eminently expedient to supply their place with private armed vessels, so happily styled by the publicists of the United States the militia of the sea, and so often and justly relied on by them as an efficient and admirable instrument of defensive warfare.

I earnestly recommend the immediate passage of a law authorizing me to accept the numerous proposals already received. . . .

A People United

In conclusion, I congratulate you on the fact that in every portion of our country there has been exhibited the most patriotic devotion to our common cause. Transportation companies have freely tendered the use of their lines for troops and supplies. . . .

Requisitions for troops have been met with such alacrity that the numbers tendering their services have in every instance greatly exceeded the demand. Men of the highest official and social position are serving as volunteers in the ranks. The gravity of age, the zeal of youth, rival each other in the desire to be foremost in the public defence, and though at no other point than the one heretofore noticed have they been stimulated by the excitement incident to actual engagement and the hope of distinction for individual deportment, they have borne, what for new troops is the most severe ordeal, patient toil, constant vigil, and all the exposure and discomfort of active service with a resolution and fortitude such as to command the approbation and justify the highest expectation of their conduct when active valor shall be required in place of steady endurance.

A people thus united and resolute cannot shrink from any sacrifice which they may be called on to make, nor can there be a reasonable doubt of their final success, however long and severe may be the test of their determination to maintain their birthright of freedom and equality as a trust which it is their first duty to transmit unblemished to their posterity. . . .

We feel that our cause is just and holy.

We protest solemnly, in the face of mankind, that we desire peace at any sacrifice, save that of honor.

In independence we seek no conquest, no aggrandizement, no cession of any kind from the States with which we have lately confederated. All we ask is to be let alone—that those who never held power over us shall not now attempt our subjugation by arms. This we will, we must resist, to the direst extremity.

The moment that this pretension is abandoned, the sword will drop from our grasp, and we shall be ready to enter into treaties of amity and commerce that cannot but be mutually beneficial.

So long as this pretension is maintained, with a firm reliance on that Divine Power which covers with its protection the just cause, we will continue to struggle for our inherent right to freedom, independence, and self-government.

VIEWPOINT 8

"No choice was left but to call out the war power of the government and so to resist force employed for its destruction by force for its preservation."

War Is Necessary to Preserve the Union

Abraham Lincoln (1809-1865)

President Abraham Lincoln's first month in office was dominated by decisions over Fort Sumter. The stronghold in Charleston, South Carolina, was one of the only federal forts not seized by the seceding states, but its soldiers were running out of food and supplies. Lincoln decided to send provisions to the fort, but before he could do so it was attacked by Southern troops on April 12, 1861—the first shots of the Civil War.

Immediately following the Confederate attack on and capture of Fort Sumter, Lincoln took several dramatic steps in response. He issued a proclamation on April 15, 1861, calling for 75,000 volunteer soldiers to suppress the rebellion, and proclaimed a naval blockade against all Confederate ports. Congress was not in session, so Lincoln called for a special session to convene on July 4. The following is taken from his address to Congress on that date.

In his speech Lincoln summarizes the events of the previous months, including those involving Fort Sumter, from his perspective as one trying to preserve the Union. He denies the legitimacy of the Confederate States' claims for independence, outlines the steps he has taken to quell the rebellion, and defines what he sees as the purpose of the war. Making little mention of slavery, he sees as the central purpose of the war to ensure the survival of the United States, and to demonstrate to the world that a constitutional republic can successfully exist amid internal crises.

Abraham Lincoln, address to Congress, July 4, 1861. Reprinted from *A Compilation of the Messages and Papers of the Presidents, 1798-1897*, edited by James D. Richardson. Washington, DC, 1896-1899.

Fellow Citizens of the Senate and House of Representatives:

Having been convened on an extraordinary occasion, as authorized by the Constitution, your attention is not called to any ordinary subject of legislation.

At the beginning of the present presidential term, four months ago, the functions of the Federal government were found to be generally suspended within the several states of South Carolina, Georgia, Alabama, Mississippi, Louisiana, and Florida, excepting only those of the Post Office Department.

Seizing Federal Property

Within these states all the forts, arsenals, dockyards, custom-houses, and the like, including the movable and stationary property in and about them, had been seized and were held in open hostility to this government, excepting only Forts Pickens, Taylor, and Jefferson, on and near the Florida coast, and Fort Sumter, in Charleston Harbor, South Carolina. The forts thus seized had been put in improved condition, new ones had been built, and armed forces had been organized and were organizing, all avowedly with the same hostile purpose.

The forts remaining in the possession of the Federal government in and near those states were either besieged or menaced by warlike preparations, and especially Fort Sumter was nearly surrounded by well-protected hostile batteries, with guns equal in quality to the best of its own and outnumbering the latter as perhaps ten to one. A disproportionate share of the Federal muskets and rifles had somehow found their way into these states, and had been seized to be used against the government. Accumulations of the public revenue lying within them had been seized for the same object. The Navy was scattered in distant seas, leaving but a very small part of it within the immediate reach of the government. Officers of the Federal Army and Navy had resigned in great numbers, and, of those resigning, a large proportion had taken up arms against the government. Simultaneously and in connection with all this the purpose to sever the Federal Union was openly avowed. In accordance with this purpose, an ordinance had been adopted in each of these states declaring the states respectively to be separated from the national Union. A formula for instituting a combined government of these states had been promulgated, and this illegal organization, in the character of Confederate States, was already invoking recognition, aid, and intervention from foreign powers.

Finding this condition of things and believing it to be an imperative duty upon the incoming executive to prevent, if possible, the consummation of such attempt to destroy the Federal Union, a choice of means to that end became indispensable. This choice was made and was declared in the inaugural address. The policy chosen looked to the exhaustion of all peaceful measures before a resort to any stronger ones. It sought only to hold the public places and property not already wrested from the government and to collect the revenue, relying for the rest on time, discussion, and the ballot box. It promised a continuance of the mails at government expense to the very people who were resisting the government, and it gave repeated pledges against any disturbance to any of the people or any of their rights. Of all that which a President might constitutionally and justifiably do in such a case, everything was forborne without which it was believed possible to keep the government on foot.

Fort Sumter

On the 5th of March, the present incumbent's first full day in office, a letter of Major [Robert] Anderson, commanding at Fort Sumter, written on the 28th of February and received at the War Department on the 4th of March, was by that department placed in his hands. This letter expressed the professional opinion of the writer that reenforcements could not be thrown into that fort within the time for his relief rendered necessary by the limited supply of provisions, and with a view of holding possession of the same, with a force of less than 20,000 good and well-disciplined men. This opinion was concurred in by all the officers of his command, and their memoranda on the subject were made enclosures of Major Anderson's letter.

The whole was immediately laid before Lieutenant General [Winfield] Scott, who at once concurred with Major Anderson in opinion. On reflection, however, he took full time, consulting with other officers, both of the Army and the Navy, and at the end of four days came reluctantly, but decidedly, to the same conclusion as before. He also stated at the same time that no such sufficient force was then at the control of the government or could be raised and brought to the ground within the time when the provisions in the fort would be exhausted. In a purely military point of view this reduced the duty of the administration in the case to the mere matter of getting the garrison safely out of the fort.

It was believed, however, that to so abandon that position under the circumstances would be utterly ruinous; that the necessity under which it was to be done would not be fully understood; that by many it would be construed as a part of a *voluntary* policy; that at home it would discourage the friends of the Union, embolden its adversaries, and go far to insure to the latter a recognition abroad; that, in fact, it would be our national destruction consummated. This could not be allowed. Starvation was not yet upon the garrison, and ere it would be reached, Fort Pickens might be reenforced. This last would be a clear indication of *policy*, and would better enable the country to accept the evacuation of Fort Sumter as a military *necessity*.

The flag that flew over Fort Sumter, damaged by Confederate fire, was unfurled over the statue of George Washington at Union Square in New York City at a public meeting on April 20, 1861. More than 100,000 people gathered to rally support for the Union and Abraham Lincoln's call for 75,000 soldiers to put down the "insurrection" of the Southern states.

An order was at once directed to be sent for the landing of the troops from the steamship *Brooklyn* into Fort Pickens. This order could not go by land but must take the longer and slower route by sea. The first return news from the order was received just one week before the fall of Fort Sumter. The news itself was that the officer commanding the *Sabine*, to which vessel the troops had been transferred from the *Brooklyn*, acting upon some quasi-armistice of the late [Buchanan] administration (and of the existence of which the present administration, up to the time the order was dispatched, had only too vague and uncertain rumors to fix attention), had refused to land the troops. To now reenforce Fort Pickens before a crisis would be reached at Fort Sumter was impossible, rendered so by the near exhaustion of provisions in the latter named fort. In precaution against such a conjuncture, the government had a few days before commenced preparing an expedition, as well-adapted as might be, to relieve Fort Sumter, which expedition was intended to be ultimately used or not, according to circumstances. The strongest anticipated case for using it was now presented, and it was resolved to send it forward.

As had been intended in this contingency, it was also resolved to notify the governor of South Carolina that he might expect an attempt would be made to provision the fort, and that if the attempt should not be resisted there would be no effort to throw in men, arms, or ammunition without further notice, or in case of an attack upon the fort. This notice was accordingly given, whereupon the fort was attacked and bombarded to its fall, without even awaiting the arrival of the provisioning expedition.

It is thus seen that the assault upon and reduction of Fort Sumter was in no sense a matter of self-defense on the part of the assailants. They well knew that the garrison in the fort could by no possibility commit aggression upon them. They knew—they were expressly notified—that the giving of bread to the few brave and hungry men of the garrison was all which would on that occasion be attempted, unless themselves, by resisting so much, should provoke more. They knew that this government desired to keep the garrison in the fort, not to assail them but merely to maintain visible possession, and thus to preserve the Union from actual and immediate dissolution, trusting, as hereinbefore stated, to time, discussion, and the ballot box for final adjustment; and they assailed and reduced the fort for precisely the reverse object—to drive out the visible authority of the Federal Union, and thus force it to immediate dissolution.

That this was their object the executive well understood; and having said to them in the inaugural address, "You can have no conflict without being yourselves the aggressors," he took pains not only to keep this declaration good but also to keep the case so free from the power of ingenious sophistry as that the world should not be able to misunderstand it. By the affair at Fort Sumter, with its surrounding circumstances, that point was reached. Then and thereby the assailants of the government began the conflict of arms, without a gun in sight or in expectancy to return their fire, save only the few in the fort, sent to that harbor years before for their own protection, and still ready to give that protection in whatever was lawful. In this act, discarding all else, they have forced upon the country the distinct issue: "Immediate dissolution or blood."

Can Democracy Survive?

And this issue embraces more than the fate of the United States. It presents to the whole family of man the question whether a constitutional republic, or democracy—a government of the people by the same people—can or cannot maintain its territorial integrity against its own domestic foes. It presents the question whether discontented individuals, too few in numbers to control administration according to organic law in any case, can always, upon the pretenses made in this case, or on any other pretenses, or arbitrarily without any pretense, break up their government and thus practically put an end to free government upon the earth. It forces us to ask—Is there in all republics this inherent and fatal weakness? Must a government of necessity be too *strong* for the liberties of its own people, or too *weak* to maintain its own existence?

So viewing the issue, no choice was left but to call out the war power of the government and so to resist force employed for its destruction by force for its preservation. . . .

Secession or Rebellion?

It might seem at first thought to be of little difference whether the present movement at the South be called "secession" or "rebellion." The movers, however, well understand the difference. At the beginning they knew they could never raise their treason to any respectable magnitude by any name which implies *violation* of law. They knew their people possessed as much of moral sense, as much of devotion to law and order, and as much pride in and reverence for the history and government of their common country as any other civilized and patriotic people. They knew they could make no advancement directly in the teeth of these strong and noble sentiments. Accordingly, they commenced by an insidious debauching of the public mind. They invented an ingenious sophism, which, if conceded, was followed by perfectly logical steps through all the incidents to the complete destruction of the Union. The sophism itself is that any state of the Union may *consistently* with the national Constitution, and therefore *lawfully* and *peacefully*, withdraw from the Union without the consent of the Union or of any other state. The little disguise that the supposed right is to be exercised only for just cause, themselves to be the sole judge of its justice, is too thin to merit any notice.

With rebellion thus sugarcoated, they have been drugging the public mind of their section for more than thirty years, and until at length they have brought many good men to a willingness to take up arms against the government the day *after* some assemblage of men have enacted the farcical pretense of taking their state out of the Union who could have been brought to no such thing the day *before*.

This sophism derives much, perhaps the whole, of its currency from the assumption that there is some omnipotent and sacred supremacy pertaining to a state—to each state of our Federal Union. Our states have neither more nor less power than that reserved to them in the Union by the Constitution, no one of them ever having been a state out of the Union. The original ones passed into the Union even before they cast off their British colonial dependence, and the new ones each came into the Union directly from a condition of dependence, excepting Texas; and even Texas, in its temporary independence, was never designated a state. The new ones only took the designation of states on coming into the Union, while that name was first adopted for the old ones in and by the Declaration of Independence. Therein the "United Colonies" were declared to be "free and independent states"; but even then the object plainly was not to declare their independence of *one another* or of the *Union*, but directly the contrary, as their mutual pledge and their mutual action before, at the time, and afterward abundantly show.

The Status of States

The express plighting of faith by each and all of the original thirteen in the Articles of Confederation, two years later, that the Union shall be perpetual is most conclusive. Having never been states, either in substance or in name, outside of the Union, whence this magical omnipotence of "state rights," asserting a claim of power to lawfully destroy the Union itself? Much is said about the "sovereignty" of the states, but the word even is not in the national Constitution, nor, as is believed, in any of the state constitutions. What is a "sovereignty" in the political sense of the term? Would it be far wrong to define it "a political community without a political superior"? Tested by this, no one of our states, except Texas, ever was a sovereignty; and even Texas gave up the character on coming into the Union, by which act she acknowledged the Constitution of the United States and the laws and treaties of the United States made in pursuance of the Constitution to be for her the supreme law of the land.

The states have their status in the Union, and they have no other legal status. If they break from this, they can only do so against law and by revolution. The Union, and not themselves separately, procured their independence and their liberty. By conquest or purchase the Union gave each of them whatever of independence and liberty it has. The Union is older than any of the states, and, in fact, it created them as states. Originally some dependent colonies made the Union, and in turn the Union threw off their old dependence for them and made them states, such as they are. Not one of them ever had a state constitution independent of the Union. Of course it is not forgotten that all the new states framed their constitutions before they entered the Union, nevertheless dependent upon and preparatory to coming into the Union.

Unquestionably the states have the powers and rights reserved to them in and by the national Constitution; but among these surely are not included all conceivable powers, however mischievous or destructive, but at most such only as were known in the world at the time as governmental powers; and certainly a power to destroy the government itself had never been known as a governmental—as a merely administrative—power. This relative matter of national power and state rights, as a principle, is no other than the principle of *generality* and *locality*. Whatever concerns the whole should be confided to the whole—to the general government—while whatever concerns only the state should be left exclusively to the state. This is all there is of original principle about it. Whether the national Constitution in defining boundaries between the two has applied the principle with exact accuracy is not to be questioned. We are all bound by that defining without question.

What is now combated is the position that secession is *consistent* with the Constitution—is *lawful* and *peaceful*. It is not contended that there is any express law for it, and nothing should ever be implied as law which leads to unjust or absurd consequences. . . .

The seceders insist that our Constitution admits of secession. They have assumed to make a national constitution of their own, in which of necessity they have either *discarded* or *retained* the right of secession, as they insist it exists in ours. If they have discarded it, they thereby admit that on principle it ought not to be in ours. If they have retained it, by their own construction of ours they show that to be consistent they must secede from one another whenever they shall find it the easiest way of settling their debts or effecting any other selfish or unjust object. The principle itself is one of disintegration and upon which no government can possibly endure.

If all the states save one should assert the power to drive that one out of the Union, it is presumed the whole class of seceder politicians would at once deny the power and denounce the act as the greatest outrage upon state rights. But suppose that precisely the same act, instead of being called "driving the one out," should be called "the seceding of the others from that one," it would be exactly what the seceders claim to do, unless, indeed, they make the point that the one, because it is a minority, may rightfully do what the others, because they are a majority, may not rightfully do. These politicians are subtle and profound on the rights of minorities. They are not partial to that power which made the Constitution and speaks from the Preamble, calling itself "We, the people."

It may well be questioned whether there is today a majority of the legally qualified voters of any state, except, perhaps, South Carolina, in favor of disunion. There is much reason to believe that the Union men are the majority in many, if not in every other one, of the so-called seceded states. The contrary has not been demonstrated in any one of them. It is ventured to affirm this even of Virginia and Tennessee; for the result of an election held in military camps, where the bayonets are all on one side of the question voted upon, can scarcely be considered as demonstrating popular sentiment. At such an election all that large class who are at once *for* the Union and *against* coercion would be coerced to vote against the Union. . . .

A People's Contest

This is essentially a people's contest. On the side of the Union it is a struggle for maintaining in the world that form and substance of government whose leading object is to elevate the condition of men; to lift artificial weights from all shoulders; to clear the paths of laudable pursuit for all; to afford all an unfettered start and a fair chance in the race of life. Yielding to partial and temporary departures, from necessity, this is the leading object of the government for whose existence we contend. . . .

Our popular government has often been called an experiment. Two points in it our people have already settled—the successful *establishing* and the successful *administering* of it. One still remains: its successful *maintenance* against a formidable internal attempt to overthrow it. It is now for them to demonstrate to the world that those who can fairly carry an election can also suppress a rebellion; that ballots are the rightful and peaceful successors of bullets, and that when ballots have fairly and constitutionally decided, there can be no successful appeal back to bullets; that there can be no successful appeal except to ballots themselves at succeeding elections. Such will be a great lesson of peace, teaching men that what they cannot take by an election neither can they take it by a war; teaching all the folly of being the beginners of a war.

Lest there be some uneasiness in the minds of candid men as to what is to be the course of the government toward the Southern states after the rebellion shall have been suppressed, the executive deems it proper to say it will be his purpose then, as ever, to be guided by the Constitution and the laws, and that he probably will have no different understanding of the powers and duties of the Federal government relatively to the rights of the states and the people under the Constitution than that expressed in the inaugural address.

He desires to preserve the government, that it may be administered for all as it was administered by the men who made it. Loyal citizens everywhere have the right to claim this of their government, and the government has no right to withhold or neglect it. It is not perceived that in giving it there is any coercion, any conquest, or any subjugation in any just sense of those terms.

The Constitution provides, and all the states have accepted the provision, that "the United States shall guarantee to every state in this Union a republican form of government." But if a state may lawfully go out of the Union, having done so it may also discard the republican form of government; so that to prevent its going

156

out is an indispensable *means* to the *end* of maintaining the guaranty mentioned; and when an end is lawful and obligatory, the indispensable means to it are also lawful and obligatory.

Using War Power

It was with the deepest regret that the executive found the duty of employing the war power in defense of the government forced upon him. He could but perform this duty or surrender the existence of the government. No compromise by public servants could in this case be a cure; not that compromises are not often proper, but that no popular government can long survive a marked precedent that those who carry an election can only save the government from immediate destruction by giving up the main point upon which the people gave the election. The people themselves, and not their servants, can safely reverse their own deliberate decisions.

As a private citizen the executive could not have consented that these institutions shall perish; much less could he in betrayal of so vast and so sacred a trust as these free people had confided to him. He felt that he had no moral right to shrink, not even to count the chances of his own life, in what might follow. In full view of his great responsibility he has so far done what he has deemed his duty. You will now, according to your own judgment, perform yours. He sincerely hopes that your views and your action may so accord with his as to assure all faithful citizens who have been disturbed in their rights of a certain and speedy restoration to them under the Constitution and the laws.

And having thus chosen our course, without guile and with pure purpose, let us renew our trust in God and go forward without fear and with manly hearts.

Chapter 3

Debates North and South

Chapter Preface

The Confederate attack on federal forces at Fort Sumter on April 12, 1861, closed the debate on some hotly contested questions. Secession was no longer threatened or argued; it was, for eleven states, a fact. War could not be prevented by a different policy or a proposed compromise; it was already here. But the onset of war raised a whole new set of questions and divisions, not only between the North and South, but also within the two sections. Neither the eleven states of the Confederacy nor the remaining twenty-three states of the United States were totally united in their respective war efforts. The political leaders of the Civil War, U.S. President Abraham Lincoln and Confederate President Jefferson Davis, each had to overcome criticism and dissension from his own side.

Lincoln during the war was criticized both for doing both too little and too much. On one side were elements within his party, known as Radical Republicans, who fervently called for the abolition of slavery and the use of black troops (steps initially opposed and eventually supported by Lincoln), and in general pushed for an aggressive war against the South. Radical Republicans dominated the Joint Committee on the Conduct of the War, which Congress established in December 1861 in response to the North's dismal military record during the war's first months. Lincoln's critics at the other end of the political spectrum consisted of those people (mostly Democrats) who questioned Lincoln's decision to go to war, who opposed the abolition of slavery, and who argued that Lincoln had become dictatorial in his actions directing the war effort. Although not as powerful in Congress as the Radical Republicans, these Peace Democrats (also called Copperheads) were well represented in state and local governments and were a constant concern for the Lincoln administration.

Jefferson Davis faced comparable divisions within the Confederacy, including criticism of his leadership. After enjoying an initial flush of military success the Confederacy ran into setbacks, and its people became increasingly disillusioned and divided over military strategy, conscription, and other issues. Ironically, the ideal of states' rights—the stated reason for the Southern states' secession and the subsequent creation of the Confederacy—became itself a source of division. Some state governors—notably Georgia's Joseph E. Brown and North Carolina's Zebulon Vance—resisted orders from Davis and refused to coordinate military efforts in order to preserve their state prerogatives.

Slavery remained a central issue for both North and South. While most of the Southern elite was united in wanting to preserve the institution, the majority of whites in the South did not own slaves, and many were not wholly dedicated to the institution and the planter class it supported. Perhaps more importantly, the defiance of the slaves themselves proved to be a significant weakness of the Confederacy during the Civil War, as historian Eric Foner writes:

> The conflict undermined the South's "peculiar institution." Their "grapevine telegraph" kept many slaves remarkably well informed about the war's progress. And the drain of white men into military service left plantations under the control of planter's wives and elderly and infirm men, whose authority slaves increasingly felt able to challenge. Reports of "demoralized" and "insubordinate" behavior multiplied throughout the South.

The issue of slavery was divisive in the North as well. Many Northerners who supported the war effort against the rebelling states did not at first support the abolition of slavery. In July 1861 Congress passed a resolution sponsored by Kentucky senator John Crittenden stating that war was being fought "to preserve the Union," not to subjugate the South or interfere with slavery. But abolitionists believed that the Civil War presented an opportunity for the United States to extinguish the institution. Many added to their moral indictments of slavery the argument that emancipating the slaves would deprive the South of its labor force, weaken the rebelling states, and hasten the end of war—an argument that gained increasing support even from people who had not been abolitionists before the war. Lincoln at first sought to placate slaveowners from the slave states that did not secede, and resisted entreaties by abolitionists to use his presidental powers to free the slaves. But, citing discouraging results on the battlefield and later stating that "we . . . must change our tactics, or risk losing the game," Lincoln finally decided to make the end of slavery an official war aim by issuing the Emancipation Proclamation, which took effect on January 1, 1863.

The following viewpoints present a small sampling of the controversies faced by the leaders of both North and South during the Civil War.

VIEWPOINT 1

"Soldiers! we congratulate you on an event which ensures the liberty of our country."

The Battle of Manassas Is a Glorious Victory for the Confederacy

Joseph E. Johnston (1807-1891)
and Pierre G.T. Beauregard (1818-1893)

The first major battle of the Civil War took place on July 21, 1861, in Virginia countryside about twenty-five miles west of Washington, D.C., on the banks of Bull Run Creek. It was called the First Battle of Bull Run by the North (a second battle would be fought in the same place the following year), and First Battle of Manassas by the Confederacy (after a nearby town). Both sides, however, agreed after the battle that it was an inspiring victory for the South and a stinging defeat for the North. Typical of the exuberant Confederate reactions was a proclamation by the two commanding Confederate generals who oversaw the battle. The proclamation, reprinted here, was issued on July 28, one week after Confederate forces had routed the invading Union army and forced its soldiers (along with numerous spectators from Washington) into a disorganized, panic retreat. The two generals praise the Confederate soldiers for their valor on the 21st, as well as during another skirmish three days earlier.

Joseph E. Johnston and Pierre G.T. Beauregard, bulletin to Confederate soldiers. Reprinted from *The Rebellion Record: A Diary of American Events, with Documents, Narratives, Illustrative Incidents, Poetry, etc., etc.*, vol. 2, edited by Frank Moore. New York: G.P. Putnam, 1862.

Soldiers of the Confederate States:—

One week ago a countless host of men, organized into an army, with all the appointments which modern art and practiced skill could devise, invaded the soil of Virginia.

Their people sounded their approach with triumph and displays of anticipated victory. Their generals came in almost regal state. Their Minister, Senators, and women came to witness the immolation of this army and the subjugation of our people, and to celebrate these with wild revelry.

It is with the profoundest emotions of gratitude to an overruling God, whose hand is manifested in protecting our homes and your liberties, that we, your generals commanding, are enabled in the name of our whole country to thank you for that patriotic courage, that heroic gallantry, that devoted daring, exhibited by you in the action of the 18th and 21st of July, by which the host of the enemy was scattered, and a signal and glorious victory was achieved.

A Complete Victory

The two affairs of the 18th and 21st were but the sustained and continued efforts of your patriotism against the constantly recurring colors of an enemy fully treble our numbers, and this effort was crowned, on the evening of the 21st, with a victory so complete, that the invaders were driven from the field, and made to fly in disorderly route back to their intrenchments, a distance of over thirty miles.

They left upon the field nearly every piece of their artillery, a large portion of their arms, equipments, baggage, stores, &c., and almost every one of their wounded and dead, amounting, together with the prisoners, to many thousands; and thus the Northern hosts were driven by you from Virginia.

Soldiers! we congratulate you on an event which insures the liberty of our country. We congratulate every man of you whose glorious privilege it was to participate in this triumph of courage and truth, to fight in the battle of Manassas. You have created an epoch in the history of liberty, and unborn nations will rise up and call you blessed. Continue this noble devotion, looking always to the protection of the just God, and, before time grows much older, we will be hailed as the deliverers of a nation of ten millions of people.

Comrades! Our brothers who have fallen have earned undying renown, and their blood, shed in our holy cause, is a precious and acceptable sacrifice to the Father of Truth and Right; their graves are beside the tomb of Washington, their spirits have joined his in

A Splendid Victory

Many Southern newspaper accounts of the first major battle of the Civil War spoke glowingly of the Confederate victory and praised Confederate president Jefferson Davis and Generals Joseph E. Johnston and Pierre G.T. Beauregard. This excerpt is from the New Orleans Crescent, *July 23, 1863.*

The battle annals of the American continent furnish no parallel to the brilliant and splendid victory won by the Southern army on Sunday last over the hired mercenaries and minions of the abolition despotism. With an inferior force, in point of numbers, we have driven back to their dens the boasting invaders of our soil, scattering them before our victorious arms as leaves are scattered before the autumn wind. The details we publish in our telegraphic column leave no doubt that we have put the enemy to utter rout, and struck him a blow from which it is impossible for him wholly to recover.

The victory is the more significant, from the fact that it is the first general engagement between the opposing forces. That the President of the Confederate States was himself in the thickest of the fight, exposed to all the perils of the battle-field, is another circumstance that adds to the joy of our triumph, and swells our triumphant note of exultation. All honor to our brave and gallant leader and President, to the brave Beauregard, the gallant Johnston, and our chivalric soldiery.

We have driven the enemy back from our soil, we have mowed down his men by the hundreds and by the thousands, we have captured his batteries, and sent him howling and panic-stricken from the field of the fight. The blow, in its moral and its physical effects, will prove of incalculable advantage to the Southern cause.

eternal communion. We will hold the soil in which the dust of Washington is mingled with the dust of our brothers. We drop one tear on their laurels, and move forward to avenge them.

Soldiers! We congratulate you on a glorious triumph and complete victory. We thank you for doing your whole duty in the service of your country.

"No delusive hope need be entertained for a solitary moment that a peace has been conquered by the result at Manassas."

Victory at Manassas Should Not Make the South Overconfident

Memphis Appeal

The First Battle of Manassas (or Bull Run) featured the first major fighting of the Civil War. It occurred several months following the South's attack on Fort Sumter and President Abraham Lincoln's subsequent call for 75,000 troops from the states to put down the Confederate rebellion. In the weeks and months following Sumter, Northern congressional leaders and newspaper editors urged the U.S. Army to quickly attack the Confederate capital, Richmond, Virginia, and crush the Confederacy in its infancy. It was partly in response to this political pressure that Union war leaders planned an invasion of Virginia. The confident belief that the South could be easily defeated was shattered after Manassas, however, when the invading Northern army, composed largely of raw recruits, was routed by Confederate forces. The battle boosted the confidence of many in the South, who argued that it showed the superior fighting ability of Southern troops over their opponents.

Memphis Appeal, July 30, 1861. Reprinted from *The Rebellion Record: A Diary of American Events, with Documents, Narratives, Illustrative Incidents, Poetry, etc., etc.*, vol. 2, edited by Frank Moore. New York: G.P. Putnam, 1862.

One exception to the general euphoria expressed in the Southern press was a July 30 editorial, reprinted here, from the *Memphis Appeal*, a Tennessee newspaper. The writer of the editorial warns against overconfidence on the part of the Confederacy, argues that the Battle of Manassas will force the Union to take the war more seriously, and points out the advantage the Union holds over the Confederacy in population.

There is a danger we fear that the Southern mind, intoxicated with its exultations over the recent great victory of our arms at Manassas, may over-estimate the present advantage as well as the ultimate consequences of that brilliant achievement.

A Great Victory

Certainly there can be no difference of opinion as to its having proved a God-send to the cause of Southern independence and true constitutional liberty. It has greatly strengthened the confidence of our people in the ability of their government to maintain itself, even at the point of the bayonet, against the marauding legions of Hessian soldiery who have been precipitated by the enemy upon our sacred soil. It has impaired the energies of the "old wreck" of the Federal Government, and has so far annihilated the confidence of its subjects in the final success of its boasted scheme of subjugation, as to work the most serious detriment to the national credit—which, according to the recent acknowledgment of a congressman, has already failed. It has given a *prestige* to the young republic of the South, just emerging, like Venus, in all the perfection of her beauty, from the foaming sea of political convulsion, which will put to naught the vaunting assertion of Northern superiority, and perhaps decide the question of foreign recognition which now trembles in the hesitating balance held by the hands of European powers. In addition to these there may be even other, though less important results flowing from it.

But to suppose that our independence is an accomplished fact, without other like desperate struggles, is palpable absurdity, the entertainment of which will prove a delusion and a snare. It is true that the forces of the enemy, outnumbering our own more than two to one, were utterly routed, and driven into a retreat styled by themselves both disgraceful and cowardly. But the defeat is not such as to turn the reckless politicians, who manage this movement, from the attempted execution of their direful purpose. Their pride has been sorely wounded, and their passion of revenge stimulated to the performance of new deeds of infamy. At any sacrifice of life or of the people's money, they will rally their routed forces and attempt with still greater desperation to retrieve their lost fortunes. Relying upon the brute force of mere numbers, the enemy are evidently determined to risk other engagements, perhaps of greater magnitude, if for nothing else than the gratification of their malignity, or the palliation of their disgrace now so manifest to the eyes of foreign powers. The vast preparations that are now being made, and the great caution taken in the efficient organization of the army for the future, with the unceremonious dismissal of incompetents, are but a few of the indications to foreshadow their increased, yet fruitless determination.

A Northern View of Manassas

Edward Everett of Massachusetts was a noted orator who gave numerous speeches on behalf of the Union cause (he was the keynote speaker the day Abraham Lincoln delivered his Gettysburg Address). In this excerpt from an article that appeared in the New York Ledger *on August 22, 1861, he argues that defeat at Manassas (Bull Run) has not significantly weakened the North.*

There probably never was a military disaster, of which the importance was more unduly magnified, than that of the 21st of July in front of Manassas. After a severe and protracted encounter between the two armies, which, it is admitted, was about to terminate in a drawn battle, if not even in favor of the United States, the Confederates were largely reinforced, a panic arose on the part of the teamsters and civilians following in the train of our forces, the alarm gradually spread to the troops, a retreat commenced, and ended in a general rout. The losses of the enemy in the mean time were equal to our own; he was unable to pursue our flying regiments, and they reoccupied, unmolested, the positions from which (from political reasons, and against the judgment of the Commander-in-chief) the premature advance was made. A month has since elapsed; the army of the United States has passed through the terrible ordeal of the return of the three months men [initial Union recruits who had enlisted for ninety days], which began simultaneously with the disaster of the 21st of July, and in spite of the disheartening effect of that disaster and the confidence it was so well calculated to inspire on the part of the Confederates, our military position is stronger now than it was before the inauspicious event.

It may be that the half million of men voted Mr. Lincoln by his obsequious parliament may not all be obtained, and certain it is that the five hundred millions of money will come in very tardily, and at great sacrifices on the part of the Government, if at all. But it is quite as evident that men and money will be secured for the prosecution of this atrocious war, even though the one be obtained by drafting, and the other by direct taxation and forced loans. We may expect, and must be prepared to encounter, an army of at least four hundred thousand men, who will be gathered at various points upon the borders of our Confederacy, seeking to force an entrance with the bayonet in less than ninety days. Our preparations for the vast campaign, unequalled by any of modern times, and scarcely overshadowed by Bonaparte's into Russia, must be commensurate with its magnitude and the importance of confronting it with successful resistance.

The population of the eleven States, comprising the Confederate Government, according to the census of 1860, is just 5,581,649. A levy of ten per cent. of this amount, which has always been regarded as not only practicable but extremely light for military purposes, would give us an army of five hundred and fifty-eight thousand men. Leaving out the disaffected portions of the country, where recruiting might prove somewhat difficult, we may safely calculate on raising 400,000 men with the greatest facility, for it is estimated that we have more than 200,000 armed and equipped in the field. The Confederate Government should at once exercise its energies in this work. While we can readily whip the enemy in an open field and fair fight, where they do not outnumber us in a proportion greater than three to two, we must not place ourselves in such a condition as to render the result the least doubtful. To make assurance doubly sure, it is our bounden duty to meet the invaders man for man, and by the adoption of a vigorous and aggressive policy make this war a brief one. An eye for an eye and a tooth for a tooth, is the maxim that should guide us through this revolution.

Prepare for the Worst

But, to resume: The point which we most desire to impress upon the minds of the people is the necessity of being prepared yet for the worst. No delusive hope need be entertained for a solitary moment that a peace has been conquered by the result at Manassas. It is only the entering wedge to such a consummation. We may still with propriety advise with Patrick Henry, when he eloquently exclaimed, "WE MUST FIGHT! I REPEAT IT, SIRS, WE MUST FIGHT!"

"The cautious policy and strategy so far pursued by our armies, if persevered in, will insure us against any serious disasters, and . . . exhaust the strength and the means of our enemy."

The Confederacy Should Adopt a Defensive Strategy

George Fitzhugh (1806-1881)

The question of military strategy was important for both the North and the South, and was often discussed in newspapers and magazines as people offered advice to their generals and leaders. One such would-be adviser was George Fitzhugh, a Virginia lawyer who is best remembered today for his books *Sociology for the South* and *Cannibals All!*, in which he argued that slavery as practiced in the South was a morally superior system to the industrial wage labor system of the North.

The following viewpoint is taken from an article Fitzhugh wrote for the January/February 1862 issue of *De Bow's Review*, a monthly magazine published in New Orleans, Louisiana, that focused on issues concerning the South. Fitzhugh disagrees with those who want the Confederacy to invade the North, arguing that defenders have the advantage over attackers in war. The Confederacy, he asserts, can win the war by successfully defending itself against Northern attack, thus weakening Union armies and stirring up division within the Northern states. He specifically argues against an invasion of Maryland as being too risky for the Confederacy.

George Fitzhugh, article in *De Bow's Review*, vol. 32, January/February 1862. Reprinted from *The Cause of the South*, edited by Paul F. Paskoff and Daniel J. Wilson, 1982.

The mob rules despotically among our enemies. Shall we instal it in supreme power at the South? So far, our President and all our officers have disregarded the senseless clamor of home-keeping people, who talk and write ignorantly, thoughtlessly and recklessly, about the conduct of the war, which they comprehend about as well as they do the Chaldaic language, or the Egyptian hieroglyphics. Out of danger's way themselves, they do not feel or care for the useless danger to which they would expose our troops. Our officers, whether volunteers or regulars, have exhibited remarkable prudence, caution, skill and sagacity. As conscientious men, they have endeavored to gain victory with little loss of life. In this they have succeeded, because they have fought the enemy at advantage, and never at disadvantage. An army acting on the defensive, in its own territory may, by retreating, choose its own position for battle. The invading army must either cease to advance, give up its project of conquest, or attack it at disadvantage, in the strong position which it has selected. Where such retreat is conducted in good order, the retreating army gathers strength daily from the surrounding country, and has little difficulty in procuring provisions, because it is always among friends whose resources have not been exhausted.

Southern Obstacles to Invasion

On the other hand, the invading army rapidly diminishes in numbers, from having daily to detail forces to keep open its line of communication with its base of operations. Besides, with it the difficulty of obtaining provisions increases with each advance. It must procure them from home, from which it is hourly receding; for if the retreating army have not entirely exhausted the supplies of the country through which it has passed, the people are unfriendly, and will not bring into the camp of their enemies the little that is left. If they send out foraging parties this still further weakens them, and exposes them to decimation in detail. Bonaparte set out for Moscow with half a million of men, and if we mistake not, had little over a hundred and fifty thousand when he arrived there. Russia, and the whole of Northern Europe, except Sweden, Norway and Lapland, is a dead level, interspersed with towns and villages. It has no natural strength, and hence, in past times conquest in Europe, with slight exceptions, has proceeded northwardly. The Confederate States present greater natural obstacles to an invading army than any equal area of country on the globe. Armies cannot march down our Atlantic coast, because of the great number of bays, inlets, creeks and rivers; nor down the interior, because of mountain ridges, impassable roads, sparse population, and scarcity of provisions.

The Mississippi is narrow, long, tedious, and easily defended, and its valley is subject to overflow. No invading army will attempt a serious invasion in that direction. It is our true policy to decoy the enemy into the interior, and then to cut them off. . . . When we have defeated and captured their armies, exhausted their treasury, and cowed their spirits by defensive warfare, it will be time for us to begin to act on the offensive and to invade their territory. The northwest is as level a country as Northern Europe, teems with provisions, and abounds with towns and villages. Its population is a spiritless rabble, who have few arms and know little of their use, and who are endowed with no sense of personal or national honor. The northeast rules them with a rod of iron, and, by its protective tariff, robs them of half the proceeds of their labor. They should welcome us as deliverers from Yankee bondage, rather than as conquerors.

Cincinnati and Philadelphia are both weak and tempting points, and when we have well whipped the enemy within our own territory, it will be time to turn our attention to those cities.

Culver Pictures Inc.

This 1861 photograph of members of the 1st Virginia Militia was taken at a time when many Southerners were highly confident of victory over the North.

We need not fear that we shall not have abundant opportunities, if we will be but prudent and cautious, to fight them at advantage. They have undertaken to conquer the South, and must advance. In Missouri, Kentucky, and northwestern Virginia, we may bide our time and opportunity, select our positions, and fight them only when it is policy to do so. They propose, too, to go to the relief of Eastern Tennessee. Let them try it; when they have marched through Kentucky it will be impossible for them to keep up communication with the North, and their invading army will fall an easy prey to our forces.

We must conquer Washington and Maryland on Virginia soil. McClellan is required by the whole North to advance. He must advance or resign. If he, or the general who succeeds him, advances, we will be sure to defeat them at Centreville, or Manassas, or at some point between Washington and Richmond. A half dozen defeats would not injure us. A single one would ruin them, and open the way to Washington and Maryland. We must break up their army before we advance into Maryland; and this they will afford us an early opportunity to effect, if we will be but patient.

Should they go into winter quarters in Washington, the North will see that the subjugation of the South is a hopeless project, and the nations of Europe will recognize our independence and break up the [Northern] blockade. The press and the people of the North see this, and promise, as a dernier resort, a series of brilliant victories, to be achieved by land and by sea within the next few weeks. They must fight us within that time on our own soil and at positions selected by ourselves, and defeat us, too, or the illusion of subjugating the South will pass off from all Northern minds. Invasion alone can subjugate a country; and after nine months of threatening and preparation the North has not advanced ten miles into the well-affected portion of our territory, and has almost lost Missouri, Kentucky, northwestern Virginia and Maryland, which offered them no resistance when the war began. The grand result of their attempted conquest has been, so far, to add a third to the numbers and strength of their enemies.

Should Maryland Be Invaded?

Many who admit that it is both perilous and useless, so far as ultimate success is concerned, to attempt now to take Washington, who see that so soon as we cross the Potomac we divide our strength, and "have an impassable river behind us and an enemy in superior force before us," contend, nevertheless, that we are in honor bound to attempt the relief of Maryland.

Marching into her territory will be sure to transfer the seat of war from Virginia and carry it into her midst. She is now comparatively well treated by the federal forces, because they are trying

171

to conciliate her favor, and retain her in the Union. When we attempt to relieve her by crossing the Potomac, we shall place her in the situation of Kentucky, Missouri, Western Virginia and Fairfax [Virginia]. The federalists will burn her farm-houses and villages and towns, and rob and lay waste her whole territory; and her own citizens, divided in their allegiance, will rise up and shed each other's blood. We can imagine no situation more deplorable than would be that of Maryland if we were now to march a part of our army into her territories. The time has not yet arrived when the federals would flee from her soil, panic stricken at our approach; and will not arrive until we have re-enacted on Virginia soil another Manassas. This we shall almost certainly have an opportunity to effect ere winter closes.

Comparing Armies

An anonymous author, writing in the December 1861 issue of the New Orleans–based magazine De Bow's Review, *argues that Confederate victory is assured because of the superior quality of Southern soldiers.*

Our soldiers are not like the miserable hirelings of Lincoln—the scum of infamy and degradation—hunted up from the dens, sewers, and filthy prisons of the North, with the low vandalism of foreign importations, picked up wherever they can be found. Yet such are the creatures our brave soldiers have to meet. Our armies are composed of men who have not volunteered for pay, nor for food and clothing; and it is even doubtful whether a solitary man can be found among them, now numbering over three hundred thousand strong, who would not be willing to serve the Government, cheerfully, if required, to the end of the war, being fed and clothed, without any pay. This is saying much; but if the test was necessary to be applied, there would surely be but few exceptions. Thus we find in our armies, even amidst all the privations incident thereto, the same spirit of union and devotion to the Confederacy which actuates those whom they have left at home; indeed, with a large number of our people, there is being manifested a general feeling to give over the effort to make money or accumulate property during the continuance of this war. Such, then, is the state of the Confederacy; with a people so united, so determined, and so cooperating, there can be no such thing as fail, and the armies of such a people are unconquerable. Its independence is certain and secure.

Should we be defeated in Maryland, our whole army, with their arms and ammunition, would be captured by the enemy. We might in a short time repair the loss of our men, but the loss of our munitions of war would inflict upon us a stunning and appalling blow. One defeat in Maryland would do us more harm than ten in Virginia. We have the selection of the battle-ground—Why choose Maryland?

We cannot conquer the North except by exhausting it, or by stirring up dissension between the northeast, East and northwest. Our victories but excite their indignation, increase their energies, stimulate them to enlist in the army, and keep down sectional and domestic broils among them. To avoid civil discord, by keeping the people engaged in foreign war, has been the common policy and practice of statesmen in all ages and in all countries. It is thus with the North. She fears the unemployed, destitute, agrarian mob of her large cities, and equally fears a rupture with the northwest. She has to choose between domestic war and war with us. She prefers the latter, and will carry on the war as long as her money or credit lasts. She will hardly be at a loss for men, as the wages she pays to her soldiers are better than those which she gives to her laborers. The prodigious expense which she is now incurring cannot be long continued, unless some rashness on our part enables her to recruit her failing strength from the spoils of the South. The cautious policy and strategy so far pursued by our armies, if persevered in, will insure us against any serious disasters, and gradually and slowly wear away and exhaust the strength and the means of our enemy.

True Character

Our soldiers and our officers have exhibited a noble specimen of the moral sublime, in the patience with which they have submitted to misconstruction, calumny and abuse. They prefer to pursue that course which is right, to that which only seems to be right. They will not sacrifice true honor to gain ephemeral reputation. They possess that lofty moral fortitude, that true courage, that can submit, even to the imputation of cowardice, rather than by failing in duty, to play the actual coward....

It is easier, far easier, to face the cannon's mouth, or mount the deadly breach, than to prefer duty to reputation.... They are solicitous, not so much for self-approbation as for the applause of the crowd, and are satisfied to do what is wrong, provided they can win the plaudits of the mob. When the future historian records the story of our war, his pen will become most eloquent as he dilates upon that wise, cautious and prudent policy, that, despite of misconstruction, and sacrificing temporary reputation to ultimate success, often won victory by avoiding battle.

"The present seems to be the most propitious time since the commencement of the war for the Confederate Army to enter Maryland."

The Confederacy Should Adopt an Offensive Strategy

Robert E. Lee (1807-1870)
and Jefferson Davis (1808-1889)

Robert E. Lee and Jefferson Davis were, respectively, the preeminent military and political leaders of the Confederacy. Lee commanded the Army of Northern Virginia from 1862 to 1865, and gained respect from both sides for his military leadership. Davis, a Mississippi plantation owner who had served in the U.S. Senate, was president of the Confederacy. A graduate of West Point and a veteran of the Mexican-American War, Davis was heavily involved in the formulation of military policy, much to the consternation of his critics.

The following viewpoint consists of two documents that shed light on one of the fateful decisions made by the Confederacy—Lee's determination to invade Maryland in September 1862, after his army had just successfully repulsed an invasion of Virginia by the Union forces led by George McClellan. The first document reprinted is from Lee's September 3 letter to Davis, in which he tells of his plans to enter Maryland. Lee argues that although such a move is risky—it leaves Richmond, Virginia, vulnerable to attack and his army is lacking in supplies—such an invasion will "harass" the enemy and perhaps encourage Maryland (a slave state) to join the Confederacy. Another consideration, not men-

Robert E. Lee, letter to Jefferson Davis dated September 3, 1862. Jefferson Davis, letter to Robert E. Lee, Braxton Bragg, and Edmund Kirby Smith dated September 7, 1862. Reprinted from *Basic History of the Confederacy*, edited by Frank E. Vandiver, 1961.

tioned in the letter, was the hope for English and French recognition of the Confederacy if it could follow up its successful defense of Virginia with a victory on Northern soil.

Part II of the viewpoint is taken from a September 7, 1862, directive from Jefferson Davis to Lee, as well as to Confederate generals Braxton Bragg and Kirby Smith, who in confluence with Lee's move were attacking the state of Kentucky. Davis's missive was meant to be read by the generals to the people of the states they were invading. It illustrates the "offensive-defensive" strategy pursued by the Confederacy at this stage of the war—the idea that although the Confederacy's ultimate goal was merely to defend itself, it could best do so by, at carefully chosen times and places, taking the war into Northern territory, thus bringing the effects of war home to its people and possibly splintering the North.

By the time Davis had written this directive, Lee was already in Maryland. The forces of Lee and McClellan clashed on September 17, 1862, at the Battle of Antietam, the bloodiest single day of fighting of the Civil War. One-third of Lee's invading army was killed, captured, or wounded; the remaining troops were forced to return to Virginia. The North's success in repelling Lee's Maryland invasion encouraged President Abraham Lincoln to make public his intention of emancipating the slaves in the South by January 1, 1863.

I

M̲r. President:

The present seems to be the most propitious time since the commencement of the war for the Confederate Army to enter Maryland. The two grand armies of the United States that have been operating in Virginia, though now united, are much weakened and demoralized. Their new levies, of which I understand sixty thousand men have already been posted in Washington, are not yet organized, and will take some time to prepare for the field. If it is ever desired to give material aid to Maryland and afford her an opportunity of throwing off the oppression to which she is now subject, this would seem the most favorable. After the enemy had disappeared from the vicinity of Fairfax Court House and taken the road to Alexandria & Washington, I did not think it would be advantageous to follow him farther. I had no intention of attacking him in his fortifications, and am not prepared to invest them. If I possessed the necessary munitions, I should be unable to supply provisions for the troops. I therefore determined while threatening the approaches to Washington, to draw the troops into Loudoun, where forage and some provisions can be obtained, menace their possession of the Shenandoah Valley, and if found practicable, to cross into Maryland.

The purpose, if discovered, will have the effect of carrying the enemy north of the Potomac, and if prevented, will not result in

A Time to Press Forward

In June and July 1862 Confederate forces successfully repulsed the attempted invasion of Virginia by the large Union Army of the Potomac under General George B. McClellan; by early July 1862, McClellan had given up his attempt to capture the Confederate capital of Richmond, Virginia. A July 7, 1862, editorial in the Charleston Mercury *in South Carolina urges that the successful defense of Richmond be followed up with aggressive military action by the Confederate armies.*

But, however we rejoice over the great victory just achieved, it is only a successful defence of Richmond, accompanied by the defeat of the best army of the North. Richmond is not the only place threatened, and there are States and cities already in the hands of the enemy. It is incumbent upon us to redeem these, either by recapture or by the obtainment of equivalents from the enemy: Until we do this, we cannot make a satisfactory peace which will secure us independence, not only in political government, but in commercial relations. Maryland, Tennessee, Kentucky and Missouri have to be redeemed. New Orleans, Memphis, Nashville and Norfolk have to be obtained, and all the ports and harbors on our coasts and rivers now held by the enemy. We, therefore, have a heavy labor yet before us, and one which energy, enterprise and activity on the part of our Government and generals and troops alone can accomplish. We cannot afford to throw away this dear bought opportunity, as we have done several before. We have been sufficiently imperilled by victories, made moral, not material, by hallucinations of prudence and preparation. They have cost us enough of property and life, to fill the land with misery and with mourning. "Masterly inactivity" and "brilliant retreats" are too expensive a species of strategy to be longer tolerated. The people of the Confederate States want action—they want a war of aggressive movement, and this is a moment for inaugurating it in the East and in the West. Rapidity on the part of the Confederate Generals, ere our own victorious army is demoralized, and before the Northern forces can recover from the great disaster they have suffered, can put us in possession of our own, or furnish the means for a satisfactory peace of real independence within a moderately brief period. But every thing depends upon the advantage taken of the late great and bloody victory. Let troops be hurried forward and strike. No breathing time to the enemy. The God of battles favors our cause.

much evil. The army is not properly equipped for an invasion of an enemy's territory. It lacks much of the material of war, is feeble in transportation, the animals being much reduced, and the men are poorly provided with clothes, and in thousands of instances are destitute of shoes. Still we cannot afford to be idle, and though weaker than our opponents in men and military equipments, must endeavor to harass, if we cannot destroy them. I am aware that the movement is attended with much risk, yet I do not consider success impossible, and shall endeavor to guard it from loss. As long as the army of the enemy are employed on this frontier I have no fears for the safety of Richmond, yet I earnestly recommend that advantage be taken of this period of comparative safety to place its defence, both by land and water, in the most perfect condition. A respectable force can be collected to defend its approaches by land, and the steamer *Richmond* I hope is now ready to clear the river of hostile vessels. . . . What occasions me most concern is the fear of getting out of ammunition. I beg you will instruct the Ordnance Department to spare no pains in manufacturing a sufficient amount of the best kind, & to be particular in preparing that for the artillery, to provide three times as much of the long range ammunition as of that for smooth bore or short range guns.

The points to which I desire the ammunition to be forwarded will be made known to the Department in time. If the Quartermaster Department can furnish any shoes, it would be the greatest relief.

We have entered upon September, and the nights are becoming cool.

II

Sirs:

It is deemed proper that you should in accordance with established usage announce by proclamation to the people of _____ the motives and purposes of your presence among them at the head of an invading army, and you are instructed in such proclamation to make known,

1ST. That the Confederate Government is waging this war solely for self-defence, that it has no design of conquest or any other purpose than to secure peace and the abandonment by the United States of its pretensions to govern a people who have never been their subjects and who prefer self-government to a Union with them.

Peace Overtures Rejected

2ND. That this Government at the very moment of its inauguration sent commissioners to Washington to treat for a peaceful adjustment of all differences, but that these commissioners were not received nor even allowed to communicate the object of their mission, and that on a subsequent occasion a communication from the President of the Confederacy to President Lincoln remained without answer, although a reply was promised by General Scott into whose hands the communication was delivered.

The invasion of Maryland in 1862 by General Robert E. Lee's Army of Northern Virginia culminated in the bloody Battle of Antietam. Although the September 17 battle was not decisively won by either side, the Confederates were compelled to retreat to Virginia after suffering more than 13,000 casualties (2,700 killed in battle), including the dead artillerymen pictured here.

3RD. That among the pretexts urged for continuance of the War is the assertion that the Confederate Government desires to deprive the United States of the free navigation of the Western Rivers although the truth is that the Confederate Congress by public act, prior to the commencement of the War, enacted that "the peaceful navigation of the Mississippi River is hereby declared free to the citizens of the States upon its borders, or upon the borders of its navigable tributaries"—a declaration to which this Government has always been and is still ready to adhere.

4TH. That now at a juncture when our arms have been successful, we restrict ourselves to the same just and moderate demand, that we made at the darkest period of our reverses, the simple demand that the people of the United States should cease to war upon us and permit us to pursue our own path to happiness, while they in peace pursue theirs.

5TH. That we are debarred from the renewal of formal proposals for peace by having no reason to expect that they would be received with the respect mutually due by nations in their intercourse, whether in peace or in war.

Taking the War to the Enemy

6TH. That under these circumstances we are driven to protect our own country by transferring the seat of war to that of an enemy who pursues us with a relentless and apparently aimless hostility: That our fields have been laid waste, our people killed, many homes made desolate, and that rapine and murder have ravaged our frontiers, that the sacred right of self defence demands that if such a war is to continue its consequences shall fall on those who persist in their refusal to make peace.

7TH. That the Confederate army therefore comes to occupy the territory of their enemies and to make it the theatre of hostilities. That with the people of _____ themselves rests the power to put an end to this invasion of their homes, for if unable to prevail on the Government of the United States to conclude a general peace, their own State Government in the exercise of its sovereignty can secure immunity from the desolating effects of warfare on the soil of the State by a separate treaty of peace which this Government will ever be ready to conclude on the most just and liberal basis.

8TH. That the responsibility thus rests on the people of _____ of continuing an unjust and aggressive warfare upon the Confederate States, a warfare which can never end in any other manner than that now proposed. With them is the option of preserving the blessings of peace, by the simple abandonment of the design of subjugating a people over whom no right of dominion has been ever conferred either by God or man.

"Read the proclamation for it is the most important of any to which the President of the United States has ever signed his name."

The Emancipation Proclamation Is a Significant Achievement

Frederick Douglass (1817-1895)

Frederick Douglass was an escaped slave who gained national and international fame as an abolitionist, lecturer, and writer. He was publisher and editor of the abolitionist newspaper *The North Star*, which later became known as *Douglass' Monthly*. Douglass viewed the Civil War as a moral crusade against slavery, and was an early advocate of both emancipation of the slaves and enlistment of black soldiers for the Union. The following is taken from the October 1862 issue of *Douglass' Monthly*, just after President Abraham Lincoln had made a preliminary announcement of his Emancipation Proclamation, which would free all the slaves in the Confederate states on January 1, 1863. Douglass criticizes Lincoln for acting too slowly to free the slaves, but ultimately praises the proclamation and calls for renewed efforts to defeat the Confederacy.

Common sense, the necessities of the war, to say nothing of the dictation of justice and humanity have at last prevailed. We shout for joy that we live to record this righteous decree. *Abraham*

Frederick Douglass, *Douglass' Monthly*, October 1862. Reprinted from *The Life and Writings of Frederick Douglass*, edited by Philip S. Foner, 1952.

Lincoln, President of the United States, Commander-in-Chief of the army and navy, in his own peculiar, cautious, forbearing and hesitating way, slow, but we hope sure, has, while the loyal heart was near breaking with despair, proclaimed and declared: *"That on the First of January, in the Year of Our Lord One Thousand, Eight Hundred and Sixty-three, All Persons Held as Slaves Within Any State or Any Designated Part of a State, The People Whereof Shall Then be in Rebellion Against the United States, Shall be Thenceforward and Forever Free."* "Free forever" oh! long enslaved millions, whose cries have so vexed the air and sky, suffer on a few more days in sorrow, the hour of your deliverance draws nigh! Oh! Ye millions of free and loyal men who have earnestly sought to free your bleeding country from the dreadful ravages of revolution and anarchy, lift up now your voices with joy and thanksgiving for with freedom to the slave will come peace and safety to your country. President Lincoln has embraced in this proclamation the law of Congress passed more than six months ago, prohibiting the employment of any part of the army and naval forces of the United States, to return fugitive slaves to their masters, commanded all officers of the army and navy to respect and obey its provisions. He has still further declared his intention to urge upon the Legislature of all the slave States not in rebellion the immediate or gradual abolishment of slavery. But read the proclamation for it is the most important of any to which the President of the United States has ever signed his name.

Reactions

Opinions will widely differ as to the practical effect of this measure upon the war. All that class at the North who have not lost their affection for slavery will regard the measure as the very worst that could be devised, and as likely to lead to endless mischief. All their plans for the future have been projected with a view to a reconstruction of the American Government upon the basis of compromise between slaveholding and non-slaveholding States. The thought of a country unified in sentiments, objects and ideas, has not entered into their political calculations, and hence this newly declared policy of the Government, which contemplates one glorious homogeneous people, doing away at a blow with the whole class of compromisers and corrupters, will meet their stern opposition. Will that opposition prevail? Will it lead the President to reconsider and retract? Not a word of it. Abraham Lincoln may be slow, Abraham Lincoln may desire peace even at the price of leaving our terrible national sore untouched, to fester on for generations, but Abraham Lincoln is not the man to reconsider, retract and contradict words and purposes solemnly proclaimed over his official signature.

The Emancipation Proclamation

The official Emancipation Proclamation was issued and signed by Abraham Lincoln on January 1, 1863. It declared the freeing of slaves in Confederate territory to be both a "necessary war measure" and an "act of justice," and made the Civil War a war to ultimately abolish slavery.

Whereas, on the 22nd day of September, in the year of our Lord 1862, a proclamation was issued by the President of the United States, containing, among other things, the following, to wit:

That on the 1st day of January, in the year of our Lord 1863, all persons held as slaves within any state or designated part of a state, the people whereof shall then be in rebellion against the United States, shall be then, thenceforward, and forever free; and the executive government of the United States, including the military and naval authority thereof, will recognize and maintain the freedom of such persons and will do no act or acts to repress such persons, or any of them, in any efforts they may make for their actual freedom.

That the executive will, on the 1st day of January aforesaid, by proclamation, designate the states and parts of states, if any, in which the people thereof, respectively, shall then be in rebellion against the United States; and the fact that any state or the people thereof shall on that day be in good faith represented in the Congress of the United States by members chosen thereto at elections wherein a majority of the qualified voters of such states shall have participated shall, in the absence of strong countervailing testimony, be deemed conclusive evidence that such state and the people thereof are not then in rebellion against the United States.

Now, therefore, I, Abraham Lincoln, President of the United States, by virtue of the power in me vested as commander in chief of the Army and Navy of the United States, in time of actual armed rebellion against the authority and government of the United States, and as a fit and necessary war measure for suppressing said rebellion, do, on this 1st day of January, in the year of our Lord 1863, and

The careful, and we think, the slothful deliberation which he has observed in reaching this obvious policy, is a guarantee against retraction. But even if the temper and spirit of the President himself were other than what they are, events greater than the President, events which have slowly wrung this proclamation from him may be relied on to carry him forward in the same direction. To look back now would only load him with heavier evils, while diminishing his ability, for overcoming those with which he now has to contend. To recall his proclamation would only increase rebel pride, rebel sense of power and would be hailed as a direct admission of weakness on the part of the Federal Government, while it would cause heaviness of heart and depression of national enthusiasm all over the loyal North and West. No, Abrain accordance with my purpose so to do, publicly proclaimed for the full period of 100 days from the day first above mentioned, order and designate as the states and parts of states wherein the people thereof, respectively, are this day in rebellion against the United States the following, to wit:

Arkansas, Texas, Louisiana (except the parishes of St. Bernard, Plaquemines, Jefferson, St. John, St. Charles, St. James, Ascension, Assumption, Terrebonne, Lafourche, St. Mary, St. Martin, and Orleans, including the city of New Orleans), Mississippi, Alabama, Florida, Georgia, South Carolina, North Carolina, and Virginia (except the forty-eight counties designated as West Virginia, and also the counties of Berkeley, Accomac, Northampton, Elizabeth City, York, Princess Anne, and Norfolk, including the cities of Norfolk and Portsmouth), and which excepted parts are for the present left precisely as if this proclamation were not issued.

And, by virtue of the power and for the purpose aforesaid, I do order and declare that all persons held as slaves within said designated states and parts of states are, and henceforward shall be, free; and that the executive government of the United States, including the military and naval authorities thereof, will recognize and maintain the freedom of said persons.

And I hereby enjoin upon the people so declared to be free to abstain from all violence, unless in necessary self-defense; and I recommend to them that, in all cases when allowed, they labor faithfully for reasonable wages.

And I further declare and make known that such persons of suitable condition will be received into the armed service of the United States to garrison forts, positions, stations, and other places, and to man vessels of all sorts in said service.

And upon this act, sincerely believed to be an act of justice, warranted by the Constitution upon military necessity, I invoke the considerate judgment of mankind and the gracious favor of Almighty God.

---

ham Lincoln will take no step backward. His word has gone out over the country and the world, giving joy and gladness to the friends of freedom and progress wherever those words are read, and he will stand by them, and carry them out to the letter. If he has taught us to confide in nothing else, he has taught us to confide in his word. The want of Constitutional power, the want of military power, the tendency of the measure to intensify Southern hate, and to exasperate the rebels, the tendency to drive from him all that class of Democrats at the North, whose loyalty has been conditioned on his restoring the union as it was, slavery and all, have all been considered, and he has taken his ground notwithstanding. The President doubtless saw, as we see, that it is not more absurd to talk about restoring the union, without hurting slavery, than restoring the union without hurting the rebels. As to exasperating the South, there can be no more in the cup than the cup will hold, and that was full already. The whole situation having been carefully scanned, before Mr. Lincoln could be made to budge an inch, he will now stand his ground. Border State influence, and the influence of half-loyal men, have been exerted and have done their worst. The end of these two influences is implied in this proclamation. Hereafter, the inspiration as well as the men and the money for carrying on the war will come from the North, and not from half-loyal border States.

The effect of this paper upon the disposition of Europe will be great and increasing. It changes the character of the war in European eyes and gives it an important principle as an object, instead of national pride and interest. It recognizes and declares the real nature of the contest, and places the North on the side of justice and civilization, and the rebels on the side of robbery and barbarism. It will disarm all purpose on the part of European Government to intervene in favor of the rebels and thus cast off at a blow one source of rebel power. All through the war thus far, the rebel ambassadors in foreign countries have been able to silence all expression of sympathy with the North as to slavery. With much more than a show of truth, they said that the Federal Government, no more than the Confederate Government, contemplated the abolition of slavery.

But will not this measure be frowned upon by our officers and men in the field? We have heard of many thousands who have resolved that they will throw up their commissions and lay down their arms, just so soon as they are required to carry on a war against slavery. Making all allowances for exaggeration there are doubtless far too many of this sort in the loyal army. Putting this kind of loyalty and patriotism to the test, will be one of the best collateral effects of the measure. Any man who leaves the field on such a ground will be an argument in favor of the proclamation, and will prove that his heart has been more with slavery than with his country. Let the army be cleansed from all such pro-slavery vermin, and its health and strength will be greatly improved. But there can be no reason to fear the loss of many officers or men by resignation or desertion. We have no doubt that the measure was brought to the attention of most of our leading Generals, and blind as some of them have seemed to be in the earlier part of the war, most of them have seen enough to convince them that there can be no end to this war that does not end slavery. At any rate, we may hope that for every pro-slavery man that shall start from the ranks of our loyal army, there will be two anti-slavery men to fill up the vacancy, and in this war one truly devoted to the cause of Emancipation is worth two of the opposite sort.

Two Necessary Conditions

Whether slavery will be abolished in the manner now proposed by President Lincoln, depends of course upon two conditions, the first specified and the second implied. The first is that the slave States shall be in rebellion on and after the first day of January 1863 and the second is we must have the ability to put down that rebellion. About the first there can be very little doubt. The South is thoroughly in earnest and confident. It has staked everything upon the rebellion. Its experience thus far in the field has rather increased its hopes of final success than diminished them. Its armies now hold us at bay at all points, and the war is confined to the border States slave and free. If Richmond were in our hands and Virginia at our mercy, the vast regions beyond would still remain to be subdued. But the rebels confront us on the Potomac, the Ohio, and the Mississippi. Kentucky, Maryland, Missouri, and Virginia are in debate on the battlefields and their people are divided by the line which separates treason from loyalty. In short we are yet, after eighteen months of war, confined to the outer margin of the rebellion. We have scarcely more than touched the surface of the terrible evil. It has been raising large quantities of food during the past summer. While the masters have been fighting abroad, the slaves have been busy working at home to supply them with the means of continuing the struggle. They will not [back] down at the bidding of this Proclamation, but may be safely relied upon till January and long after January. A month or two will put an end to general fighting for the winter. When the leaves fall we shall hear again of bad roads, winter quarters and spring campaigns. The South which has thus far withstood our arms will not fall at once before our pens. All fears for the abolition of slavery arising from this apprehension may be dismissed. Whoever, therefore, lives to see the first day of next January, should Abraham Lincoln be then alive and President of the United States, may confidently look in the morning papers for the final proclamation, granting freedom, and freedom forever, to all slaves within the rebel States. On the next point nothing need be said. We have full power to put down the rebellion. Unless one man is more than a match for four, unless the South breeds braver and better men than the North, unless slavery is more precious than liberty, unless a just cause kindles a feebler enthusiasm than a wicked and villainous one, the men of the loyal States will put down this rebellion and slavery, and all the sooner will they put down that rebellion by coupling slavery with that object. Tenderness towards slavery has been the loyal weakness during the war. Fighting the slaveholders with one hand and holding the slaves with the other, has been fairly tried and has failed. We have now inaugurated a wiser and better policy, a policy which is better for the loyal cause than an hundred thousand armed men. The Star Spangled Banner is now the harbinger of Liberty and the millions in bondage, inured to hardships, accustomed to toil, ready to suffer, ready to fight, to dare and to die, will rally under that banner wherever they see it gloriously unfolded to the breeze. Now let the Government go forward in its mission of Liberty as the only condition of peace and union, by weeding out the army and navy of all such officers as the late Col. [Dixon] Miles, whose sympathies are now known to have been with the rebels. Let only the men who assent heartily to the wisdom and the justice of the anti-slavery policy of the Government be lifted into command; let the black man have an arm as well as a heart in this war, and the tide of battle which has thus far only waved backward and forward, will steadily set in our favor. The rebellion suppressed, slavery abolished, and America will, higher than ever, sit as a queen among the nations of the earth.

Now for the work. During the interval between now and next January, let every friend of the long enslaved bondman do his utmost in swelling the tide of anti-slavery sentiment, by writing, speaking, money and example. Let our aim be to make the North a unit in favor of the President's policy, and see to it that our voices and votes, shall forever extinguish that latent and malignant sentiment at the North, which has from the first cheered on the rebels in their atrocious crimes against the union, and has systematically sought to paralyze the national arm in striking down the slaveholding rebellion. We are ready for this service or any other, in this, we trust the last struggle with the monster slavery.

VIEWPOINT 6

"You cannot abolish slavery by the sword; still less by proclamations."

The Emancipation Proclamation Is a Worthless Act

Clement L. Vallandigham (1820-1871) and Jefferson Davis (1808-1889)

Abraham Lincoln's Emancipation Proclamation, on January 1, 1863 (following a preliminary proclamation on September 22, 1862), declared all the slaves in rebelling states to be free. The Proclamation, while highly praised by abolitionists, provoked criticism in both the North and the South. The following two-part viewpoint is taken from the views of a leading Northern dissenter and the president of the Confederacy, both of whom are harshly critical of the Proclamation.

Part I is by Clement L. Vallandigham, a Democratic representative from Ohio and leader of the "Copperheads," who opposed the war. In a January 14, 1863, speech delivered in the House of Representatives, he argues that the Emancipation Proclamation will not end slavery. It will, he predicts, prevent ending the Civil War by a peaceful compromise with the South—something he had long advocated. Part II is by Jefferson Davis, a former senator from Mississippi who was the first and only president of the Confederacy. In a special message to the Confederate Congress on January 12, 1863, Davis argues that Lincoln's actions fully justify the Confederacy's decision to leave the United States, and make restoration of the Union impossible.

From Clement L. Vallandigham, speech before Congress, January 14, 1863, *Appendix to the Congressional Globe*, 1863. Jefferson Davis, message to Confederate Congress, January 12, 1863. Reprinted from *Jefferson Davis, Constitutionalist: His Letters, Papers and Speeches*, edited by Dunbar Rowland, 1923, courtesy of the Mississippi Department of Archives and History.

I

Now, sir, on the 14th of April [1861], I believed that coercion would bring on war, and war disunion. More than that, I believed, what you all in your hearts believe to-day, that the South could never be conquered—never. And not that only, but I was satisfied—and you of the abolition party have now proved it to the world—that the secret but real purpose of the war was to abolish slavery in the States. In any event, I did not doubt that whatever might be the momentary impulses of those in power, and whatever pledges they might make in the midst of the fury for the Constitution, the Union, and the flag, yet the natural and inexorable logic of revolutions would, sooner or later, drive them into that policy, and with it to its final but inevitable result, the change of our present democratical form of government into an imperial despotism. . . .

And now, sir, I recur to the state of the Union to-day. . . .

You have not conquered the South. You never will. It is not in the nature of things possible; much less under your auspices. But money you have expended without limit, and blood poured out like water. Defeat, debt, taxation, sepulchers, these are your trophies. In vain the people gave you treasure and the soldier yielded up his life. "Fight, tax, emancipate, let these," said the gentleman from Maine, (Mr. Pike,) at the last session, "be the trinity of our salvation." Sir, they have become the trinity of your deep damnation. The war for the Union is, in your hands, a most bloody and costly failure. The President confessed it on the 22d of September, solemnly, officially, and under the broad seal of the United States. And he has now now repeated the confession. The priests and rabbis of abolition taught him that God would not prosper such a cause. War for the Union was abandoned; war for the negro openly begun, and with stronger battalions than before. With what success? Let the dead at Fredericksburg and Vicksburg answer. . . .

The Great Question

And now, sir, I come to the great and controlling question within which the whole issue of union or disunion is bound up: is there "an irrepressible conflict" between the slaveholding and non-slaveholding States? . . . If so, then there is an end of all union and forever. You cannot abolish slavery by the sword; still less by proclamations, though the President were to "proclaim" every month. Of what possible avail was his proclamation of September? Did the South submit? Was she even alarmed? And yet he has now fulmined another "bull against the comet"—*bru-*

188

tum fulmen [irrational threat]—and, threatening servile insurrection with all its horrors, has yet coolly appealed to the judgment of mankind, and invoked the blessing of the God of peace and love! But declaring it a military necessity, an essential measure of war to subdue the rebels, yet, with admirable wisdom, he expressly exempts from its operation the only States and parts of States in the South where he has the military power to execute it.

Neither, sir, can you abolish slavery by argument. As well attempt to abolish marriage or the relation of paternity. The South is resolved to maintain it at every hazard and by ever sacrifice; and if "this Union cannot endure part slave and part free," then it is already and finally dissolved. . . .

But I deny the doctrine. It is full of disunion and civil war. It is disunion itself. Whoever first taught it ought to be dealt with as not only hostile to the Union, but an enemy of the human race. Sir, the fundamental idea of the Constitution is the perfect and eternal compatibility of a union of States "part slave and part free;" else the Constitution never would have been framed, nor the Union founded; and seventy years of successful experiment have approved the wisdom of the plan. In my deliberate judgment, a confederacy made up of slaveholding and non-slaveholding States is, in the nature of things, the strongest of all popular governments. African slavery has been, and is, eminently conservative. It makes the absolute political equality of the white race everywhere practicable. It dispenses with the English order of nobility, and leaves every white man, North and South, owning slaves or owning none, the equal of every other white man. It has reconciled universal suffrage throughout the free States with the stability of government. I speak not now of its material benefits to the North and West, which are many and more obvious. But the South, too, has profited many ways by a union with the non-slaveholding States. Enterprise, industry, self-reliance, perseverance, and the other hardy virtues of a people living in a higher latitude and without hereditary servants, she has learned or received from the North. Sir, it is easy, I know, to denounce all this, and to revile him who utters it. Be it so. The English is, of all languages, the most copious in words of bitterness and reproach. "Pour on: I will endure.". . .

Whoever hates negro slavery more than he loves the Union, must demand separation at last. I think that you can never abolish slavery by fighting. Certainly you never can till you have first destroyed the South, and then . . . converted this Government into an imperial despotism. And, sir, whenever I am forced to a choice between the loss to my own country and race, of personal and political liberty with all its blessings, and the involuntary domestic servitude of the negro, I shall not hesitate one moment to choose the latter alternative. The sole question to-day is between the Union with slavery, or final disunion, and, I think, anarchy and despotism. I am for the Union. It was good enough for my fathers. It is good enough for us and our children after us.

II

The public journals of the North have been received, containing a proclamation, dated on the 1st day of the present month [January 1863], signed by the President of the United States, in which he orders and declares all slaves within ten of the States of the Confederacy to be free, except such as are found within certain districts now occupied in part by the armed forces of the enemy. We may well leave it to the instincts of that common humanity which a beneficent Creator has implanted in the breasts of our fellowmen of all countries to pass judgment on a measure by which several millions of human beings of an inferior race, peaceful and contented laborers in their sphere, are doomed to extermination, while at the same time they are encouraged to a general assassination of their masters by the insidious recommendation "to abstain from violence unless in necessary self-defense." Our own detestation of those who have attempted the most execrable measure recorded in the history of guilty man is tempered by profound contempt for the impotent rage which it discloses. So far as regards the action of this Government on such criminals as may attempt its execution, I confine myself to informing you that I shall, unless in your wisdom you deem some other course more expedient, deliver to the several State authorities all commissioned officers of the United States that may hereafter be captured by our forces in any of the States embraced in the proclamation, that they may be dealt with in accordance with the laws of those States providing for the punishment of criminals engaged in exciting servile insurrection. The enlisted soldiers I shall continue to treat as unwilling instruments in the commission of these crimes, and shall direct their discharge and return to their homes on the proper and usual parole.

The Designs of Lincoln

In its political aspect this measure possesses great significance, and to it in this light I invite your attention. It affords to our whole people the complete and crowning proof of the true nature of the designs of the party which elevated to power the present occupant of the Presidential chair at Washington and which sought to conceal its purpose by every variety of artful device and by the perfidious use of the most solemn and repeated pledges on every possible occasion. . . .

The people of this Confederacy, then, cannot fail to receive this proclamation as the fullest vindication of their own sagacity in

Jefferson Davis was the first and only president of the Confederate States of America.

foreseeing the uses to which the dominant party in the United States intended from the beginning to apply their power, nor can they cease to remember with devout thankfulness that it is to their own vigilance in resisting the first stealthy progress of approaching despotism that they owe their escape from consequences now apparent to the most skeptical. This proclamation will have another salutary effect in calming the fears of those who have constantly evinced the apprehension that this war might end by some reconstruction of the old Union or some renewal of close political relations with the United States. These fears have never been shared by me, nor have I ever been able to perceive on what basis they could rest. But the proclamation affords the fullest guarantee of the impossibility of such a result; it has established a state of things which can lead to but one of three possible consequences—the extermination of the slaves, the exile of the whole white population from the Confederacy, or absolute and total separation of these States from the United States.

This proclamation is also an authentic statement by the Government of the United States of its inability to subjugate the South by force of arms, and as such must be accepted by neutral nations, which can no longer find any justification in withholding our just claims to formal recognition. It is also in effect an intimation to the people of the North that they must prepare to submit to a separation, now become inevitable, for that people are too acute not to understand a restoration of the Union has been rendered forever impossible by the adoption of a measure which from its very nature neither admits of retraction nor can coexist with union.

"If the freedom of speech and of the press are to be suspended in time of war, then the essential element of popular government to effect a change of policy in the constitutional mode is at an end."

Lincoln's Actions Violate Constitutional Liberties

Ohio Democratic Convention

Throughout the Civil War Abraham Lincoln came under criticism from many people for actions that they believed violated the U.S. Constitution. One such action was the arrest of Clement L. Vallandigham, a Democratic representative from Ohio who was perhaps the most prominent of Northern political dissenters (known as "Copperheads") during the Civil War. He made numerous speeches against Lincoln's policies and urged peace negotiations with the Confederacy. In May 1863 he was arrested in Ohio and tried by the army for treason. After being found guilty of "weakening the power of the Government" in putting down "an unlawful rebellion," he was sentenced to imprisonment—a sentence commuted by Lincoln to banishment to the Confederacy.

Vallandigham was the most famous of the thousands of people in the North arrested for hindering the Union war effort during the Civil War; his case provoked much public controversy and at least two petitions to the president. The first petition was sent by a group of Democrats from Albany, New York, on May 19, 1863. A month later Lincoln replied to their call for the release of Vallandigham with a famous letter in which he argued his actions were justified, given the national crisis the United States was facing. "Must I shoot the simple-minded soldier boy who deserts,

From James L. Vallandigham, *A Life of Clement L. Vallandigham*. Baltimore: Turnbull Bros., 1872.

while not touching a hair on the wily agitator who induces him to desert?" he asked in his response, which was widely reprinted as a pamphlet.

Many people remained unconvinced—including the group of Ohio Democrats, who on June 26, 1863, sent Lincoln the letter and set of resolutions reprinted in this viewpoint. Responding in part to statements Lincoln had made in his June 19 letter, the Ohio politicians argue that the arrest of Vallandigham, whom they had just nominated for governor, is unjustifiable. They contend that freedom of speech and of the press are indispensable in wartime as in peace. The petitioners also criticize Lincoln for his decision to suspend the right of habeas corpus (which forbids government from the arbitrary arrest of individuals without showing just cause to the courts), arguing that only Congress, not the president, has the power to make such a decision.

———

To His Excellency, the President of the United States:—The undersigned having been appointed a committee, under the authority of the resolutions of the State Convention held at the City of Columbus, Ohio, on the 11th inst., to communicate with you on the subject of the arrest and banishment of Clement L. Vallandigham, most respectfully submit the following as the resolutions of that Convention bearing upon the subject of this communication, and ask of your Excellency their earnest consideration. And they deem it proper to state that the Convention was one in which all parts of the State were represented, and one of the most respectable as to numbers and character, one of the most earnest and sincere in the support of the Constitution and the Union, ever held in that State.

[The resolutions—some of which appear below—were inserted into the letter here.]

The Resolutions

That the arrest, imprisonment, and pretended trial and actual banishment of C.L. Vallandigham, a citizen of the State of Ohio, not belonging to the land or naval forces of the United States, nor to the militia in actual service, by alleged military authority, for no other pretended crime than that of uttering words of legitimate criticism upon the conduct of the Administration in power, and of appealing to the ballot-box for a change of policy—said arrest and military trial taking place where the courts of law are open and unobstructed, and for no act done within the sphere of active military operations in carrying on the war—we regard as a palpable violation of the provisions of the Constitution of the United States.

That Clement L. Vallandigham was, at the time of his arrest, a prominent candidate for nomination by the Democratic party for the office of Governor of the State; that the Democratic party was fully competent to decide whether he was a fit man for that nomination, and that the attempt to deprive them of that right by his arrest and banishment was an unmerited imputation upon their intelligence and loyalty, as well as a violation of the Constitution.

That we respectfully, but most earnestly, call upon the President of the United States to restore Clement L. Vallandigham to his home in Ohio, and that a committee of one from each congressional district of the State, to be selected by the presiding officer of this convention, is hereby appointed to present this application to the President.

The undersigned, in the discharge of the duty assigned them, do not think it necessary to reiterate the facts connected with the arrest, trial, and banishment of Mr. Vallandigham—they are well known to the President, and are of public history—nor to enlarge upon the positions taken by the Convention, nor to recapitulate the CONSTITUTIONAL PROVISIONS which it is believed have been violated: they have been stated at length, and with clearness, in the resolutions which have been recited. The undersigned content themselves with a brief reference to other suggestions pertinent to the subject.

They do not call upon your Excellency as suppliants, praying the revocation of the order banishing Mr. Vallandigham as a favor; but by the authority of a Convention representing a majority of the citizens of the State of Ohio, they respectfully ask it as a right due to an American citizen in whose personal injury the sovereignty and dignity of the people of Ohio as a free State have been offended. And this duty they perform the more cordially from the consideration that, at a time of great national emergency, pregnant with danger to our Federal Union, it is all-important that the true friends of the Constitution and the Union, however they may differ as to *the mode* of administering the Government, and the measures most likely to be successful in the maintenance of the Constitution and the restoration of the Union, should not be thrown into conflict with each other.

The arrest, unusual trial, and banishment of Mr. Vallandigham, have created wide-spread and alarming disaffection among the people of the State, not only endangering the harmony of the friends of the Constitution and the Union, and tending to disturb the peace and tranquillity of the State, but also impairing that confidence in the fidelity of your Administration to the great landmarks of free government essential to a peaceful and successful enforcement of the laws of Ohio.

You are reported to have used, in a public communication on this subject, the following language:

> It gave me pain when I learned that Mr. Vallandigham had been arrested—that is, I was pained that there should have seemed to be a necessity for arresting him; and that it will afford me great pleasure to discharge him so soon as I can by any means believe the public safety will not suffer by it.

The undersigned assure your Excellency, from our personal knowledge of the feelings of the people of Ohio, that the public safety will be far more endangered by continuing Mr. Vallandigham in exile than by releasing him. It may be true that persons differing from him in political views may be found in Ohio, and elsewhere, who will express a different opinion; but they are certainly mistaken.

Mr. Vallandigham may differ with the President, and even with some of his own political party, as to the true and most effectual means of maintaining the Constitution and restoring the Union; but this difference of opinion does not prove him to be unfaithful to his duties as an American citizen. If a man, devotedly attached to the Constitution and the Union, conscientiously believes that, from the inherent nature of the Federal compact, the war, in the present condition of things in this country, can not be used as a means of restoring the Union; or that a war to subjugate a part of the States, or a war to revolutionise the social system in a part of the States, could not restore, but would inevitably result in the final destruction of both the Constitution and the Union—is he not to be allowed the right of an American citizen to appeal to the judgment of the people for a change of policy by the constitutional remedy of the ballot-box?

During the war with Mexico many of the political opponents of the Administration then in power thought it their duty to oppose and denounce the war, and to urge before the people of the country that it was unjust and prosecuted for unholy purposes. With equal reason it might have been said of them that their discussions before the people were calculated to "discourage enlistments," "to prevent the raising of troops," and to "induce desertions from the army," and "leave the Government without an adequate military force to carry on the war."

If the freedom of speech and of the press are to be suspended in time of war, then the essential element of popular government to effect a change of policy in the constitutional mode is at an end. The freedom of speech and of the press is indispensable, and necessarily incident to the nature of popular government itself. If any inconvenience or evils arise from its exercise, they are unavoidable.

196

On this subject you are reported to have said, further:

> It is asserted, in substance, that Mr. Vallandigham was by a military commander seized and tried for no other reason than words addressed to a public meeting in criticism of the course of the Administration, and in condemnation of the military order of the General. Now, if there be no mistake about this—if there was no other reason for the arrest—then I concede that the arrest was wrong. But the arrest, I understand, was made for a very different reason. Mr. Vallandigham avows his hostility to the war on the part of the Union; and his arrest was made because he was laboring with some effect to prevent the raising of troops, to encourage desertions in the army, and to leave the rebellion without an adequate military force to suppress it. He was not arrested because he was damaging the political prospects of the Administration, or the personal interest of the Commanding General, but because he was damaging the army, upon the existence and vigor of which the life of the nation depends. He was warring upon the military, and this gave the military constitutional jurisdiction to lay hands upon him. If Mr. Vallandigham was not damaging the military power of the country, then his arrest was made on a mistake of facts, which I would be glad to correct on reasonable satisfactory evidence.

In answer to this, permit us to say, first, that neither the charge, nor the specifications in support of the charge on which Mr. Vallandigham was tried, impute to him the act of either laboring to prevent the raising of troops, or to encourage desertions from the army. Secondly, no evidence on the trial was offered with a view to support, or even tended to support, any such charge. In what instance and by what act did he either discourage enlistments or encourage desertions from the army? Who is the man who was discouraged from enlisting, and who was encouraged to desert, by any act of Mr. Vallandigham? If it be assumed that perchance some person might have been discouraged from enlisting, or that some person might have been encouraged to desert on account of hearing Mr. Vallandigham's views as to the policy of the war as a means of restoring the Union, would that have laid the foundation for his conviction and banishment? If so, upon the same grounds every political opponent of the Mexican War might have been convicted and banished from the country.

When gentlemen of high standing and extensive influence, including your Excellency, opposed in the discussions before the people the policy of the Mexican War, were they "warring upon the military," and did this "give the military constitutional jurisdiction to lay hands upon" them? And finally, the charge in the specifications upon which Mr. Vallandigham was tried, entitled him to a trial before the civil tribunals, according to the express provisions of the late Acts of Congress, approved by yourself, of July 17, 1862, and March 3, 1863, which were manifestly designed

197

to supersede all necessity or pretext for arbitrary military arrests.

The undersigned are unable to agree with you in the opinion you have expressed, that the Constitution is different in time of insurrection or invasion from what it is in time of peace and public security. The Constitution provides for no limitation upon, or exceptions to, the guarantees of personal liberty, except as to the writ of *habeas corpus*. Has the President, at the time of invasion or insurrection, the right to engraft limitations or exceptions upon these constitutional guarantees whenever, in his judgement, the public safety requires it?

Arrested for Defending the Constitution

War opponent Clement L. Vallandigham wrote the following letter to Ohio Democrats following his military arrest in May 1863. He argues that his arrest was caused by his public defenses of the Constitution against what he views as tyrannical acts by the federal government under President Abraham Lincoln.

I am here in a military bastile for no other offence than my political opinions, and the defence of them and of the rights of the people, and of your constitutional liberties. Speeches made in the hearing of thousands of you in denunciation of the usurpations of power, infractions of the Constitution and laws, and of military despotism, were the sole cause of my arrest and imprisonment. I am a Democrat—for Constitution, for law, for the Union, for liberty—this is my only "crime." For no disobedience to the Constitution; for no violation of law; for no word, sign or gesture of sympathy with the men of the South, who are for disunion and Southern independence, but in obedience to *their* demand as well as the demand of Northern Abolition disunionists and traitors, I am here in bonds to-day.

True it is, the article of the Constitution which defines the various powers delegated to Congress, declares that the "privilege of the writ of *habeas corpus* shall not be suspended unless where, in case of rebellion or invasion, the public safety may require it." But this qualification or limitation upon this restriction upon the powers of Congress has no reference to, or connection with, the other constitutional guarantees of personal liberty. Expunge from the Constitution this limitation upon the power of Congress to suspend the writ of *habeas corpus*, and yet the other guarantees of personal liberty would remain unchanged.

Although a man might not have a constitutional right to have an immediate investigation made as to the legality of his arrest upon *habeas corpus*, yet his "right to a speedy and public trial by an impartial jury of the State and District wherein the crime shall have been committed," will not be altered; neither will his right to the exemption from "cruel and unusual punishments;" nor his right to be secure in his person, houses, papers and effects against any unreasonable seizures and searches; nor his right to be deprived of life, liberty or property, without due process of law; nor his right not to be held to answer for a capital or otherwise infamous offence unless on presentment or indictment of a grand jury, be in anywise changed.

And certainly the restriction upon the power of Congress to suspend the writ of *habeas corpus* in time of insurrection or invasion, could not affect the guarantee that the freedom of speech and of the press shall not be abridged. It is sometimes urged that the proceedings in the civil tribunals are too tardy and ineffective for cases arising in times of insurrection or invasion. It is a full reply to this to say, that arrests by civil process may be equally as expeditious and effective as arrests by military orders.

True, a summary trial and punishment are not allowed in the civil courts. But if the offender be under arrest and imprisoned, and not entitled to a discharge under a writ of *habeas corpus*, before trial, what more can be required for the purposes of the Government? The idea that all the constitutional guarantees of personal liberty are suspended throughout the country at a time of insurrection or invasion in any part of it, places us upon a sea of uncertainty, and subjects the life, liberty and property of every citizen to the mere will of a military commander, or what he may say he considers the public safety requires. Does your Excellency wish to have it understood that you hold that the rights of every man throughout this vast country are subject to be annulled whenever you may say that you consider the public safety requires it, in time of invasion or insurrection? You are further reported as having said that the constitutional guarantees of personal liberty have "no application to the present case we have in hand, because the arrests complained of were not made for treason—that is, not for the treason defined in the Constitution, and upon the conviction of which the punishment is death—nor yet were they made to hold persons to answer for capital or otherwise infamous crime; nor were the proceedings following in any constitutional or criminal sense legal prosecutions. The arrests were made on totally different grounds, and the proceedings following accorded with the grounds of the arrests," &c. The conclusion to be drawn from this position of your Excellency is, that where a man is liable to a "criminal prosecution," or is charged with a crime known to the laws of the land, he is clothed with all the constitutional guarantees for his safety and security from wrong and injustice; but where he is not liable to a "criminal prosecution," or charged with any crime known to the laws, if the President or any military commander shall say that he considers that the public safety requires it, this man may be put outside of the pale of the constitutional guarantees, and arrested without charge of crime, imprisoned without knowledge what for, and any length of time, or be tried before a court-martial and sentenced to any kind of punishment unknown to the laws of the land which the President or the military commander may see proper to impose.

Did the Constitution intend to throw the shield of its securities around the man liable to be charged with treason as defined by it, and yet leave the man not liable to any such charge unprotected by the safeguard of personal liberty and personal security? Can a man not in the military or naval service, nor within the field of the operations of the army, be arrested and imprisoned without any law of the land to authorise it? Can a man thus in civil life be punished without any law defining the offence and prescribing the punishment? If the President or a court-martial may prescribe one kind of punishment unauthorised by law, why not any other kind? Banishment is an unusual punishment, and unknown to our laws. If the President has the right to prescribe the punishment of banishment, why not that of death and confiscation of property? If the President has the right to change the punishment prescribed by the court-martial from imprisonment to banishment, why not from imprisonment to torture upon the rack, or execution upon the gibbet?

If an indefinable kind of constructive treason is to be introduced and engrafted upon the Constitution, unknown to the laws of the land, and subject to the will of the President whenever an insurrection or invasion shall occur in any part of this vast country, what safety or security will be left for the liberties of the people?

The "constructive treason" that gave the friends of freedom so many years of toil and trouble in England, was inconsiderable compared to this. The precedents which you make will become a part of the Constitution for your successors, if sanctioned and acquiesced in by the people now.

The people of Ohio are willing to co-operate zealously with you in every effort warranted by the Constitution to restore the Union of the States, but they cannot consent to abandon those fundamental principles of civil liberty which are essential to their existence as a free people.

In their name we ask that, by a revocation of the order of his banishment, Mr. Vallandigham may be restored to the enjoyment of those rights of which they believe he has been unconstitutionally deprived.

VIEWPOINT 8

"The military arrests and detentions, which have been made . . . have been for prevention, *and not for* punishment.*"*

Extraordinary Measures in Wartime Are Justified

Abraham Lincoln (1809-1865)

Abraham Lincoln, as president of the United States from 1861 to 1865, took unprecedented actions over the course of the Civil War that greatly expanded the power of the presidency. He declared the Southern states to be in a state of insurrection, proclaimed a naval blockade, and raised troops, all without prior congressional authorization. Perhaps his most controversial move was to suspend the constitutional right of habeas corpus, enabling the U.S. government to arrest and detain opponents of the Civil War without holding a trial or military hearing. The Constitution provided for the suspension of habeas corpus "in cases of rebellion," but opponents of Lincoln argued that suspending it was the prerogative of Congress, not the president.

Thousands of people were arrested as war opponents, the most famous of whom was Clement L. Vallandigham. A Democratic representative from Ohio, Vallandigham was arrested in May 1863 and convicted by a military tribunal of hindering the war effort. Lincoln commuted his sentence from imprisonment to banishment to the Confederacy, but Vallandigham still became a focal point for Lincoln's critics. Lincoln personally responded to two petitions calling for Vallandigham's release—one from a group of Democrats from Albany, New York, and a second from Democratic petitions from Ohio. In his reply to the Ohio Democrats, made on June 29, 1863, and reprinted here, Lincoln defends his actions—including the arrest of Vallandigham (Mr. V.

Abraham Lincoln, letter to Democratic congressmen from Ohio, dated June 29, 1863. Reprinted from *The Collected Works of Abraham Lincoln*, edited by Roy P. Basler, 1953.

in Lincoln's letter)—as necessary to win the war. He closes his letter with an offer to release Vallandigham if the petitioners will agree to some propositions in support of the war effort—an offer the petitioners later responded to by saying they "were not authorized to enter into any bargains, terms, contracts, or conditions with the President of the United States to procure the release of Mr. Vallandigham."

Gentlemen: The resolutions of the Ohio Democratic State convention which you present me, together with your introductory and closing remarks, being in position and argument, mainly the same as the resolutions of the Democratic meeting at Albany, New-York, I refer you to my response to the latter, as meeting most of the points in the former. This response you evidently used in preparing your remarks, and I desire no more than that it be used with accuracy. In a single reading of your remarks I only discovered one inaccuracy in matter which I suppose you took from that paper. It is when you say "The undersigned are unable to agree with you in the opinion you have expressed that the constitution is different in time of insurrection or invasion from what it is in time of peace & public security." A recurrence to the paper will show you that I have not expressed the opinion you suppose. I expressed the opinion that the constitution is different, *in its application* in cases of Rebellion or Invasion, involving the Public Safety, from what it is in times of profound peace and public security; and this opinion I adhere to, simply because, by the constitution itself, things may be done in the one case which may not be done in the other.

I dislike to waste a word on a merely personal point; but I must respectfully assure you that you will find yourselves at fault should you ever seek for evidence to prove your assumption that I "opposed, in discussions before the people, the policy of the Mexican war."

The Constitution and War

You say "Expunge from the constitution this limitation upon the power of congress to suspend the writ of Habeas corpus, and yet the other guarranties of personal liberty would remain unchanged." Doubtless if this clause of the constitution, improperly called, as I think, a limitation upon the power of congress, were expunged, the other guarranties would remain the same; but the question is, not how those guarranties would stand, with that clause *out* of the constitution, but how they stand with that clause remaining in it—in cases of Rebellion or Invasion, involving the public Safety. If the liberty could be indulged, of expunging that clause letter & spirit, I really think the constitutional argument

---

Vallandigham's Arrest Justified

Abraham Lincoln's reply to a petition from Erastus Corning and other New York Democrats calling for Clement L. Vallandigham's release was widely reproduced in newspapers and pamphlets. In the following excerpts from Lincoln's June 12, 1863, letter to Corning, the president defends his actions.

He was not arrested because he was damaging the political prospects of the administration or the personal interests of the commanding general but because he was damaging the army, upon the existence and vigor of which the life of the nation depends. He was warring upon the military and this gave the military constitutional jurisdiction to lay hands upon him. If Mr. Vallandigham was not damaging the military power of the country, then his arrest was made on mistake of fact, which I would be glad to correct on reasonably satisfactory evidence. . . .

Long experience has shown that armies cannot be maintained unless desertion shall be punished by the severe penalty of death. The case requires, and the law and the Constitution sanction, this punishment. Must I shoot a simpleminded soldier boy who deserts, while I must not touch a hair of a wily agitator who induces him to desert? This is none the less injurious when effected by getting a father, or brother, or friend into a public meeting, and there working upon his feelings till he is persuaded to write the soldier boy that he is fighting in a bad cause, for a wicked administration of a contemptible government, too weak to arrest and punish him if he shall desert. I think that, in such a case, to silence the agitator and save the boy is not only constitutional but withal a great mercy.

If I be wrong on this question of constitutional power, my error lies in believing that certain proceedings are constitutional when, in cases of rebellion or invasion, the public safety requires them, which would not be constitutional when, in absence of rebellion or invasion, the public safety does not require them; in other words, that the Constitution is not in its application in all respects the same in cases of rebellion or invasion involving the public safety as it is in times of profound peace and public security. The Constitution itself makes the distinction, and I can no more be persuaded that the government can constitutionally take no strong measures in time of rebellion, because it can be shown that the same could not be lawfully taken in time of peace, than I can be persuaded that a particular drug is not good medicine for a sick man because it can be shown not to be good food for a well one.

would be with you. My general view on this question was stated in the Albany response, and hence I do not state it now. I only add that, as seems to me, the benefit of the writ of Habeas corpus, is the great means through which the guarranties of personal liberty are conserved, and made available in the last resort; and corroborative of this view, is the fact that Mr. V. in the very case in question, under the advice of able lawyers, saw not where else to go but to the Habeas Corpus. But by the constitution the benefit of the writ of Habeas corpus itself may be suspended when in cases of Rebellion or Invasion the public Safety may require it.

You ask, in substance, whether I really claim that I may override all the guarrantied rights of individuals, on the plea of conserving the public safety—when I may choose to say the public safety requires it. This question, divested of the phraseology calculated to represent me as struggling for an arbitrary personal prerogative, is either simply a question *who* shall decide, or an affirmation that *nobody* shall decide, what the public safety does require, in cases of Rebellion or Invasion. The constitution contemplates the question as likely to occur for decision, but it does not expressly declare who is to decide it. By necessary implication, when Rebellion or Invasion comes, the decision is to be made, from time to time; and I think the man whom, for the time, the people have, under the constitution, made the commander-in-chief, of their Army and Navy, is the man who holds the power, and bears the responsibility of making it. If he uses the power justly, the same people will probably justify him; if he abuses it, he is in their hands, to be dealt with by all the modes they have reserved to themselves in the constitution.

The earnestness with which you insist that persons can only, in times of rebellion, be lawfully dealt with, in accordance with the rules for criminal trials and punishments in times of peace, induces me to add a word to what I said on that point, in the Albany response. You claim that men may, if they choose, embarrass those whose duty it is, to combat a giant rebellion, and then be dealt with in turn, only as if there was no rebellion. The constitution itself rejects this view. The military arrests and detentions, which have been made, including those of Mr. V. which are not different in principle from the others, have been for *prevention*, and not for *punishment*—as injunctions to stay injury, as proceedings to keep the peace—and hence, like proceedings in such cases, and for like reasons, they have not been accompanied with indictments, or trials by juries, nor, in a single case by any punishment whatever, beyond what is purely incidental to the prevention. The original sentence of imprisonment in Mr. V.'s case, was to prevent injury to the Military service only, and the modification of it was made as a less disagreeable mode to him, of securing the same prevention.

I am unable to perceive an insult to Ohio in the case of Mr. V. Quite surely nothing of the sort was or is intended. I was wholly unaware that Mr. V. was at the time of his arrest a candidate for the democratic nomination for Governor until so informed by your reading to me the resolutions of the convention. I am grateful to the State of Ohio for many things, especially for the brave soldiers and officers she has given in the present national trial, to the armies of the Union.

Why Clement Vallandigham Was Arrested

You claim, as I understand, that according to my own position in the Albany response, Mr. V. should be released; and this because, as you claim, he has not damaged the military service, by discouraging enlistments, encouraging desertions, or otherwise; and that if he had, he should have been turned over to the civil authorities under recent acts of congress. I certainly do not *know* that Mr. V. has specifically, and by direct language, advised against enlistments, and in favor of desertion, and resistance to drafting. We all know that combinations, armed in some instances, to resist the arrest of deserters, began several months ago; that more recently the like has appeared in resistance to the enrolment preparatory to a draft; and that quite a number of assassinations have occurred from the same animus. These had to be met by military force, and this again has led to bloodshed and death. And now under a sense of responsibility more weighty and enduring than any which is merely official, I solemnly declare my belief that this hindrance, of the military, including maiming and murder, is due to the course in which Mr. V. has been engaged, in a greater degree than to any other cause; and is due to him personally, in a greater degree than to any other one man. These things have been notorious, known to all, and of course known to Mr. V. Perhaps I would not be wrong to say they originated with his special friends and adherents. With perfect knowledge of them, he has frequently, if not constantly made speeches, in congress, and before popular assemblies; and if it can be shown that, with these things staring him, in the face, he has ever uttered a word of rebuke, or counsel against them, it will be a fact greatly in his favor with me, and one of which, as yet I, am totally ignorant. When it is known that the whole burthen of his speeches has been to stir up men against the prosecution of the war, and that in the midst of resistance to it, he has not been known, in any instance, to counsel against such resistance, it is next to impossible to repel the inference that he has counselled directly in favor of it. With all this before their eyes the convention you represent have nominated Mr. V. for Governor of Ohio;

205

The Constitution and Self-Preservation

In a speech in the United States Senate on April 21, 1862, Benjamin Wade, an Ohio Republican senator, questions the loyalty of those in the Senate and elsewhere who argue that the Constitution limits the actions the country and its president can take in times of crisis.

That man is not quite honest who . . . argues constitutional questions in this Senate, and invokes the Constitution in behalf of the rights of every man precisely as he would in times of peace where there were isolated cases of delinquency, and where it was safe to bring a man to trial. The man who says it, and would have you proceed with these traitors precisely as you would in time of peace is endeavoring to deceive the public. Can you prosecute a traitor south of Mason and Dixon's line? As the old saying is, you might as well try the devil in hell, and summon as jurors his chief angels. It is impracticable; it cannot be done. . . .

Do you think that we will stand by, yielding to your argument, while you fetter our legs, and bind our arms with the Constitution of the United States that you may stab it to death? Is that your idea of the Constitution, that it is made to tie the hands of honest men from its defense, while traitors may stab it to the heart? That is the use you would make of the Constitution of the United States. Sir, I say again, I have no scruples about the Constitution of the United States as wielded against traitors in this time of violent revolution. You have seen that the ordinary course of the common law and of the Constitution cannot be followed. Shall the Constitution lie down and die? Must we give up all our glorious principles that were defended by it because traitors have assailed it in such a way that they have prevented its operation? Sir, folly like that would deserve the ignominious fate which would inevitably follow so foolish a course.

and both they and you, have declared the purpose to sustain the national Union by all constitutional means. But, of course, they and you, in common, reserve to yourselves to decide what are constitutional means; and, unlike the Albany meeting, you omit to state, or intimate, that in your opinion, an army is a constitutional means of saving the Union against a rebellion; or even to intimate that you are conscious of an existing rebellion being in progress with the avowed object of destroying that very Union. At the same time your nominee for Governor, in whose behalf you appeal, is known to you, and to the world, to declare against the use of an army to suppress the rebellion. Your own attitude, therefore, encourages desertion, resistance to the draft and the like, because it teaches those who incline to desert, and to escape the draft, to believe it is your purpose to protect them, and to hope that you will become strong enough to do so. After a short personal intercourse with you gentlemen of the committee, I can not say I think you desire this effect to follow your attitude; but I assure you that both friends and enemies of the Union look upon it in this light. It is a substantial hope, and by consequence, a real strength to the enemy. If it is a false hope, and one which you would willingly dispel, I will make the way exceedingly easy. I send you duplicates of this letter, in order that you, or a majority of you, may if you choose, indorse your names upon one of them, and return it thus indorsed to me, with the understanding that those signing, are thereby committed to the following propositions, and to nothing else.

Propositions and an Offer

1. That there is now a rebellion in the United States, the object and tendency of which is to destroy the national Union; and that in your opinion, an army and navy are constitutional means for suppressing that rebellion.

2. That no one of you will do any thing which in his own judgment, will tend to hinder the increase, or favor the decrease, or lessen the efficiency of the army or navy, while engaged in the effort to suppress that rebellion; and,

3. That each of you will, in his sphere, do all he can to have the officers, soldiers, and seamen of the army and navy, while engaged in the effort to suppress the rebellion, paid, fed, clad, and otherwise well provided and supported.

And with the further understanding that upon receiving the letter and names thus indorsed, I will cause them to be published, which publication shall be within itself, a revocation of the order in relation to Mr. V.

It will not escape observation that I consent to the release of Mr. V. upon terms, not embracing any pledge from him, or from others as to what he will, or will not do. I do this because he is not present to speak for himself, or to authorize others to speak for him; and because I should expect that on his returning, he would not put himself practically in antagonism with the position of his friends. But I do it chiefly because I thereby prevail on other influential gentlemen of Ohio to so define their position, as to be of immense value to the Army—thus more than compensating for the consequences of any mistake in allowing Mr. V. to return; and so that, on the whole, the public safety will not have suffered by it. Still, in regard to Mr. V. and all others, I must hereafter as heretofore, do so much as the public safety may seem to require.

Chapter 4

Black Soldiers in the Civil War

Chapter Preface

An important development in the Civil War was the recruitment of black soldiers by the North. Some leaders such as black abolitionist Frederick Douglass advocated such a step when the war began, but their views were not initially shared by the Lincoln administration or Northern public opinion. Many blacks, including escaped slaves, were employed by the Union army as laborers, yet they remained unwanted as soldiers. But as the costs and length of the war became apparent, an increasing number of people advocated the use of black soldiers as a way to both strengthen the North (by augmenting its armed forces) and weaken the South (by encouraging slaves to escape and depriving the South of slave labor). Abraham Lincoln's Emancipation Proclamation of 1863 made special reference to the enlistment of black soldiers, and Northern recruiting of blacks began in earnest in the spring of that year.

The new recruits faced numerous obstacles and prejudices, including less pay than white soldiers, no opportunity to become commissioned officers, and a reluctance by some white Union commanders to put them into combat. But several notable battles—especially the assault on Fort Wagner, South Carolina, by the Massachusetts 54th Regiment, and the fighting of black regiments in the battles of Port Hudson and Milliken's Bend, Louisiana—convinced most white doubters that blacks could be capable soldiers. Ultimately 180,000 blacks served in Northern armies, about one-fifth of the nation's population of military-age black men.

The following viewpoints examine the debates surrounding black soldiers in the Union Army. Ironically, given the importance of slavery to the Confederacy and the Southern historical fear of slave revolts, some people within the Confederacy also advocated the recruiting of black soldiers. Upon the urging of Robert E. Lee, among others, the Confederate government finally decided to authorize the use of black soldiers in March 1865—too late to influence the war.

VIEWPOINT 1

"Why does the Government reject the Negro? Is he not a man?"

The Union Should Enlist Black Soldiers

Frederick Douglass (1817-1895)

Frederick Douglass was born a slave in Maryland and escaped to Massachusetts in 1838 at the age of twenty, where he became a famous abolitionist lecturer and writer. Douglass was publisher and editor of the abolitionist newspaper *The North Star*, later known as *Douglass' Monthly*, in which he wrote numerous articles championing abolition, women's rights, and other social causes.

When the Civil War began Douglass continued to lecture and write in support of emancipation and the enlistment of blacks as soldiers in the Union Army. The following viewpoint is taken from an article published in the September 1861 issue of *Douglass' Monthly*. Douglass notes the lack of military success of the North and questions why blacks are not being enlisted as soldiers. He argues that the Union is risking defeat by neglecting a valuable resource.

What upon earth is the matter with the American Government and people? Do they really covet the world's ridicule as well as their own social and political ruin? What are they thinking about, or don't they condescend to think at all? So, indeed, it would seem from their blindness in dealing with the tremendous issue now upon them. Was there ever any thing like it before? They are

Frederick Douglass, *Douglass' Monthly*, September 1861. Reprinted from *The Life and Writings of Frederick Douglass*, edited by Philip S. Foner, 1952.

sorely pressed on every hand by a vast army of slaveholding rebels, flushed with success, and infuriated by the darkest inspirations of a deadly hate, bound to rule or ruin. Washington, the seat of Government, after ten thousand assurances to the contrary, is now positively in danger of falling before the rebel army. Maryland, a little while ago considered safe for the Union, is now admitted to be studded with the materials for insurrection, and which may flame forth at any moment.—Every resource of the nation, whether of men or money, whether of wisdom or strength, could be well employed to avert the impending ruin. Yet most evidently the demands of the hour are not comprehended by the Cabinet or the crowd. Our Presidents, Governors, Generals and Secretaries are calling, with almost frantic vehemence, for men.—"Men! men! send us men!" they scream, or the cause of the Union is gone, the life of a great nation is ruthlessly sacrificed, and the hopes of a great nation go out in darkness; and yet these very officers, representing the people and Government, steadily and persistently refuse to receive the very class of men which have a deeper interest in the defeat and humiliation of the rebels, than all others.—Men are wanted in Missouri—wanted in Western Virginia, to hold and defend what has been already gained; they are wanted in Texas, and all along the sea coast, and though the Government has at its command a class in the country deeply interested in suppressing the insurrection, it sternly refuses to summon from among the vast multitude a single man, and degrades and insults the whole class by refusing to allow any of their number to defend with their strong arms and brave hearts the national cause. What a spectacle of blind, unreasoning prejudice and pusillanimity is this! The national edifice is on fire. Every man who can carry a bucket of water, or remove a brick, is wanted; but those who have the care of the building, having a profound respect for the feeling of the national burglars who set the building on fire, are determined that the flames shall only be extinguished by Indo-Caucasian hands, and to have the building burnt rather than save it by means of any other. Such is the pride, the stupid prejudice and folly that rules the hour.

Why does the Government reject the Negro? Is he not a man? Can he not wield a sword, fire a gun, march and countermarch, and obey orders like any other? Is there the least reason to believe that a regiment of well-drilled Negroes would deport themselves less soldier-like on the battle field than the raw troops gathered up generally from the towns and cities of the State of New York? We do believe that such soldiers, if allowed now to take up arms in defence of the Government, and made to feel that they are hereafter to be recognized as persons having rights, would set the highest example of order and general good behavior to their fellow soldiers, and in every way add to the national power.

If persons so humble as we can be allowed to speak to the President of the United States, we should ask him if this dark and terrible hour of the nation's extremity is a time for consulting a mere vulgar and unnatural prejudice? We should ask him if national preservation and necessity were not better guides in this emergency than either the tastes of the rebels, or the pride and prejudices of the vulgar? We would tell him that General [Andrew] Jackson in a slave State fought side by side with Negroes at New Orleans [against the British in the War of 1812], and like a true man, despising meanness, he bore testimony to their bravery at the close of the war. We would tell him that colored men in Rhode Island and Connecticut performed their full share in the war of the [American] Revolution, and that men of the same color, such as the noble Shields Green, Nathaniel Turner and Denmark Vesey stand ready to peril every thing at the command of the Government. We would tell him that this is no time to fight with one

After the Union Army decided to accept black soldiers, Frederick Douglass traveled throughout the country speaking to potential recruits. Two of his sons were among the first to enlist.

hand, when both are needed; that this is no time to fight only with your white hand, and allow your black hand to remain tied.

Whatever may be the folly and absurdity of the North, the South at least is true and wise. The Southern papers no longer indulge in the vulgar expression, "free n——rs." That class of bipeds are now called "colored residents." The Charleston papers say:

> The colored residents of this city can challenge comparison with their class, in any city or town, in loyalty or devotion to the cause of the South. Many of them individually, and without ostentation, have been contributing liberally, and on Wednesday evening, the 7th inst., a very large meeting was held by them, and a Committee appointed to provide for more efficient aid. The proceedings of the meeting will appear in results hereinafter to be reported.

It is now pretty well established, that there are at the present moment many colored men in the Confederate army doing duty not only as cooks, servants and laborers, but as real soldiers, having muskets on their shoulders, and bullets in their pockets, ready to shoot down loyal troops, and do all that soldiers may to destroy the Federal Government and build up that of the traitors and rebels. There were such soldiers at [the First Battle of] Manassas, and they are probably there still. There is a Negro in the army as well as in the fence, and our Government is likely to find it out before the war comes to an end. That the Negroes are numerous in the rebel army, and do for that army its heaviest work, is beyond question. They have been the chief laborers upon those temporary defences in which the rebels have been able to mow down our men. Negroes helped to build the batteries at Charleston. They relieve their gentlemanly and military masters from the stiffening drudgery of the camp, and devote them to the nimble and dexterous use of arms. Rising above vulgar prejudice, the slaveholding rebel accepts the aid of the black man as readily as that of any other. If a bad cause can do this, why should a good cause be less wisely conducted? We insist upon it, that one black regiment in such a war as this is, without being any more brave and orderly, would be worth to the Government more than two of any other; and that, while the Government continues to refuse the aid of colored men, thus alienating them from the national cause, and giving the rebels the advantage of them, it will not deserve better fortunes than it has thus far experienced.—Men in earnest don't fight with one hand, when they might fight with two, and a man drowning would not refuse to be saved even by a colored hand.

VIEWPOINT 2

"If this Union cannot be preserved by the white man, . . . there are no conditions upon which it can be saved."

The Union Should Not Enlist Black Soldiers

Garrett Davis (1801-1872)

Early proposals to arm and train blacks for the Union Army met with vociferous opposition, especially from representatives of the slave states that remained in the Union (Missouri, Kentucky, Delaware, and Maryland) who did not want to see their own authority over their slaves jeopardized. One example of opposition comes from the following speech by Garrett Davis, a longtime Kentucky representative and senator. The U.S. Senate, on July 9, 1861, was debating a resolution authorizing the president to accept "persons of African descent" into the service of the United States "for the purpose of constructing intrenchments, or performing camp service, or any other labor, or any war service for which they may be found competent." Davis in his speech objects to the last provision, arguing that while accepting blacks into military service as workers was acceptable, accepting them as soldiers was not. He argues that such a move would alienate Union supporters in the border states. Davis also claims that the racial characteristics of blacks make them unacceptable soldiers.

I have myself never considered secession a remedy for any evil. I do not now consider it a remedy for any evil, but to have brought upon the country all existing evils; and that, if an accom-

From Garrett Davis, speech to U.S. Senate, July 9, 1861, *Congressional Globe*, 1861.

plished fact, it would prove the fruitful mother of many other evils, of which we have yet had no experience. For my own State, for the South, for the North, for the East, and the West, I have no hope, if secession is triumphant and permanent dissolution takes place. I am for a reconstruction of the Union. I believe the only principle and means by which that reconstruction is possible, is by the employment of the full, legitimate military power of the country, and not by arming slaves and attempting to form a military force of them. . . .

Blacks Can Be Workers, Not Soldiers

From the debate that has sprung up in this Chamber on this subject, it appears to me that there are only two principal matters in the measure proposed about which there is much difference of opinion. The one is the employment of the negro in all camp and military labor, and the other is placing arms in his hands, and forming him into a portion of the soldiery of the United States in the war. To the first proposition I have no objection, and never had any, but to the second I am utterly opposed, and will ever be opposed. . . .

I never heard any Union man in my State or out of it object to the use and the appropriation of negroes by the United States Government, just as other property is applied to their military purposes. The whole of their remonstrance and protest has been against making a discrimination between that and other property by the laws of Congress or by the policy of the war, as the President or his generals might carry it on. When a general is commanding in the field, and he has occasion for the labor of horses and oxen, what does he do? He impresses them into the service of the Army of the United States, and nobody objects. Just so, if that general may need the services of negroes for the purpose of fortifying, or ditching, or rendering any other labor in his camp, or any service whatever, especially that kind which would shield and protect and save the life of the white soldier, I think that general in command would be perfectly authorized so to employ the negro, and I have never heard any man object to such employment; certainly I never made any such objection as that myself. And all this would be done by order of the President, or by our generals commanding, without any act of Congress to authorize it. But when the general has done with the negro, and the negro is no longer useful in his camp for the purpose of labor, or for any other useful purpose, let him be discharged, sent away like other property. I protest against placing arms in his hands and making a soldier of him; and to that line of policy I never will give my consent; nor will my people, although it may be regarded as a matter of very little importance in this Senate what they or I think in relation to this or any other measure of policy of the dominant party. If the State of Kentucky was polled upon the proposition of placing arms in the hands of negroes, I have no doubt to-day that nine hundred and ninety-nine out of every thousand, yea, I believe that the thousandth man would vote against it, and enter up his most solemn remonstrance against it.

Library of Congress

In the early years of the Civil War, blacks were employed in the Union Army as laborers and grave diggers, but not as soldiers.

Has it come to this, Mr. President, that we cannot command white soldiers enough to fight our battles to put down this rebellion? Whenever we authorize by law of Congress the enrollment of negro soldiers for that purpose, we admit that the white man is whipped in the contest, and that he cannot come out conqueror without making an auxiliary of the negro. I protest against any such degrading position as that. Our countrymen are not reduced to it; and sooner than the white men, the citizens and sovereigns of the United States, would submit to so humiliating an admission as that, one million of additional soldiers would be ready to rush to the battle-field. I believe that if this measure was passed it would weaken our Army; it would weaken the cause of the Union and of the legitimate Government in this contest tenfold as much as it would strengthen it.

Sir, I know the soldiery of the Northwest. They want no negro auxiliaries in this war; they would feel themselves degraded fighting by their side. They feel that the white race are amply strong in numbers, in courage, in all the elements of a martial people, to bring this contest to a close without the ignominy of enlisting the negro as a fellow-soldier. I deny that in the revolutionary war there ever was any considerable organization of negroes. I deny that in the war of 1812 there was ever any organization of negro slaves. I admit that through both those wars, and in the Mexican war, and also in the present war, there have been negro slaves that were waiters upon masters in the armies in whose hands in battle arms have been placed, and who used those arms; but they were in only a very few and exceptional cases an organized soldiery. . . .

I know the negro well; I know his nature. He is, until excited, mild and gentle; he is affectionate and faithful, too; but when his passions have been inflamed and thoroughly aroused, you find him a fiend, a latent tiger fierceness in his heart, and when he becomes excited by a taste of blood he is a demon. Such is the nature of the race; and there never was a servile insurrection in the world where it did not manifest that nature. In the Southampton insurrection a few years ago in Virginia [the 1831 Nat Turner rebellion] the negroes displayed the nature which I have imputed to them. I admit that they do not spring to acts of cruelty and ferocity at once. They have to be schooled awhile to prepare them; they come to such acts step by step, as they did in the island of St. Domingo [Haiti, the site of a violent slave revolt against the French colonial government in the 1790s]. . . .

Sir, there is not a man in this body nor in the land that is more deeply devoted to the restoration of the Union than I am, or one who is more attached to the Union and to the Constitution which forms the government of the United States. But when you offer to me and my people a policy and ask us, will you take our measures; will you take general confiscation of the property of all the disloyal; abolition of slavery, the slaves to remain in their localities; will you agree to our arming them, and making them soldiers to fight the battle of the Constitution, which Constitution guarantied them as property to their owners; will you take all these atrocities? We answer, never! never! never! All we ask, is that the just power of the Government of the United States shall be brought into full requisition to suppress this rebellion. The Union men of the slave States are as ready to cooperate in that just and constitutional war as are the Union men of the free States; but they require that the Constitution—the bond of our Union, the ark of our liberties, without which there can be no freedom in this land—shall be held intact and religiously preserved throughout all the storms of the conflict. They ask no exemption of their property from the same law, the same policy, and the same military measures that you would deal out to any other property. I have a few slaves, and my county possesses upwards of seven thousand. If it were necessary to-morrow, to prevent the consummation of this revolution and the disruption of the Union, that those seven thousand slaves should be manumitted, there is not one of them belonging to a Union man who would not be surrendered just as cheerfully as sacrifice for so great an end ever was made by a loyal heart to the cause of his country. But we believe and know that there is no such necessity; there is no such sacrifice required at our hands. On the other hand, we believe and know that the policy so madly urged in the two Houses of Congress by some of the extreme men is fatal, or eminently mischievous to the purposes they profess to have in view. Instead of weakening and subduing the rebels, it would strengthen them. . . .

No Necessity for Black Soldiers

If this Union cannot be preserved by the white man, making him the soldier and the hero of the battle for the Union, there are no conditions upon which it can be saved. But, sir, it can be rescued upon that noble condition; it ought not to be attempted on any other. If you put arms in the hands of the negroes and make them feel their power and impress them with their former slavery, wrongs, and injustice, and arm them, as [General David] Hunter promises, to the number of fifty thousand, you will whet their fiendish passions, make them the destroying scourge of the cotton States, and you will bring upon the country a condition of things what will render restoration hopeless. There is no necessity for it; there can be none. Exhaust the energies, the patriotism, and the resources of the white man; at least tax them further, and yet further, and whenever the time comes and you demonstrate to slave-holding Union men that by the sacrifice of their slaves the Union can be restored and the Constitution can be preserved, and that there shall be but one American empire whose arch shall span the continent from ocean to ocean, and that sacrifice will be unhesitatingly made.

But there is no such stress upon us. It is an inglorious, ignoble, and a cowardly admission that there is any such stress or necessity as that. Why, sir, do you not perceive that the Englishman, the Frenchman, and the Spaniard are already beginning to contemn and spit upon you? Yesterday, or before this rebellion, the name of American might have stood against the world; now it is so poor that none will even do it reverence. That contempt and degradation of our country, that ignoble impress will go on rapidly increasing—yes, sir, it will go on irretrievably to its miserable, degrading consummation, whenever you agree to call in regiments, brigades, divisions, and army corps of negroes into the field. I implore you to use the negro for no such purpose. Wherever you can make him labor, wherever you can make him useful without putting arms in his hands, employ him; there can be no just objection to it. In a particular state of the case, where there was a small corps or a large corps hard pressed, and there were negroes about, and they could be made to swab the cannon, to load the cannon, or fire guns, and to use the cutlass, or any other weapon, in such an emergency, use him; but do not make occasion to use him. Do not organize him as a part of our Army.

VIEWPOINT 3

"I claim that the raising of black regiments for the war would be highly impolitic and uncalled for under the present state of affairs."

Blacks Should Stay Neutral in the War

R.H. Vashon (dates unkown)

Even before blacks were welcomed into the Union Army or state militias, black leaders were canvassing the free population of the North, calling for the formation of black military regiments. However, not all blacks agreed that such a move was wise. One such doubter was R.H. Vashon, a member of a prominent black abolitionist family. In the following viewpoint, which first appeared in the *Anglo-African*, a New York journal of opinion, on September 28, 1861, he criticizes the movement for black enlistment. He argues that the cause of the Union is not the cause of blacks, be they free people in the North or slaves in the South. Blacks, he concludes, should maintain a policy of neutrality in the war, and wait to see which side takes steps to emancipate slaves first—a step he says could just as easily happen in the South as in the North.

MR. EDITOR:

The duty of the black man at this critical epoch is a question of much importance, deeply interesting the friends of liberty, both white and black. The most imposing feature of this duty, I am told, is in relation to military organizations. This question, I am told, is forced upon us by our eminent, educated, far-sighted

R.H. Vashon, article in the *Anglo-African*, September 28, 1861. Reprinted from *Letters and Discussions on the Formation of Colored Regiments* by Alfred M. Green, 1862.

leaders, who, anxious for our elevation and zealous for our reputation, in connection with our white brothers would have us write our names side by side with them upon the immortal book of fame, won by well-contested and desperate encounters upon the battle-field. Claiming that any omission on our part to exhibit that patriotism so noticeable in the whites, will, when history shall record the doings of this memorable country, leave our names without one deed of patriotism or expressed desire for the success of the cause of liberty; not one laurel to entwine the brows of those whose valor like blazing stars upon the battle-field would, no doubt, have eclipsed those whom we now are satisfied to acknowledge as superiors and protectors. Is this all wisdom, this mode of reasoning; or is it a mistaken idea, called into existence by a desire for fame? Is it a demanding necessity that the world will decide belongs to us to meet, thus to prove our manhood and love of liberty? Have not two centuries of cruel and unrequited servitude in this country, alone entitled the children of this generation to the rights of men and citizens? Have we not done our share towards creating a national existence for those who now enjoy it to our degradation, ever devising evil for our suffering, heart-crushed race?

Who that will carefully note the many historical reminiscences, made mention of by those who are ready to do justice to us, can doubt our bravery? Who that has heard of the many privations, hair-breadth escapes, and the unflinching determination of our enslaved brethren seeking the free shores of Canada, can doubt our love of liberty? True patriotism does not consist in words alone, neither do patriotic demonstrations always contribute to the end alone, independent of material aid. I do not suppose any people have been taxed heavier or more than the poor colored people for the cause of liberty, with such small results to themselves. Now, if we have contributed our share to support and establish a government, that we are not entitled to a share in the benefits thereof, what becomes our duty when that government is menaced by those they have cherished at the expense of our blood, toil and degradation?

Let your own heart answer this question, and no regiments of black troops will leave their bodies to rot upon the battle-field beneath a Southern sun—to conquer a peace based upon the perpetuity of human bondage—stimulating and encouraging the inveterate prejudice that now bars our progress in the scale of elevation and education.

Black Regiments Uncalled For

I claim that the raising of black regiments for the war would be highly impolitic and uncalled for under the present state of affairs, knowing, as we do, the policy of the Government in relation to colored men. It would show our incompetency to comprehend the nature of the differences existing between the two sections now at variance, by lending our aid to either party. By taking such measures we invite injustice at the hands of those we prefer to serve; we would contribute to the African colonization scheme, projected a half century ago, by ridding the country of that element [free blacks] so dangerous to the charming institution of negro slavery.

A Call for Equal Pay

Even after the Emancipation Proclamation, some blacks resisted joining the Union Army because of unequal pay and treatment. In a February 29, 1864, address, J.P. Campbell, an official of the African Methodist Episcopal Church, argues that blacks should as a matter of principle join the Union Army only under the condition of equal pay between white and black soldiers.

We ask, then, that the same pay, bounty, pensions, rights and privileges be given to black men that are given to white men, and they will go to the war. . . .

We ask for equal pay and bounty, not because we set a greater value upon money than we do upon human liberty, compared with which money is mere trash; but we contend for equal pay and bounty upon the principle that if we receive equal pay and bounty when we go into the war, we hope to receive equal rights and privileges when we come out of the war. If we go in equal in pay, we hope to come out equal in enfranchisement.

Is that an unreasonable hope or an unjust claim? It takes as much to clothe and feed the black man's wife as it does the white man's wife. It takes as much money to go to market for the black man's little boys and girls as it does for the white man's little boys and girls. We have yet to learn why it is that the black soldier should not receive the same compensation for labor in the service of his country that the white soldier receives. There is no financial embarrassment, as in the case of Mr. Jefferson Davis' government at Richmond. Our great and good financier, Mr. Salmon P. Chase, Secretary of the Treasury, has money enough to carry on the war, and some millions of gold and silver to sell. Give us equal pay, and we will go to the war—not pay on mercenary principles, but pay upon the principles of justice and equity.

Entertaining the sentiment and determination that they do, would it not be unjust in them to accept our service? Would we still invite them to cap the climax by forcing us to the cannon's mouth to save the destruction of those whose whole existence should be merged in with their country's weal and woe? That death should be the readiest sacrifice patriotic citizens could offer to uphold the people's hope, the people's palladium, no one should deny. But what do we enjoy, that should inspire us with those feelings towards a government that would sooner consign five millions of human beings to never-ending slavery than wrong one slave master of his human property? Does not the contemplation of so flagrant a wrong cause your blood to boil with Christian indignation, or bring tears to the eyes of your broken-hearted old men, whose heads, now silvered by time or bleached by sorrow, can no longer shoulder the weightier responsibilities of a young man's calling?

Not only that. Any public demonstration (for this could not well be done in a corner) would only embarrass the present administration, by stirring up old party prejudices which would cause the loss of both sympathy and treasure, which the government cannot well afford to lose at present. By weakening the arm of the government, we strengthen that of the slave power, who would soon march through these States without fear of forcible resistance.

It would be contrary to Christian humanity to permit so flagrant an outrage in silence to be perpetrated upon any people, especially a class who have known naught else but wrong at their hands, whom they would so gloriously serve in time of danger to their own liberties and sacred rights, preferring now their services to uphold a Government leagued with perdition, upon which the doom of death is written, unless they repent, in letters so plain that he who runs may read. Let us weigh well this thing before taking steps which will not only prove disastrous to the cause we would help, but bring suffering and sorrows upon those left to mourn unavailingly our loss.

A Call for Neutrality

I maintain that the principle of neutrality is the only safe one to govern us at this time. When men's lives are in their hands, and so little inducement as there is for us to cast ourselves into the breach, our work for the present lies in quite a different channel from assuming war responsibilities uninvited, with no promised future in store for us—a dilemma inviting enmity and destruction to the few, both North and South, among our people, enjoying partial freedom.

The slave's only hope—his only help—is his suffering brother at the North. When we are removed, the beacon light which directs and assists the panting fugitive is darkened and obscured—his once bright hope, that gave comfort to him as he pressed on to liberty's goal, is shadowed o'er forever. Our own precipitous, unwise zeal must never be the cause to stay the car of freedom, but ever let it roll onward and upward until earth and heaven united shall become one garden of paradisal freedom, knowing no color, no clime, but all one people, one language, one Father, Almighty God.

Once under army discipline, subject to the control of government officers or military leaders, could we dictate when and where the blow should be struck? Could we enter upon Quixotic crusades of our own projecting, independent of the constituted authorities, or these military chiefs? Will the satisfaction of again hearing a casual mention of our heroic deeds upon the field of battle, by our own children, doomed for all that we know to the same inveterate, heart-crushing prejudice that we have come up under, and die leaving as a legacy unto our issue—all from those for whom you would so unwittingly face the cannon's mouth to secure to them a heritage denied you and yours?

Is this country ready and anxious to initiate a new era for down-trodden humanity, that you now so eagerly propose to make the sacrifice of thousands of our ablest men to encourage and facilitate the great work of regeneration? No! no!! Your answer must be: No!!! No black regiments, unless by circumstances over which we have no option, no control; no initiatory war measures, to be adopted or encouraged by us. Our policy must be neutral, ever praying for the success of that party determined to initiate first the policy of justice and equal rights.

Wait and See What Happens

Who can say that in another twelve months' time the policy of the South will not change in our favor, if the assistance of England or France will by it be gained, rather than submit to northern dictation or subjugation? Did that idea ever suggest itself to your mind? Strange things happen all the while. Look back for the last twenty-four months, and ask yourself if you could have foretold what to-day you are so well informed has actually transpired when coming events cast their shadows before?

In these days, principle is supplanted by policy, and interest shapes policy, I find by daily observation, both in high and low places. Although to many the above idea may seem idle and delusory, inconsistent with the present spirit and suicidal policy of the South, yet I for one would feel justified in entertaining it equally with the idea that the North would proclaim a general emancipation so long as she supposed it a possibility to reclaim the disaffected States of the Southern Confederacy.

And, if an impossibility, what would all proclamations to that effect avail?

I believe with the act of emancipation adopted and proclaimed by the South, both England and France, (and in fact I might safely say all Europe,) would not only recognize their independence, but would render them indirectly material aid and sympathy.

To get the start of the northern slave-worshippers, as they are sometimes termed, who can say that, as a last resort, these rebel leaders have not had that long in contemplation, knowing that should they succumb to this government through force of circumstances, or the uncertain chances of war, their lives would be valueless only as a warning to future generations.

Then, why may we not hope that such is their ultimatum in case of a series of defeats—the liberation of four millions of our poor, heart-crushed, enslaved race. One or two large battles will decide the future policy of both the contending parties—the sooner it comes the sooner we will know our fate. It is in that scale it hangs.

Then let us do our duty to each other—use care in all our public measures—be not too precipitous, but in prayer wait and watch the salvation of God.

VIEWPOINT 4

"The prejudiced white men, North or South, never will respect us until they are forced to do it by deeds of our own."

Blacks Should Fight for the North

Alfred M. Green (dates unknown)

Alfred M. Green was a black schoolteacher and lecturer in Philadelphia. When the Civil War broke out in 1861 he became involved in promoting the organization of black military units, despite the fact that such units were not then accepted in the Union Army. The following is an article by Green that was first published in the *Anglo-African*, a New York journal, on October 19, 1861. Green, responding to an article opposing black enlistment that had appeared in a previous issue of the *Anglo-American*, argues that the Civil War presents an opportunity for blacks to make their presence felt in the war, to free the slaves, and to prove their worth as American citizens. Green later arranged to have this exchange of views and several other articles printed in a pamphlet in Philadelphia in 1862.

M R. EDITOR:

In your issue of September 28th, appears an able and elaborate article on the "Formation of Colored Regiments." I have no desire for contention at a time like this with those who differ honorably from me in opinion; but I think it just, once in a while, to speak out and let the world know where we stand on the great issues of

From a letter of Alfred M. Green to the editor of the *Anglo-African*, October 19, 1861. Reprinted from *Letters and Discussions on the Formation of Colored Regiments* by Alfred M. Green, 1862.

the day, for it is only by this means that we can succeed in arousing our people from a mistaken policy of inactivity, at a time when the world is rushing like a wild tornado in the direction of universal emancipation. The inactivity that is advocated is the principle that has ever had us left behind, and will leave us again, unless we arouse from lethargy and arm ourselves as men and patriots against the common enemy of God and man. For six months I have labored to arouse our people to the necessity of action, and I have the satisfaction to say not without success. I have seen companies organized and under the most proficient modern drill in that time. I have seen men drilled among our sturdy-going colored men of the rural districts of Pennsylvania and New Jersey, in the regular African Zouave drill, that would make the hearts of secession traitors or prejudiced northern Yankees quake and tremble for fear.

Now I maintain that for all practical purposes, whatever be the turn of the war, preparation on our part, by the most efficient knowledge of the military art and discipline, is one of the most positive demands of the times. No nation ever has or ever will be emancipated from slavery, and the result of such a prejudice as we are undergoing in this country, but by the sword, wielded too by their own strong arms. It is a foolish idea for us to still be nursing our past grievances to our own detriment, when we should as one man grasp the sword—grasp this most favorable opportunity of becoming inured to that service that must burst the fetters of the enslaved and enfranchise the nominally free of the North. We admit all that has been or can be said about the meanness of this government towards us—we are fully aware that there is no more soul in the present administration on the great moral issues involved in the slavery question and the present war, than has characterized previous administrations; but, what of that; it all teaches the necessity or our making ourselves felt as a people, at this extremity of our national government, worthy of consideration, and of being recognized as a part of its own strength. Had every State in the Union taken active steps in the direction of forming regiments of color, we should now, instead of numbering eight regiments or about eight thousand five hundred men, have numbered seventy-five thousand—besides awakening an interest at home and abroad, that no vacillating policy of the half-hearted semi-secessionists of the North could have suppressed.

It would have relieved the administration of so much room for cavil on the slavery question and colored men's right to bear arms, &c. It is a strange fact that now, when we should be the most united and decided as to our future destiny; when we should all have our shoulders to the wheel in order to enforce the doctrine we have ever taught of self-reliance, and ourselves striking blows

A Union Army recruiting poster. Black soldiers in the Civil War served in segregated regiments under white officers.

for freedom; that we are most divided, most inactive, and in many respects most despondent of any other period of our history. Some are wasting thought and labor, physical and intellectual, in counseling emigration, (which I have nothing against when done with proper motives); others are more foolishly wasting time and means in an unsuccessful war against it; while a third class, and the most unfortunate of the three, counsel sitting still to see the salvation of God. Oh, that we could see that God will help no one that refuses to help himself; that God will not even help a sinner that will not first help himself. Stretch forth thy hand, said the Saviour to the man with a withered hand. He did so and was healed. Take up thy bed and walk, said he, and the man arose; go and wash, said he to the blind man, and he did it. How many are the evidences of this kind. God is saying to us to-day, as plainly as events can be pointed out, stretch forth thy hand; but we sit idly, with our hands folded, while the whole world, even nations thousands of miles distant across the ocean, are maddened by the fierceness of this American strife, which after all is nothing less than God's means of opening the way for us to free ourselves by the assistance of our own enslavers, if we will do it.

Can we be still or idle under such circumstances. If ever colored men plead for rights or fight for liberty, now of all others is the time. The prejudiced white men, North or South, never will respect us until they are forced to do it by deeds of our own. Let us draw upon European sentiment as well as unbiased minds in our own country, by presenting an undaunted front on the side of freedom and equal rights; but we are blindly mistaken if we think to draw influence from any quarter by sitting still at a time like this. The world must know we are here, and that we have aims, objects and interests in the present great struggle.

Without this we will be left a hundred years behind this gigantic age of human progress and development. I never care to reply to such views as those which set up the plea of previous injustice or even of present injustice done to us, as a reason why we should stand still at such a time as this. I have lived long enough to know that men situated like ourselves must accept the least of a combination of difficulties; if, therefore, there is a chance for us to get armed and equipped for active military service, that is one point gained which never could be gained in a time of peace and prosperity in this country: and that could have been done months ago, and can now be done in a few weeks, if we adopt the measure of united effort for its accomplishment.

Does any one doubt the expediency of our being armed and under military discipline, even if we have always been sufferers at the hands of those claiming superiority? But enough of this. As to public demonstrations of this kind weakening the arm of the Federal Government, I must say that I was prepared to hear that remark among Democratic Union-savers, but I am startled to hear it from among our own ranks of unflinching abolitionists.

Indeed, sir, the longer the government shirks the responsibility of such a measure, the longer time she gives the rebel government to tamper with the free colored people of the South, and prompt and prepare their slaves for shifting the horrors of Saint Domingo [Haiti] from the South to the North; and, in such an event, could we rid ourselves from the responsibility of entering the field, more than any other Northern men whom the government chose to call into active service?

Could we more effectually exercise proper discretion, without arms, without drill, without union, than by availing ourselves of all these at the present time, looking boldly forward to that auspicious moment?

The South (as I have said in an article written for the Philadelphia "Press," and copied into several popular journals) can mean nothing less than emancipation, by the act of her having thousands of free colored men, as well as slaves, even now under the best military discipline. England and France of course would favor such a project, should the South thus snatch the key to a termination of this rebellion from the hands of the Federal Government. But how much better off would we be, sitting here like Egyptian mummies, till all this was done, and then drafted and driven off, undisciplined, to meet well-disciplined troops, who will then truly be fighting for freedom; and while we could have no other motive than to help conquer a peace for the "*Union still*" in its perfidious unregenerate state? Tell me not that it will be optional with us, in the event of emancipation by the South, whether we fight or not. On the contrary, there is no possible way to escape it but to either commit suicide or run away to Africa, for even the climate of Canada, in such an event, would not be cool enough to check the ardor of fighting abolitionists against the hell-born prejudice of the North, and the cowardly black man, would sit here quietly with his arms folded, instead of taking advantage of the times, till even the emancipated slaves of the South, rigorous in their majesty, force him to rise and flee to Canada to save his unsavory bacon. Let us then, sir, hear no more of these measures of actual necessity inaugurating a "dilemma, inviting enmity, and destruction to the few, both North and South, among our people enjoying partial freedom." That is a work that cannot be accomplished by loyal patriotic efforts to prepare a hundred thousand men to do service for God, for freedom, for themselves. Sitting still, shirking the responsibility God has thrown upon our shoulders, alone can engender such a dilemma.

Your correspondent also asks whether: "Once under army discipline, subject to the control of the government officers or military orders, we could dictate when and where the blow should be struck. Could we enter upon Quixotic crusades of our own projecting, independent of the constituted authorities or these military chiefs?" Sir, it appears to me that, under whatever changes of governmental policy, our favor would be courted more under such circumstances, and our dictation received with more favor and regard, both by the authorities, chiefs, and the people at large, than by our weak, effeminate pleadings for favor on the merits or our noble ancestry, rather than nerving our own arms and hearts for a combat that we have long half-heartedly invited by our much groanings and pleadings at a throne of grace.

The issue is here; let us prepare to meet it with manly spirit; let us say to the demagogues of the North who would prevent us now from proving our manhood and foresight in the midst of all these complicated difficulties, that we will be armed, we will be schooled in military service, and if our fathers were cheated and disfranchised after nobly defending the country, we, their sons, have the manhood to defend the right and the sagacity to detect the wrong; time enough to secure to ourselves the primary interest we have in the great and moving cause of the great American rebellion.

VIEWPOINT 5

"All negroes and mulattoes who shall be engaged in war . . . against the Confederate States . . . shall, when captured . . . be delivered to the authorities of the State or States in which they shall be captured."

Captured Black Soldiers Should Be Treated As Criminals

Confederate Congress

In May 1863 the Confederate Congress, acting upon the recommendations of Confederate president Jefferson Davis, passed a series of resolutions responding to the Emancipation Proclamation and the use of black soldiers in Union forces. They declared that the North's use of black soldiers constituted the promotion of slave revolts—a capital offense in the South—and that officers of black regiments were to be executed and black soldiers were to be delivered to the state governments. The resolutions made little distinction between black soldiers who were escaped slaves and those who were not. On the battlefield the actions of Confederate soldiers toward their black opponents were even more harsh—most notoriously at Fort Pillow, Tennessee, where Confederate forces under Nathan B. Forrest killed hundreds of black soldiers after they had surrendered.

From resolutions of the Confederate Congress, May 1863. Reprinted from *The American Conflict: A History of the Great Rebellion in the United States of America* by Horace Greeley, 1867.

Resolved, by the Congress of the Confederate States of America, In response to the message of the President, transmitted to Congress at the commencement of the present session, That, in the opinion of Congress, the commissioned officers of the enemy ought *not* to be delivered to the authorities of the respective States, as suggested in the said message, but all captives taken by the Confederate forces ought to be dealt with and disposed of by the Confederate Government.

SEC. 2. That, in the judgment of Congress, the proclamations of the President of the United States, dated respectively September 22d, 1862, and January 1st, 1863, and the other measures of the Government of the United States and of its authorities, commanders, and forces, designed or tending to emancipate slaves in the Confederate States, or to abduct such slaves, or to incite them to insurrection, or to employ negroes in war against the Confederate States, or to overthrow the institution of African Slavery, and bring on a servile war in these States, would, if successful, produce atrocious consequences, and they are inconsistent with the spirit of those usages which, in modern warfare, prevail among civilized nations; they may, therefore, be properly and lawfully repressed by retaliation.

Retaliation for the Use of Black Soldiers

SEC. 3. That in every case wherein, during the present war, any violation of the laws or usages of war among civilized nations shall be, or has been, done and perpetrated by those acting under the authority of the Government of the United States, on the persons or property of citizens of the Confederate States, or of those under the protection or in the land or naval service of the Confederate States, or of any State of the Confederacy, the President of the Confederate States is hereby authorized to cause full and ample retaliation to be made for every such violation, in such manner and to such extent as he may think proper.

SEC. 4. That every White person, being a commissioned officer, or acting as such, who, during the present war, shall command negroes or mulattoes in arms against the Confederate States, or who shall arm, train, organize, or prepare negroes or mulattoes for military service against the Confederate States, or who shall voluntarily aid negroes or mulattoes in any military enterprise, attack, or conflict, in such service, shall be deemed as inciting servile insurrection, and shall, if captured, be put to death, or be otherwise punished at the discretion of the court.

SEC. 5. Every person, being a commissioned officer, or acting as such in the service of the enemy, who shall, during the present

Subject to Death

Confederate secretary of war James A. Seddon, in a November 30, 1862, letter to General Pierre G. Beauregard, outlines a policy of executing captured black soldiers as criminals guilty of breaking slave insurrection laws.

Slaves in flagrant rebellion are subject to death by the laws of every slave holding State, and did circumstances admit, without too great delays, and Military inconveniences, might be handed over to the civil tribunals for condemnation. They cannot be recognized in any way as soldiers subject to the rules of war and to trial by Military Courts, yet for example, and to repress any spirit of insubordination, it is deemed essential that slaves in armed insurrection should meet condign punishment, summary execution must therefore be inflicted on those taken . . . under circumstances indicative beyond doubt of actual rebellion. To guard however against the possible abuse of this grave power under the immediate excitement of capture, or through over zeal on the part of subordinate officers, it is deemed judicious that the discretion of deciding and giving the order of execution should be reposed in the General Commanding the Special Locality of the capture.

war, excite, attempt to excite, or cause to be excited, a servile insurrection, or who shall incite, or cause to be incited, a slave to rebel, shall, if captured, be put to death, or be otherwise punished at the discretion of the court.

SEC. 6. Every person charged with an offense punishable under the preceding resolutions shall, during the present war, be tried before the military court attached to the army or corps by the troops of which he shall have been captured, or by such other military court as the President may direct, and in such manner and under such regulations as the President shall prescribe; and, after conviction, the President may commute the punishment in such manner and on such terms as he may deem proper.

SEC. 7. All negroes and mulattoes who shall be engaged in war, or be taken in arms against the Confederate States, or shall give aid or comfort to the enemies of the Confederate States, shall, when captured in the Confederate States, be delivered to the authorities of the State or States in which they shall be captured, to be dealt with according to the present or future laws of such State or States.

"I know that a colored man ought to run no greater risques than a white."

Captured Black Soldiers Should Be Treated as Prisoners of War

Hannah Johnson (dates unknown)

Hannah Johnson was the mother of a member of the 54th Massachusetts Regiment, one of the first black regiments to be organized in the North, and which had distinguished itself in the attack on Fort Wagner in South Carolina on July 18, 1863. Johnson wrote to Lincoln on July 31, telling of her fears that her son, if captured, would be sold as a slave. She argues the Confederacy should treat its black prisoners of war the same as it treats its white prisoners, and urges the president to retaliate against Confederate prisoners if such was not the case. Lincoln never responded to her letter, but on the previous day he had issued a statement promising to retaliate against Confederate prisoners if black prisoners were denied their rights as prisoners of war.

Excellent Sir My good friend says I must write to you and she will send it My son went in the 54th regiment. I am a colored woman and my son was strong and able as any to fight for his country and the colored people have as much to fight for as any. My father was a Slave and escaped from Louisiana before I was born morn forty years agone I have but poor edication but I

Hannah Johnson, letter to Abraham Lincoln, July 31, 1863. Reprinted from *Free at Last*, edited by Ira Berlin et al., 1992.

never went to schol, but I know just as well as any what is right betwcen man and man. Now I know it is right that a colored man should go and fight for his country, and so ought to a white man. I know that a colored man ought to run no greater risques than a white, his pay is no greater his obligation to fight is the same. So why should not our enemies be compelled to treat him the same, Made to do it.

A Plea for Fair Treatment

My son fought at Fort Wagoner but thank God he was not taken prisoner, as many were   I thought of this thing before I let my boy go but then they said Mr. Lincoln will never let them sell our colored soldiers for slaves, if they do he will get them back quck he will rettallyate and stop it. Now Mr Lincoln dont you think you oght to stop this thing and make them do the same by the colored men   they have lived in idleness all their lives on stolen labor and made savages of the colored people, but they now are so furious because they are proving themselves to be men, such as have come away and got some edication. It must not be so. You must put the rebels to work in State prisons to making shoes

A New General Order

On July 30, 1863, President Abraham Lincoln issued the following policy of retaliation against any failure of the Confederacy to treat captured black soldiers as prisoners of war.

It is the duty of every Government to give protection to its citizens, of whatever class, color, or condition, and especially to those who are duly organized as soldiers in the public service. The law of nations, and the usages and customs of war, as carried on by civilized powers, permit no distinction as to color in the treatment of prisoners of war as public enemies. To sell or enslave any captured person, on account of his color, and for no offense against the laws of war, is a relapse into barbarism, and a crime against the civilization of the age.

The Government of the United States will give the same protection to all its soldiers; and if the enemy shall sell or enslave any one because of his color, the offense shall be punished by retaliation upon the enemy's prisoners in our possession.

It is therefore ordered that, for every soldier of the United States killed in violation of the laws of war, a Rebel soldier shall be executed; and for every one enslaved by the enemy or sold into Slavery, a Rebel soldier shall be placed at hard labor on public works, and continued at such labor until the other shall be released and receive the treatment due to a prisoner of war.

and things, if they sell our colored soldiers, till they let them all go. And give their wounded the same treatment. it would seem cruel, but their no other way, and a just man must do hard things sometimes, that shew him to be a great man. They tell me some do you will take back the Proclamation, don't do it. When you are dead and in Heaven, in a thousand years that action of yours will make the Angels sing your praises I know it. Ought one man to own another, law for or not, who made the law, surely the poor slave did not. so it is wicked, and a horrible Outrage, there is no sense in it, because a man has lived by robbing all his life and his father before him, should he complain because the stolen things found on him are taken. Robbing the colored people of their labor is but a small part of the robbery   their souls are almost taken, they are made bruits of often. You know all about this

Will you see that the colored men fighting now, are fairly treated. You ought to do this, and do it at once, Not let the thing run along   meet it quickly and manfully, and stop this, mean cowardly cruelty. We poor oppressed ones, appeal to you, and ask fair play. Yours for Christs sake

Hannah Johnson.

CHAPTER 5

The War Ends

Chapter Preface

Historians now recognize July 3, 1863, as a major turning point in the Civil War. On that date the Confederacy suffered two significant setbacks. In Gettysburg, Pennsylvania, a Confederate division of 15,000 soldiers led by Virginia general George E. Pickett launched a famed frontal charge against Union troops and lost two-thirds of its men—thus ending the Battle of Gettysburg and the last significant offensive incursion against the North. On the same day, Confederate general John C. Pemberton asked Union general Ulysses S. Grant for terms of the surrender of Vicksburg, Mississippi, a seemingly impregnable Confederate fortress on the Mississippi River that had been kept under siege for the previous six weeks by Union forces. The formal surrender of Vicksburg the next day left the North in control of the Mississippi River, and the Confederacy effectively split in two.

People in the North expressed hopes that the war would soon end. However, despite these significant Northern victories, the war would last for nearly two more years, with thousands more casualties to come on both sides. The Civil War became a war of attrition. The South, under Generals Robert E. Lee and Joseph E. Johnson, entrenched its armies in defensive positions and tried to create a military stalemate in the hope that the North would tire of the casualties and other costs of the war. The North, under Generals Grant and William T. Sherman, tried to break the Southern will to fight, not only by defeating Confederate armies, but by campaigns, such as Sherman's march through Georgia in 1864, aimed at destroying Southern resources and morale.

For both sides the presidential election of 1864 loomed as a crucial event. Southerners rested their hopes on elements within the Democratic Party who called for an armistice between the two sides. Lincoln steadfastly refused to accept anything less than full surrender of the South. His reelection victory over former general George B. McClellan was another bitter disappointment for the Confederacy.

VIEWPOINT 1

"At no time . . . has this state been other than willing to terminate . . . a war unnecessary in its origin, fraught with horror and suffering . . . and necessarily dangerous to the liberties of all in its continuance."

The North Should Negotiate for Peace

New Jersey State Legislature

Over the course of the Civil War the North faced internal division between those who supported and those who opposed the fighting. As casualties mounted and Union armies suffered defeats in the early years of the war, increasing numbers of people questioned whether to continue the war. Dissent in the North increased following Abraham Lincoln's Emancipation Proclamation, as some people argued that instead of a battle to save the Union, lives were being sacrificed for a new cause they did not believe in.

In March 1863 the state legislature of New Jersey passed a series of resolutions protesting the course of the Civil War and calling for peace. The resolutions, reprinted here, are typical of many critics of the Civil War and especially the administration of Abraham Lincoln. The legislature cites resolutions passed by Congress on July 25, 1861, stating the purpose of the war to be solely the preservation of the Union and not the abolition of slavery, and argues for a return to that policy. While not specifically endorsing the principle of secession, the resolutions call for peace negotiations between the North and the South with the purpose of ending the conflict.

Resolutions of the New Jersey State Legislature, March 1863. Reprinted from *The Rebellion Record: A Diary of American Events, with Documents, Narratives, Illustrative Incidents, Poetry, etc., etc.,* Supplement, vol. 1, edited by Frank Moore. New York: G.P. Putnam, 1864.

1. *Be it resolved by the Senate and General Assembly of the state of New Jersey*, that this state, in promptly answering the calls made by the President of the United States, at and since the inauguration of the war, for troops and means to assist in maintaining the power and dignity of the Federal government, believed and confided in the professions and declarations of the President of the United States, in his inaugural address, and in the resolutions passed by Congress on the 25th day of July, 1861, in which, among other things, it was declared "that the war is not waged for conquest or subjugation, or interfering with the rights or established institutions of the states but to maintain and defend the supremacy of the Constitution, with the rights and equality under it unimpaired, and that as soon as these objects shall be accomplished the war ought to cease"; and that, relying upon these assurances, given under the sanctity of official oaths, this state freely, fully, and without delay or conditions contributed to the assistance of the Federal government her sons and her means.

2. *And be it resolved*, that this state, having waited for the redemption of the sacred pledges of the President and Congress with a patience and forbearance only equaled in degree by the unfaltering and unswerving bravery and fidelity of her sons, conceives it to be her solemn duty, as it is her unquestioned right, to urge upon the President and Congress, in the most respectful but decided manner, the redemption of the pledges under which the troops of this state entered upon, and to this moment have continued in, the contest.

And inasmuch as no conditions have delayed nor hesitation marked her zeal in behalf of the Federal government, even at times when party dogmas were dangerously usurping the place of broad national principles and executive and congressional faith; and as the devotion of this state to the sacred cause of perpetuating the Union and maintaining the Constitution has been untainted in any degree by infidelity, bigotry, sectionalism, or partisanship, she now, in view of the faith originally plighted, of the disasters and disgrace that have marked the steps of a changed and changing policy, and of the imminent dangers that threaten our national existence, urges upon the President and Congress a return and adherence to the original policy of the administration as the only means, under the blessing of God, by which the adhering states can be reunited in action, the Union restored, and the nation saved.

3. *And be it resolved*, that it is the deliberate sense of the people of this state that the war power within the limits of the Constitution is ample for any and all emergencies, and that all assumption

of power, under whatever plea, beyond that conferred by the Constitution is without warrant or authority, and if permitted to continue without remonstrance will finally encompass the destruction of the liberties of the people and the death of the republic; and therefore, to the end that in any event the matured and deliberate sense of the people of New Jersey may be known and declared, we their representatives in Senate and General Assembly convened, do, in their name and in their behalf, make unto the Federal government this our solemn protest:

Against a war waged with the insurgent states for the accomplishment of unconstitutional or partisan purposes;

Against a war which has for its object the subjugation of any of the states, with a view to their reduction to territorial condition;

Against proclamations from any source by which, under the plea of "military necessity," persons in states and territories sustaining the Federal government, and beyond necessary military lines, are held liable to the rigor and severity of military laws;

Against the domination of the military over the civil law in states, territories, or districts not in a state of insurrection;

Against all arrests without warrant; against the suspension of the writ of habeas corpus in states and territories sustaining the Federal government, "where the public safety does not require it"; and against the assumption of power by any person to suspend such writ, except under the express authority of Congress;

Against the creation of new states by the division of existing

The 1864 Democratic Platform

The Democratic Party, meeting in Chicago in 1864, nominated former Union general George B. McClellan for president. He was forced to distance himself from the party platform, which featured the following passage arguing that the Civil War was a failure and calling for a "cessation of hostilities" at "the earliest practicable moment."

Resolved, That this Convention does explicitly declare, as the sense of the American people, that, after four years of failure to restore the Union by the experiment of war, during which, under the pretense of a military necessity of a war power higher than the Constitution, the Constitution itself has been disregarded in every part, and public liberty and private right alike trodden down, and the material prosperity of the country essentially impaired, justice, humanity, liberty, and the public welfare demand that immediate efforts be made for a cessation of hostilities, with a view to an ultimate Convention of all the States, or other peaceable means, to the end that, at the earliest practicable moment, peace may be restored on the basis of the Federal Union of the States.

ones, or in any other manner not clearly authorized by the Constitution; and against the right of secession as practically admitted by the action of Congress in admitting as a new state a portion of the state of Virginia [West Virginia];

Against the power assumed in the proclamation of the President made January 1, 1863, by which all the slaves in certain states and parts of states are forever set free; and against the expenditures of the public moneys for the emancipation of slaves or their support at any time, under any pretense whatever;

Against any and every exercise of power upon the part of the Federal government that is not clearly given and expressed in the Federal Constitution—reasserting that "the powers not delegated to the United States by the Constitution, nor prohibited by it to the states, are reserved to the states respectively, or to the people."

4. *And be it resolved*, that the unequaled promptness with which New Jersey has responded to every call made by the President and Congress for men and means has been occasioned by no lurking animosity to the states of the South or the rights of her people; no disposition to wrest from them any of their rights, privileges, or property, but simply to assist in maintaining, as she has ever believed and now believes it to be her duty to do, the supremacy of the Federal Constitution; and while abating naught in her devotion to the Union of the states and the dignity and power of the Federal government, at no time since the commencement of the present war has this state been other than willing to terminate, peacefully and honorably to all, a war unnecessary in its origin, fraught with horror and suffering in its prosecution and necessarily dangerous to the liberties of all in its continuance.

5. *And be it resolved*, that the legislature of the state of New Jersey believes that the appointment of commissioners upon the part of the Federal government to meet commissioners similarly appointed by the insurgent states, to convene in some suitable place for the purpose of considering whether any and, if any, what plan may be adopted, consistent with the honor and dignity of the national government, by which the present civil war may be brought to a close, is not inconsistent with the integrity, honor, and dignity of the Federal government, but as an indication of the spirit which animates the adhering states, would in any event tend to strengthen us in the opinion of other nations; and hoping, as we sincerely do, that the Southern states would reciprocate the peaceful indications thus evinced, and believing, as we do, that under the blessing of God, great benefits would arise from such a conference, we most earnestly recommend the subject to the consideration of the government of the United States and request its cooperation therein.

VIEWPOINT 2

"We consider the . . . introduction of the so-called Peace Resolutions as wicked, weak, and cowardly, tending to aid by their sympathy the rebels seeking to destroy the republic."

The North Should Not Negotiate for Peace

Eleventh New Jersey Volunteers

Throughout most of the Civil War the people of the North were divided over the war's ultimate aims, and indeed over whether to continue the war at all. As the conflict dragged on through 1862 and 1863 with no immediate end in sight, a significant number of political leaders (called "Copperheads" by their opponents) argued that the North should negotiate peace with the South. One stronghold of such sentiment was the state legislature of New Jersey, which in March 1863 debated and passed a series of resolutions criticizing President Abraham Lincoln and calling for a halt to the fighting. The resolutions, printed in several local newspapers, prompted members of a volunteer regiment from New Jersey to issue their own set of resolutions, reprinted here, protesting the actions of the state legislature and reiterating their

Resolutions of the Eleventh New Jersey Volunteers, 1863. Reprinted from *The Rebellion Record: A Diary of American Events, with Documents, Narratives, Illustrative Incidents, Poetry, etc., etc.,* Supplement, vol. 1, edited by Frank Moore. New York: G.P. Putnam, 1864.

willingness to fight until Confederate surrender. The victory of Abraham Lincoln over his Democratic opponent, former general George B. McClellan, in the 1864 presidential election was widely seen as an endorsement of Lincoln's war policies and of the views expressed in this viewpoint.

Whereas, the legislature of our native state, a state hallowed by the remembrance of the battles of Princeton, Trenton, and Monmouth, fields stained by the blood of our forefathers in the establishment of our government, has sought to tarnish its high honor and bring upon it disgrace by the passage of resolutions tending to a dishonorable peace with armed rebels seeking to destroy our great and beneficent government, the best ever designed for the happiness of the many; and

Whereas, we, her sons, members of the Eleventh Regiment, New Jersey Volunteers, citizens representing every section of the state, have left our homes to endure the fatigues, privations, and dangers incident to a soldier's life, in order to maintain our republic in its integrity, willing to sacrifice our lives to that object; fully recognizing the impropriety of a soldier's discussion of the legislative functions of the state, yet deeming it due to ourselves that the voice of those who offer their all in their country's cause be heard when weak and wicked men seek its dishonor.

Therefore,

Resolved, that the Union of the states is the only guarantee for the preservation of our liberty and independence, and that the war for the maintainance of that Union commands *now*, as it ever has done, our best efforts and our heartfelt sympathy.

Cowardly Resolutions

Resolved, that we consider the passage or even the introduction of the so-called Peace Resolutions as wicked, weak, and cowardly, tending to aid by their sympathy the rebels seeking to destroy the republic.

Resolved, that we regard as traitors alike the foe in arms and the secret enemies of our government who, at home, foment disaffection and strive to destroy confidence in our legally chosen rulers.

Resolved, that the reports spread broadcast throughout the North, by secession sympathizers, prints, and voices, that the army of which we esteem it a high honor to form a part is demoralized and clamorous for peace on any terms are the lying utterances of traitorous tongues and do base injustice to our noble

244

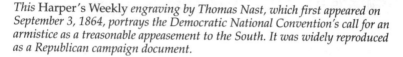

This Harper's Weekly *engraving by Thomas Nast, which first appeared on September 3, 1864, portrays the Democratic National Convention's call for an armistice as a treasonable appeasement to the South. It was widely reproduced as a Republican campaign document.*

comrades who have never faltered in the great work, and are now not only willing but anxious to follow their gallant and chivalric leader against the strongholds of the enemy.

Resolved, that we put forth every effort, endure every fatigue, and shrink from no danger, until, under the gracious guidance of a kind Providence, every armed rebel shall be conquered, and traitors at home shall quake with fear, as the proud emblem of our national independence shall assert its power from North to South, and crush beneath its powerful folds all who dared to assail its honor, doubly hallowed by the memory of the patriot dead.

VIEWPOINT 3

"You know the woe, the horrors, and the suffering, cannot be described by words; . . . we ask you to take these things into consideration."

Sherman's War Tactics Are Inhumane

James M. Calhoun (1811-1875), E.E. Rawson (1818-1893), and S.C. Wells (dates unknown)

One of the significant developments of the Civil War was the military strategy devised and implemented by Union general William T. Sherman. Placed in charge of Union forces west of the Mississippi by Ulysses S. Grant in March 1864, Sherman determined that the war and its effects needed to be fully brought to bear on the Southern people. Historian William L. Barney writes in *A Reader's Companion to American History*:

> More than any other Civil War commander, Sherman grasped the brutal logic of total war. In such a war, civilian morale and economic resources are just as much military targets as the enemy's armies. For Sherman, war unleashed the fury of hell, and he refused to sentimentalize the killing and pillaging required for victory.

An example of Sherman's concept of total warfare can be seen in his actions following the capture of Atlanta, Georgia, on September 2, 1864. Sherman decided not to remain and occupy the city, but to burn all of its military assets and take his troops on a march through Georgia. He gave an order that all civilians evacuate the city. On September 11, James M. Calhoun, the mayor of Atlanta, and two members of his city council wrote Sherman a letter, reprinted here, telling him of the hardships his order caused, and asking him to reconsider.

Letter of James M. Calhoun, E.E. Rawson, and S.C. Wells to William T. Sherman, dated September 11, 1864. Reprinted from William T. Sherman, *Memoirs of Gen. W.T. Sherman*, 1875.

Major-General W.T. Sherman.

Sir: We the undersigned, Mayor and two of the Council for the city of Atlanta, for the time being the only legal organ of the people of the said city, to express their wants and wishes, ask leave most earnestly but respectfully to petition you to reconsider the order requiring them to leave Atlanta.

Appalling Hardships

At first view, it struck us that the measure would involve extraordinary hardship and loss, but since we have seen the practical execution of it so far as it has progressed, and the individual condition of the people, and heard their statements as to the inconveniences, loss, and suffering attending it, we are satisfied that the amount of it will involve in the aggregate consequences appalling and heart-rending.

Many poor women are in advanced state of pregnancy, others now having young children, and whose husbands for the greater part are either in the army, prisoners, or dead. Some say: "I have such a one sick at my house; who will wait on them when I am gone?" Others say: "What are we to do? We have no house to go to, and no means to buy, build, or rent any; no parents, relatives, or friends, to go to." Another says: "I will try and take this or that article of property, but such and such things I must leave behind, though I need them much.". . .

We only refer to a few facts, to try to illustrate in part how this measure will operate in practice. As you advanced, the people north of this fell back; and before your arrival here, a large portion of the people had retired south, so that the country south of this is already crowded, and without houses enough to accommodate the people, and we are informed that many are now staying in churches and other out-buildings.

This being so, how is it possible for the people still here (mostly women and children) to find any shelter? And how can they live through the winter in the woods—no shelter or subsistence, in the midst of strangers who know them not, and without the power to assist them much, if they were willing to do so?

This is but a feeble picture of the consequences of this measure. You know the woe, the horrors, and the suffering, cannot be described by words; imagination can only conceive of it, and we ask you to take these things into consideration.

A Plea to Reconsider

We know your mind and time are constantly occupied with the duties of your command, which almost deters us from asking

247

your attention to this matter, but thought it might be that you had not considered this subject in all of its awful consequences, and that on more reflection you, we hope, would not make this people an exception to all mankind, for we know of no such instance ever having occurred—surely never in the United States—and what has this *helpless* people done, that they should be driven from their homes, to wander strangers and outcasts, and exiles, and to subsist on charity?

Ruins of a railroad roundhouse in Atlanta. The destruction of the city was caused both by Union bombardment and by Confederate attempts to destroy resources and prevent them from falling into Union hands.

We do not know as yet the number of people still here; of those who are here, we are satisfied a respectable number, if allowed to remain at home, could subsist for several months without assistance, and a respectable number for a much longer time, and who might not need assistance at any time.

In conclusion, we most earnestly and solemnly petition you to reconsider this order, or modify it, and suffer this unfortunate people to remain at home, and enjoy what little means they have.

Respectfully submitted:

James M. Calhoun, *Mayor*.
E.E. Rawson, *Councilman*.
S.C. Wells, *Councilman*.

VIEWPOINT 4

"You might as well appeal against the thunder-storm as against these terrible hardships of war."

War Is Necessarily Inhumane

William T. Sherman (1820-1891)

William T. Sherman was, after Ulysses S. Grant, the second most important Union general of the Civil War. The Ohio-born West Point graduate and Mexican-American War veteran had been the superintendent of the state military academy in Alexandria, Louisiana, before the Civil War. He resigned when Louisiana seceded and rejoined the U.S. Army, rising from colonel at the First Battle of Bull Run (Manassas) in 1861 to commanding general of Union forces west of the Mississippi River in 1864. He won his most important victory in September of that year when his army captured Atlanta, Georgia. Wanting to move his troops on, and not wishing to see Atlanta and its factories fall back into the hands of the Confederacy, he determined to burn the city, and ordered its inhabitants evacuated.

Sherman received several letters of protest over his decision to evacuate Atlanta, including one from the mayor and two members of the city council, who asked Sherman to take into account the hardships he was causing. Sherman replied in a September 12, 1864, letter that is reprinted here. The letter reveals Sherman's thoughts about the nature of war, which he argues is inherently cruel and cannot be refined into something humane. The only way suffering in the South can stop, he asserts, is for its people to end their rebellion.

Letter of William T. Sherman to James M. Calhoun, E.E. Rawson, and S.C. Wells, dated September 12, 1864. Reprinted from William T. Sherman, *Memoirs of Gen. W.T. Sherman*, 1875.

James M. Calhoun, *Mayor*, E.E. Rawson *and* S.C. Wells, *representing City Council of Atlanta.*

Gentlemen: I have your letter of the 11th, in the nature of a petition to revoke my orders removing all the inhabitants from Atlanta. I have read it carefully, and give full credit to your statements of the distress that will be occasioned, and yet shall not revoke my orders, because they were not designed to meet the humanities of the case, but to prepare for the future struggles in which millions of good people outside of Atlanta have a deep interest. We must have peace, not only at Atlanta, but in all America. To secure this, we must stop the war that now desolates our once happy and favored country. To stop war, we must defeat the rebel armies which are arrayed against the laws and Constitution that all must respect and obey. To defeat those armies, we must prepare the way to reach them in their recesses, provided with the arms and instruments which enable us to accomplish our purpose. Now, I know the vindictive nature of our enemy, that we may have many years of military operations from this quarter; and, therefore, deem it wise and prudent to prepare in time. The use of Atlanta for warlike purposes is inconsistent with its character as a home for families. There will be no manufactures, commerce, or agriculture here, for the maintenance of families, and sooner or later want will compel the inhabitants to go. Why not go now, when all the arrangements are completed for the transfer, instead of waiting till the plunging shot of contending armies will renew the scenes of the past month? Of course, I do not apprehend any such thing at this moment, but you do not suppose this army will be here until the war is over. I cannot discuss this subject with you fairly, because I cannot impart to you what we propose to do, but I assert that our military plans make it necessary for the inhabitants to go away, and I can only renew my offer of services to make their exodus in any direction as easy and comfortable as possible.

War Is Cruel

You cannot qualify war in harsher terms than I will. War is cruelty, and you cannot refine it; and those who brought war into our country deserve all the curses and maledictions a people can pour out. I know I had no hand in making this war, and I know I will make more sacrifices to-day than any of you to secure peace. But you cannot have peace and a division of our country. If the United States submits to a division now, it will not stop, but will go on until we reap the fate of Mexico, which is eternal war. The United States does and must assert its authority, wherever it once had power; for, if it relaxes one bit to pressure, it is gone, and I believe that such is the national feeling. This feeling assumes various shapes, but always comes back to that of Union. Once admit the Union, once more acknowledge the authority of the national Government, and, instead of devoting your houses and streets and roads to the dread uses of war, I and this army become at once your protectors and supporters, shielding you from danger, let it come from what quarter it may. I know that a few individuals cannot resist a torrent of error and passion, such as swept the South into rebellion, but you can point out, so that we may know those who desire a government, and those who insist on war and its desolation.

A Demonstration of Power

In a letter dated November 6, 1864, William T. Sherman proposes to his commanding officer, Ulysses S. Grant, a march through Georgia—a move aimed not at defeating Confederate armies but at destroying both Confederate economic resources and the people's will to fight.

I propose to act in such manner against the material resources of the south as utterly to negative [Jefferson] Davis's boasted threat and promises of protection. If we can march a well-appointed army right through his territory, it is a demonstration to the world—foreign and domestic—that we have a power which Davis cannot resist. This may not be war, . . . ; nevertheless, it is overwhelming to my mind that there are thousands of people abroad and in the south who will reason thus: If the north can march an army right through the south, it is proof positive that the north can prevail in this contest, leaving only open the question of its willingness to use that power. Now, Mr. Lincoln's election, (which is assured,) coupled with the conclusion thus reached, makes a complete logical whole. Even without a battle, the results, operating upon the minds of sensible men, would produce fruits more than compensating for the expense, trouble, and risk.

You might as well appeal against the thunder-storm as against these terrible hardships of war. They are inevitable, and the only way the people of Atlanta can hope once more to live in peace and quiet at home, is to stop the war, which can only be done by admitting that it began in error and is perpetuated in pride.

We don't want your negroes, or your horses, or your houses, or your lands, or any thing you have, but we do want and will have a just obedience to the laws of the United States. That we will have, and, if it involves the destruction of your improvements, we cannot help it.

You have heretofore read public sentiment in your newspapers, that live by falsehood and excitement; and the quicker you seek for truth in other quarters, the better. I repeat then that, by the original compact of Government, the United States had certain rights in Georgia, which have never been relinquished and never will be; that the South began war by seizing forts, arsenals, mints, customhouses, etc., etc., long before Mr. Lincoln was installed, and before the South had one jot or tittle of provocation. I myself have seen in Missouri, Kentucky, Tennessee, and Mississippi, hundreds and thousands of women and children fleeing from your armies and desperadoes, hungry and with bleeding feet. In Memphis, Vicksburg, and Mississippi, we fed thousands upon thousands of the families of rebel soldiers left on our hands, and whom we could not see starve. Now that war comes home to you, you feel very different. You deprecate its horrors, but did not feel them when you sent car-loads of soldiers and ammunition, and moulded shells and shot, to carry war into Kentucky and Tennessee, to desolate the homes of hundreds and thousands of good people who only asked to live in peace at their old homes, and under the Government of their inheritance. But these comparisons are idle. I want peace, and believe it can only be reached through union and war, and I will ever conduct war with a view to perfect and early success.

When Peace Comes

But, my dear sirs, when peace does come, you may call on me for any thing. Then will I share with you the last cracker, and watch with you to shield your homes and families against danger from every quarter.

Now you must go, and take with you the old and feeble, feed and nurse them, and build for them, in more quiet places, proper habitations to shield them against the weather until the mad passions of men cool down, and allow the Union and peace once more to settle over your old homes at Atlanta. Yours in haste,

W.T. Sherman, *Major-General commanding.*

VIEWPOINT 5

"Operating in the interior of our own country, . . . nothing is now needed to render our triumph certain but the exhibition of our own unquenchable resolve."

The South Should Never Surrender

Jefferson Davis (1808-1889)

Jefferson Davis was the first and only president of the Confederate States of America. A Mississippi planter with a distinguished record of public service prior to the Civil War, he proved to be an uninspiring war leader of the South. Historian T. Harry Williams writes in *The Union Sundered*:

> Davis possessed many fine abilities, but most of them were not the qualities that make a war leader great. . . . His intellectualism dominated his language. His state papers and public addresses were admirable exercises in logic, but they were cold and unmoving. Davis could reach men's minds but not their hearts.

The following viewpoint is taken from his last presidential address to the people of the Confederacy. When it was given, on April 4, 1865, the military situation of the Confederacy was crumbling. The day before, Davis had been forced to abandon the Confederate capital of Richmond, Virginia, as Union troops, after years of trying, finally occupied the city. In his address he argues that the conflict has entered a "new phase" of guerrilla warfare, and pledges that the Confederate armies will continue to fight.

Jefferson Davis, presidential message to the people of the Confederacy, April 4, 1865.
Reprinted from *Jefferson Davis, Constitutionalist: His Letters, Papers and Speeches*, edited by Dunbar Rowland, 1923, courtesy of the Mississippi Department of Archives and History.

To the People of the Confederate States of America:

The general in chief of our army has found it necessary to make such movements of the troops as to uncover the capital and thus involve the withdrawal of the government from the city of Richmond.

It would be unwise, even were it possible, to conceal the great moral as well as material injury to our cause that must result from the occupation of Richmond by the enemy. It is equally unwise and unworthy of us, as patriots engaged in a most sacred cause, to allow our energies to falter, our spirits to grow faint, or our efforts to become relaxed under reverses, however calamitous. While it has been to us a source of national pride that for four years of unequaled warfare we have been able, in close proximity to the center of the enemy's power, to maintain the seat of our chosen government free from the pollution of his presence; while the memories of the heroic dead who have freely given their lives to its defense must ever remain enshrined in our hearts; while the preservation of the capital, which is usually regarded as the evidence to mankind of separate existence, was an object very dear to us, it is also true, and should not be forgotten, that the loss which we have suffered is not without compensation.

For many months the largest and finest army of the Confederacy, under the command of a leader whose presence inspires equal confidence in the troops and the people, has been greatly trammeled by the necessity of keeping constant watch over the approaches to the capital, and has thus been forced to forego more than one opportunity for promising enterprises.

The hopes and confidence of the enemy have been constantly excited by the belief that their possession of Richmond would be the signal for our submission to their rule and relieve them from the burden of war which, as their failing resources admonish them, must be abandoned if not speedily brought to a successful close.

It is for us, my countrymen, to show by our bearing under reverses how wretched has been the self-deception of those who have believed us less able to endure misfortune with fortitude than to encounter danger with courage.

We have now entered upon a new phase of a struggle the memory of which is to endure for all ages and to shed ever increasing luster upon our country. Relieved from the necessity of guarding cities and particular points, important but not vital to our defense, with our army free to move from point to point and strike in detail the detachments and garrisons of the enemy; operating in the interior of our own country, where supplies are more accessible and where the foe will be far removed from his own base and cut off from all succor in case of reverse, nothing is now needed to

A Battle to the End

Jefferson Davis's defiance against surrender was shared by members of McGowan's Brigade, a noted contingent of South Carolina volunteers, who wrote the following resolution as the Civil War was nearing its end.

To submit to our enemies now, would be more infamous than it would have been in the beginning. It would be cowardly yielding to power what was denied upon principle. It would be to yield the cherished right of self-government, and to acknowledge ourselves wrong in the assertion of it; to brand the names of our slaughtered companions as traitors; to forfeit the glory already won; to lose the fruits of all the sacrifices made and the privations endured; to give up independence now nearly gained, and bring certain ruin, disgrace and eternal slavery upon our country. Therefore, unsubdued by past reverses, and unawed by future dangers, we declare our determination to battle to the end, and not to lay down our arms until independence is secured. Is life so dear, or peace so sweet, as to be purchased at the price of chains and slavery? Forbid it Heaven!

render our triumph certain but the exhibition of our own unquenchable resolve. Let us but will it, and we are free; and who, in the light of the past, dare doubt your purpose in the future?

Animated by that confidence in your spirit and fortitude, which never yet has failed me, I announce to you, fellow countrymen, that it is my purpose to maintain your cause with my whole heart and soul; that I will never consent to abandon to the enemy one foot of the soil of any one of the states of the Confederacy; that Virginia, noble state, whose ancient renown has [been] eclipsed by her still more glorious recent history; whose bosom has been bared to receive the main shock of this war; whose sons and daughters have exhibited heroism so sublime as to render her illustrious in all time to come; that Virginia, with the help of the people and by the blessing of Providence, shall be held and defended, and no peace ever be made with the infamous invaders of her homes by the sacrifice of any of her rights or territory.

If by stress of numbers we should ever be compelled to a temporary withdrawal from her limits, or those of any other border state, again and again will we return, until the baffled and exhausted enemy shall abandon in despair his endless and impossible task of making slaves of a people resolved to be free.

Let us not then [d]espond, my countrymen, but, relying on the never failing mercies and protecting care of our God, let us meet the foe with fresh defiance, with unconquered and unconquerable hearts.

VIEWPOINT 6

"A partisan war may be continued . . . causing individual suffering and the devastation of the country, but I see no prospect by that means of achieving a separate independence."

The South Should Cease Fighting

Robert E. Lee (1807-1870)

Robert E. Lee was the leading Confederate general of the Civil War. After numerous successes in the early years of the conflict, in early 1864 Lee's Army of Northern Virginia became locked in conflict with Union forces under Ulysses S. Grant. Grant took advantage of his superiority in numbers and supplies to continually pound Lee's army. By March 1865, with his forces having been reduced by deaths and desertions from 75,000 in 1864 to 25,000, lacking in food and ammunition, and pinned down by Grant, Lee decided to surrender. On April 9, 1865, at the village of Appomattox Court House, Virginia, Lee formally surrendered to Grant. While some Confederate forces remained on the field in Texas, North Carolina, and elsewhere, Lee's surrender is viewed by many as the end of the Civil War. Lee wrote to Confederate president Jefferson Davis on April 12, announcing and explaining his decision to cease fighting.

Lee, officially a paroled prisoner of war, returned to his wartime residence in Richmond, Virginia (his prewar home in Arlington, Virginia, next to Washington, D.C., had been made a cemetery for the Union dead). On April 20, he wrote one more letter to Davis, which is reprinted here. In this letter he argues that the morale of his army was low, that many men were deserting, and that the

Robert E. Lee, letter to Jefferson Davis, dated April 20, 1865. Reprinted from *The Wartime Papers of R.E. Lee*, edited by Clifford Dowdey, copyright 1961 by the Commonwealth of Virginia.

surrounding countryside could no longer support an army. Lee concludes that fighting could be continued but there is no longer hope of victory, and he therefore recommends that Davis take measures to end the war. Davis refused to surrender, and was finally captured by Union forces in Georgia in May.

Mr. President:

The apprehensions I expressed during the winter, of the moral condition of the Army of Northern Virginia, have been realized. The operations which occurred while the troops were in the entrenchments in front of Richmond and Petersburg were not marked by the boldness and decision which formerly characterized them. Except in particular instances, they were feeble; and a want of confidence seemed to possess officers and men. This condition, I think, was produced by the state of feeling in the country, and the communications received by the men from their homes, urging their return and the abandonment of the field. The movement of the enemy on the 30th March to Dinwiddie Court House was consequently not as strongly met as similar ones had been. Advantages were gained by him which discouraged the troops, so that on the morning of the 2d April, when our lines between the Appomattox and Hatcher's Run were assaulted, the resistance was not effectual: several points were penetrated and large captures made. At the commencement of the withdrawal of the army from the lines on the night of the 2d, it began to disintegrate, and straggling from the ranks increased up to the surrender on the 9th. On that day, as previously reported, there were only seven thousand eight hundred and ninety-two (7892) effective infantry. During the night, when the surrender became known, more than ten thousand men came in, as reported to me by the Chief Commissary of the Army. During the succeeding days stragglers continued to give themselves up, so that on the 12th April, according to the rolls of those paroled, twenty-six thousand and eighteen (26,018) officers and men had surrendered. Men who had left the ranks on the march, and crossed James River, returned and gave themselves up, and many have since come to Richmond and surrendered. I have given these details that Your Excellency might know the state of feeling which existed in the army, and judge of that in the country. From what I have seen and learned, I believe an army cannot be organized or supported in Virginia, and as far as I know the condition of affairs, the country east of the Mississippi is morally and physically

A Fond Farewell

General Robert E. Lee's last orders to his troops were given on April 10, 1865, the day after he surrendered to Ulysses S. Grant at Appomattox Court House, Virginia.

After four years of arduous service, marked by unsurpassed courage and fortitude, the Army of Northern Virginia has been compelled to yield to overwhelming numbers and resources.

I need not tell the brave survivors of so many hard fought battles, who have remained steadfast to the last, that I have consented to the result from no distrust of them.

But feeling that valor and devotion could accomplish nothing that would compensate for the loss that must have attended the continuance of the contest, I determined to avoid the useless sacrifice of those whose past services have endeared them to their countrymen.

By the terms of the agreement officers and men can return to their homes. . . . You will take with you the satisfaction that proceeds from the consciousness of duty faithfully performed, and I earnestly pray that a Merciful God will extend to you His blessing and protection.

With an increasing admiration of your constancy and devotion to your country, and a grateful remembrance of your kind and generous considerations for myself, I bid you all an affectionate farewell.

---

unable to maintain the contest unaided with any hope of ultimate success. A partisan war may be continued, and hostilities protracted, causing individual suffering and the devastation of the country, but I see no prospect by that means of achieving a separate independence. It is for Your Excellency to decide, should you agree with me in opinion, what is proper to be done. To save useless effusion of blood, I would recommend measures be taken for suspension of hostilities and the restoration of peace.

I am with great respect, yr obdt svt

R.E. Lee
Genl

CHAPTER 6

Historians Debate: Who Freed the Slaves?

Chapter Preface

One of the most obvious and significant changes wrought by the Civil War was the end of slavery. A noted turning point of the war was Abraham Lincoln's decision to use his powers as military commander-in-chief to declare "forever free" all slaves in any state in rebellion against the United States. First announced in preliminary form on September 22, 1862, the Emancipation Proclamation was officially signed by the president on January 1, 1863. For many years afterward that date was celebrated by American blacks as the Day of Jubilee—the day Lincoln freed the slaves.

In addition to his signing of the Emancipation Proclamation, Lincoln is credited by many historians for his leadership during the Civil War, his determination to prevent the division of the nation, and his ability to inspire people by his speeches. While Lincoln prior to the war eschewed the abolitionist agenda of immediate and total abolition as extreme and unconstitutional, he was morally opposed to slavery. "Lincoln was the supreme combination of principle and pragmatism," writes historian T. Harry Williams, and this combination helped both preserve the Union and make the abolitionist dream a reality.

Some historians, however, have questioned the importance of Abraham Lincoln in the nation's turn from slavery. They have pointed to the Emancipation Proclamation's limited scope, noting it declared slaves to be free only in the Confederacy—not in loyal slave states—and even then excluded Confederate areas then under Northern military control. Some historians, including Vincent Harding, have argued that the view of Lincoln as the Great Emancipator is largely a myth, and that he was instead a product of his times and shared many of the racist ideas of his fellow white Americans. Harding and other historians have contended that the main forces behind emancipation were not the decisions of Lincoln, but rather the actions of relatively unknown and anonymous slaves in the South. Tens of thousands of them fled behind Union lines and assisted the North as spies, laborers, and soldiers. Their actions, Harding and others have argued, compelled Lincoln and the rest of the United States goverment to respond, however slowly, to the slaves' demands for freedom.

In the following pair of viewpoints, two historians examine the Civil War and the end of slavery. They provide an interesting contrast between the perspective that momentous events are the product of great leaders, and the idea that such developments are decided by the actions of ordinary people.

VIEWPOINT 1

"If [Lincoln] had never lived, it seems safe to say that we would not have had a Thirteenth Amendment in 1865."

Lincoln Freed the Slaves

James M. McPherson (1943-)

James M. McPherson is Edwards Professor of American History at Princeton University in New Jersey. He is the author of many books on the Civil War and Reconstruction, including *Marching Toward Freedom: Blacks in the Civil War* and *Abraham Lincoln and the Second American Revolution*. His book *Battle Cry of Freedom: The Civil War Era* won a Pulitzer Prize in history.

The following viewpoint is taken from a paper prepared and delivered by McPherson for the American Historical Association at a 1993 panel discussion commemorating the 130th anniversary of the Emancipation Proclamation. McPherson criticizes the arguments made by some historians, that the slaves in America were primarily responsible for their own emancipation. He argues that such a reading of history denies due credit to Abraham Lincoln. Lincoln's campaign for president in 1860, his election, his actions at the start of the Civil War, his leadership for the duration of the conflict, and his reelection in 1864 were all pivotal for victory for the North and the end of slavery in the United States, McPherson contends, and the ultimate end of slavery was a consistent goal of Lincoln's political vision and career.

If we were to go out on the streets of almost any town in America and ask "Who freed the slaves?," probably nine out of ten respondents would unhesitatingly answer, "Abraham Lincoln." Most of them would cite the Emancipation Proclamation as the

James McPherson, "Who Freed the Slaves?" *Reconstruction*, vol. 2, no. 3, 1994.

key document. Some of the more reflective and better informed respondents would add the Thirteenth Amendment and point to Lincoln's important role in its adoption. And a few might qualify their answer by noting that without military victory the Emancipation Proclamation would never have been adopted, or at least would not have applied to the states where most of the slaves were held. But, of course, Lincoln was commander-in-chief of Union armies, so the credit for their victories would belong mainly to him. The answer would still be the same: Lincoln freed the slaves.

Elitist History?

In recent years, though, this answer has been challenged as another example of elitist history, of focusing only on the actions of great white males and ignoring the actions of the overwhelming majority of the people, who also make history. If we were to ask our question of professional historians, we would receive a reply quite different from that described above. For one thing, it would not be simple or clear cut. Many of them would answer along the lines of "On the one hand . . . but on the other." They would speak of ambivalence, ambiguity, nuances, paradox, irony. They would point to Lincoln's gradualism, his slow and apparently reluctant decision for emancipation, his revocation of emancipation orders by Generals John C. Frémont and David Hunter, his exemption of border states and parts of the Confederacy from the Emancipation Proclamation, his statements seemingly endorsing white supremacy. They would say that the whole issue is more complex than it appears—in other words, many historians, as is their wont, would not give a straight answer to the question.

But of those who did, a growing number would reply, as did an historian speaking to the Civil War Institute at Gettysburg: "THE SLAVES FREED THEMSELVES." They saw the Civil War as a potential war for abolition well before Lincoln did. By voting with their feet for freedom—by escaping from their masters to Union military camps in the South—they forced the issue of emancipation on the Lincoln administration. By creating a situation in which northern officials would either have to return them to slavery or acknowledge their freedom, these "contrabands," as they came to he called, "acted resolutely to place their freedom—and that of their posterity—on the wartime agenda." Union officers, then Congress, and finally Lincoln decided to confiscate this human property belonging to the enemy and put it to work for the Union in the form of servants, teamsters, laborers, and eventually soldiers in northern armies. Weighed in the scale of the Civil War, these 190,000 black soldiers and sailors (and probably a larger number of black army laborers) tipped the balance in favor of

Union victory. Even deep in the Confederate interior remote from the fighting fronts, with the departure of masters and overseers to the army, "leaving women and old men in charge, the balance of power gradually shifted in favor of slaves, undermining slavery on farms and plantations far from the line of battle."

Abraham Lincoln was assassinated April 14, 1865, after Congress had adopted the Thirteenth Amendment banning slavery in the United States, but before the constitutional amendment was ratified by the states.

The foremost exponent of the black self-emancipation theme is the historian and theologian Vincent Harding whose book *There Is a River: The Black Struggle for Freedom in America*, published in 1981, has become almost a Bible for the argument. "While Lincoln continued to hesitate about the legal, constitutional, moral, and military aspects of the matter," Harding writes, "the relentless movement of the self-liberated fugitives into the Union lines" soon "approached and surpassed every level of force previously known. . . . Making themselves an unavoidable military and political issue . . . this overwhelming human movement . . . of self-freed men and women . . . took their freedom into their own hands." The Emancipation Proclamation, when it finally and belatedly came, merely "confirmed and gave ambiguous legal standing to the freedom which black people had already claimed through their own surging, living proclamations."

During the past decade this self-emancipation theme has become so pervasive among social historians that it has virtually achieved the status of the orthodox interpretation. The largest

263

scholarly enterprise on the history of emancipation and the transition from a slave to a free society during the Civil War era, the Freedmen and Southern Society Project at the University of Maryland, has stamped its imprimatur on this interpretation. The slaves, write the editors of this project, were "the prime movers in securing their own liberty." The Columbia University historian Barbara J. Fields gave wide publicity to this thesis. On camera in the PBS television documentary "The Civil War" and in an essay in the lavishly illustrated volume accompanying the series, she insisted that "freedom did not come to the slaves from words on paper, either the words of Congress or those of the President, but from the initiative of the slaves" themselves. "It was they who taught the nation that it must place the abolition of slavery at the head of its agenda. . . . The slaves themselves had to make their freedom real."

Lincoln and Myth

Two important corollaries of the self-emancipation thesis are the arguments, first, that Lincoln hindered more than he helped the cause, and second, that the image of him as the great Emancipator is a myth created by whites to deprive blacks of credit for achieving their own freedom and making their own history. This "reluctant ally of black freedom," Harding remarks, "played an actively conservative role in a situation which . . . needed to be pushed toward its most profound revolutionary implications." Lincoln repeatedly "placed the preservation of the white Union above the death of black slavery"; even as late as August 1852, when he wrote his famous letter to Horace Greeley stating that "if I could save the Union without freeing any slave, I would do it," he was, Harding writes, "still trapped in his own obsession with saving the white Union at all costs, even the cost of continued black slavery." By exempting one-third of the South from the Emancipation Proclamation, Barbara Fields observes, "Lincoln was more determined to retain the goodwill of the slave owners than to secure the liberty of the slaves." Despite Lincoln, though, "no human being alive could have held back the tide that swept toward freedom" by 1863. Nevertheless, Harding laments, "while the concrete historical realities of the time testified to the costly, daring, courageous activities of hundreds of thousands of black people breaking loose from slavery and setting themselves free, the myth gave the credit for this freedom to a white republican president." By this myth, "the independent, radical action of the black movement toward freedom . . . was diminished, and the coerced, ambiguous role of a white deliverer . . . gained preeminence." University of Pennsylvania historian Robert Engs goes even farther; he thinks the "fiction" that "'Massa Lincoln' freed the slaves" was a sort of tacit conspiracy among whites to convince blacks that "white America, personified by Abraham Lincoln, had *given* them their freedom [rather] than allow them to realize the empowerment that their taking of it implied. The poor, uneducated freedman fell for that masterful propaganda stroke. But so have most of the rest of us, black and white, for over a century!"

How valid are these statements? First, we must recognize the considerable degree of truth in the main thesis. By coming into Union lines, by withdrawing their labor from Confederate owners, by working for the Union army and fighting as soldiers in it, slaves did play an active part in achieving their own freedom and, for that matter, in preserving the Union. Like workers, immigrants, women, and other so-called "non-elites," the slaves were neither passive victims nor pawns of powerful white males who loom so large in our traditional image of American history. They, too, played a part in determining their own destiny; they, too, made a history that historians have finally discovered. That is all to the good. But by challenging the "myth" that Lincoln freed the slaves, proponents of the self-emancipation thesis are in danger of creating another myth—that he had little to do with the destruction of slavery. It may turn out, upon close examination, that the traditional answer to the question "Who Freed the Slaves?" is closer to being the right answer than is the new and currently more fashionable answer.

First, one must ask what was the *sine qua non* of emancipation in the 1860s—the essential condition, the absolute prerequisite, the one thing without which it would not have happened. The clear answer is: the war. Without the Civil War there would have been no confiscation act, no Emancipation Proclamation, no Thirteenth Amendment (not to mention the Fourteenth and Fifteenth), certainly no self-emancipation, and almost certainly no end of slavery for several more decades at least. Slavery had existed in North America for more than two centuries before 1861, but except for a tiny fraction of slaves who fought in the Revolution, or escaped, or bought their freedom, there had been no self-emancipation during that time. Every slave insurrection or insurrection conspiracy failed in the end. On the eve of the Civil War, plantation agriculture was more profitable, slavery more entrenched, slave owners more prosperous, and the "slave power" more dominant within the South if not in the nation at large than it had ever been. Without the war, the door to freedom would have remained closed for an indeterminate length of time.

Lincoln and Secession

What brought war and opened that door? The answer, of course, is complex as well as controversial. A short and simple summary is that secession and the refusal of the United States government to recognize the legitimacy of secession brought on the war. In both of these matters Abraham Lincoln moves to center stage. Seven states seceded and formed the Confederacy because he won election to the presidency on an antislavery platform; four more seceded after shooting broke out when he refused to evacuate Fort Sumter; the shooting escalated to full-scale war because he called out troops to suppress rebellion. The common denominator in all the steps that opened the door to freedom was the decision making of Abraham Lincoln acting as antislavery political leader, president-elect, president, and commander-in-chief.

The statement quoted above, that Lincoln "placed the preservation of the white Union above the death of black slavery," while true in a narrow sense, is highly misleading when shorn of its context. From 1854, when he returned to politics, until nominated for president in 1860, the dominant, unifying theme of Lincoln's career was opposition to the expansion of slavery as the vital first step toward placing it on the course of ultimate extinction. A student of Lincoln's oratory has estimated that he gave 175 political speeches during those six years. The "central message" of these speeches showed Lincoln to be a "one-issue" man—the issue being slavery. Repeatedly, Lincoln denounced slavery as a "monstrous injustice," "an unqualified evil to the negro, to the white man, to the soil, and to the State." He attacked his main political rival, Stephen A. Douglas, for his "*declared* indifference" to the moral wrong of slavery. Douglas "*looks to no end of the institution of slavery,*" said Lincoln. "That is the real issue. That is the issue that will continue in this country when these poor tongues of Judge Douglas and myself shall be silent. It is the eternal struggle between these two principles—right and wrong—throughout the world. . . . One is the common right of humanity and the other the divine right of kings. . . . No matter in what shape it comes, whether from the mouth of a king who seeks to bestride the people of his own nation and live by the fruit of their labor, or from one race of men as an apology for enslaving another race, it is the same tyrannical principle." The principles of the Declaration of Independence and the principle of slavery, said Lincoln, "cannot stand together. . . . Our republican robe is soiled" by slavery. "Let us repurify it. . . . Let us readopt the Declaration of Independence, and with it, the practices, and policy, which harmonize with it. . . . If we do this, we shall not only have saved the Union; but we shall have so saved it, as to make, and to keep it, forever worthy of the saving."

Southerners read Lincoln's speeches; they knew by heart his words about the house divided and the ultimate extinction of slavery. Lincoln's election in 1860 was a sign that they had lost control of the national government; if they remained in the Union, they feared that ultimate extinction of their way of life would be their destiny. That is why they seceded. It was not merely Lincoln's election, but his election as a *principled opponent of slavery on moral grounds* that precipitated secession. Militant abolitionists critical of Lincoln for falling short of their own standard nevertheless recognized this truth.

No longer would the slave power rule the nation, said Frederick Douglass. "Lincoln's election has vitiated their authority, and broken their power." "We have passed the Rubicon," said Wendell Phillips. "For the first time in our history the *slave* has chosen a President of the United States." Without Lincoln's election, southern states would not have seceded in 1861, the war would not have come when and as it did, the door of emancipation would not have been opened as it was. Here, certainly, was an event that qualifies as a *sine qua non*, and it proceeded more from the ideas and agency of Abraham Lincoln than from any other single cause.

But, we must ask, would not the election of *any* Republican in 1860 have precipitated secession? Probably not, if the candidate had been Edward Bates, who might conceivably have won the election but had not even an outside chance of winning the nomination. Yes, almost certainly, if William H. Seward had been the nominee. Seward's earlier talk of a "higher law" and an "irrepressible conflict" had given him a more radical reputation than Lincoln. But Seward might not have won the election. More to the point, if he had won, seven states would undoubtedly have seceded. But Seward would have favored compromises and concessions to keep others from going out and perhaps to lure those seven back in. Most important of all, he would have evacuated Fort Sumter and thereby extinguished the spark that threatened to flame into war. As it was, Seward did his best to compel Lincoln into concessions and evacuation. But Lincoln stood firm. When Seward flirted with the notion of supporting the Crittenden Compromise, which would have repudiated the Republican platform by permitting the expansion of slavery, Lincoln stiffened the backbones of Seward and other key Republican leaders. "Entertain no proposition for a compromise in regard to the *extension* of slavery," he wrote to them. "The tug has to come, & better now, than any time hereafter." Crittenden's compromise "would lose everything we gained by the election." The proposal for concessions, Lincoln pointed out, "acknowledges that slavery has equal rights with liberty, and surrenders all we have contended for. . . . We have just carried an election on principles fairly stated to the people. Now we are told in advance, the government shall be broken up, unless we surrender to those we have beaten. . . . If we

267

Lincoln's Strategy

Writing in the May/June 1994 issue of Civil War Times Illustrated, Caesar A. Roy argues that Abraham Lincoln deserves great credit for freeing the slaves. Roy, a former regional director of the Food and Drug Administration lectures frequently on black Americans and the Civil War.

It has become increasingly vogue for modern-day African-Americans to disdain their slave ancestors' unshaken belief in Abraham Lincoln as the "Great Emancipator."

Many distinguished contemporary black Americans, including some prominent black historians, are prone to portray Lincoln as nothing more than an astute and able politician. They contend his only interest in abolishing slavery was to the extent such an action would help achieve his primary goal of preserving the integrity of the status quo Union. . . .

Abraham Lincoln *was* an able and astute politician, but more than any other person in the world in his time, he understood the extremely complex nature of the slavery problem.

He was not a radical abolitionist in the mold of Wendell Phillips, Horace Greeley or Frederick Douglass, but his sentiments regarding slavery were similar to theirs. In a letter dated April 6, 1859, he wrote, "He who would be no slave, must consent to have no slave. Those who deny freedom to others, deserve it not for themselves; and under a just God, cannot long retain it." In a speech to some Indiana soldiers he said, "Whenever I hear anyone arguing for slavery, I feel a strong impulse to see it tried on him personally."

A reader who keeps those remarks in mind can look at the historical record and see that early in his political life Lincoln developed a clear strategy for ending slavery, a strategy he never wavered from throughout his years in the Executive Mansion. His prescription for the country's sickness—slavery—was analogous to modern-day physicians' approaches to treating cancers of the flesh: first they take steps to prevent the spread of the disease, then they treat the symptoms of the disease, and finally they destroy the malignant tissues. They must be deliberate and cautious during each of these phases to assure the treatment does not harm the patient. . . .

It is clear his strategy was directed at eradicating slavery while taking care not to destroy the country in the process. And while some may question Lincoln's timetable for eradicating the institution, there can be no question about his objective.

surrender, it is the end of us. They will repeat the experiment upon us *ad libitum*. A year will not pass, till we shall have to take Cuba as a condition upon which they will stay in the Union."

It is worth emphasizing here that the common denominator in these letters from Lincoln to Republican leaders was slavery. To be sure, on the matters of slavery where it already existed and enforcement of the fugitive slave provision of the Constitution, Lincoln was willing to reassure the South. But on the crucial issue of 1860, slavery in the territories, he refused to compromise, and this refusal kept his party in line. Seward, or any other man who might conceivably have been elected president in 1860, would have pursued a different course. This sheds a different light on the assertion that Lincoln "placed the preservation of the white Union above the death of black slavery." The Crittenden Compromise did indeed place preservation of the Union above the death of slavery. So did Seward; so did most white Americans during the secession crisis. But that assertion does *not* describe Lincoln. He refused to yield the core of his antislavery philosophy to stay the breakup of the Union. As Lincoln expressed it in a private letter to his old friend Alexander Stephens, "You think slavery is *right* and ought to be extended; while we think it is *wrong* and ought to be restricted. That I suppose is the rub." It was indeed the rub. Even more than in his election to the presidency, Lincoln's refusal to compromise on the expansion of slavery or on Fort Sumter proved decisive. If any other man had been in his position, the course of history—and of emancipation—would have been different. Here again we have without question a *sine qua non*.

It is quite true, of course, that once the war started, Lincoln moved more slowly and reluctantly toward making it a war for emancipation than black leaders, abolitionists, radical Republicans, and the slaves themselves wanted him to move. He did reassure southern whites that he had no intention and no constitutional power to interfere with slavery in the states. In September 1861 and May 1862, he revoked orders by Generals Frémont and Hunter freeing the slaves of Confederates in their military districts. In December 1861 he forced Secretary of War Cameron to delete a paragraph from his annual report recommending the freeing and arming of slaves. And though Lincoln signed the confiscation acts of August 1861 and July 1862 that provided for freeing some slaves owned by Confederates, this legislation did not come from his initiative. The initiative was taken out in the field by slaves who escaped to Union lines and officers like General Benjamin Butler who accepted them as "contraband of war."

All of this appears to support the thesis that slaves emancipated themselves and that Lincoln's image as an emancipator is a myth. But let us take a closer look. It seems clear today, as it did to people in 1861, that no matter how many thousands of slaves came into Union lines, the ultimate fate of the millions who did not, as well as the fate of the institution of slavery itself, depended on the outcome of the war. If the North won, slavery would be weakened if not destroyed; if the Confederacy won, slavery would survive and perhaps grow stronger from the postwar territorial expansion of an independent and confident slave power. Thus Lincoln's emphasis on the priority of Union had positive implications for emancipation, while precipitate or premature actions against slavery might jeopardize the cause of Union and therefore boomerang in favor of slavery.

Lincoln's chief concern in 1861 was to maintain a united coalition of War Democrats and border-state Unionists as well as Republicans in support of the war effort. To do this he considered it essential to define the war as being waged solely for Union, which united this coalition, and not a war against slavery, which would fragment it. When General Frémont issued his emancipation edict in Missouri, on August 30, 1861, the political and military efforts to prevent Kentucky, Maryland, and Missouri from seceding and to cultivate Unionists in western Virginia and eastern Tennessee were at a crucial stage, balancing on a knife edge. If he had let Frémont's order stand, explained Lincoln to his old friend Senator Orville Browning of Illinois, it would have been "popular in some quarters, and would have been more so if it had been a general declaration of emancipation." But this would have lost the war by driving Kentucky into secession. "I think to lose Kentucky is nearly the same as to lose the whole game. Kentucky gone, we can not hold Missouri, nor, as I think, Maryland. These all against us, and the job on our hands is too large for us. We would as well consent to separation at once, including the surrender of this capitol."

There is no reason to doubt the sincerity and sagacity of this statement. Lincoln's greatest skills as a political leader were his sensitivity to public opinion and his sense of timing. He understood that while a majority of Republicans by the spring of 1862 favored a war against slavery, a decided majority of his Union coalition did not. During those spring months he alternately coaxed and prodded border-state Unionists toward recognition of the inevitable escalation of the conflict into a war against slavery and toward acceptance of his plan for compensated emancipation in their states. He warned southern Unionists and northern Democrats that he could not fight this war "with elder-stalk squirts, charged with rose water. . . . This government cannot much longer play a game in which it stakes all, and its enemies stake nothing. Those enemies must understand that they cannot experiment for ten years trying to destroy the government, and if they fail still come back into the Union unhurt."

The Military Necessity of Emancipation

Lincoln's meaning, though veiled, was clear; he was about to add the weapon of emancipation to his arsenal. When he penned these warnings, in July 1862, he had made up his mind to issue an emancipation proclamation. Whereas a year earlier, even three months earlier, Lincoln had believed that avoidance of the emancipation issue was necessary to maintain that knife-edge balance in the Union coalition, things had now changed. The war had escalated in scope and fury, mobilizing all the resources of both sides, including the slave labor force of the Confederacy. The imminent prospect of Union victory in the spring had been shredded by Robert E. Lee's successful counteroffensive in the Seven Days. The risks of alienating the border states and northern Democrats were now outweighed by the opportunity to energize the Republican majority and to mobilize part of the slave population for the cause of Union—and freedom. Lincoln was now convinced that emancipation was "a military necessity, absolutely essential to the preservation of the Union." "The slaves," he told his cabinet, were "undeniably an element of strength to those who had their service, and we must decide whether that element should be with us or against us." Lincoln had earlier hesitated to act against slavery in the states because the Constitution protected it there. But most slaves were the property of enemies waging war against the United States, and "the rebels," said Lincoln, "could not at the same time throw off the Constitution and invoke its aid. . . . Decisive and extensive measures must be adopted. . . . We [want] the army to strike more vigorous blows. The Administration must set an example, and strike at the heart of the rebellion"—slavery. Montgomery Blair, speaking for the forces of conservatism in the North and border states, warned of the consequences among these groups of an emancipation proclamation. But Lincoln was done conciliating these elements. He had tried to make the border states see reason; now "we must make the forward movement" without them. "They will acquiesce, if not immediately, soon." As for the northern Democrats, "their clubs would be used against us take what course we might."

Why Lincoln Moved Slowly

In 1864, speaking to a visiting delegation of abolitionists, Lincoln explained why he had moved more slowly against slavery than they had urged. Having taken an oath to preserve and defend the Constitution, which protected slavery, "I did not consider that I had a *right* to touch the 'State' institution of 'Slavery' until all other measures for restoring the Union had failed. . . . The moment came when I felt that slavery must die that the nation might live! . . . Many of my strongest supporters urged *Emancipation* before I thought it indispensable, and, I may say, before I thought the country ready for it. It is my conviction that, had the proclamation been issued even six months earlier than it was, public sentiment would not have sustained it."

Lincoln actually could have made a case that the country had not been ready for the Emancipation Proclamation in September 1862, even in January 1863. Democratic gains in the northern congressional elections in the fall of 1862 resulted in part from a voter backlash against the preliminary Emancipation Proclamation. The crisis in morale in the Union armies and swelling Copperhead strength during the winter of 1863 grew in part from a resentful conviction that Lincoln had unconstitutionally transformed the purpose of the war from restoring the Union to freeing the slaves. Without question, this issue bitterly divided the North and threatened fatally to erode support for the war effort—the very consequence Lincoln had feared in 1861 and that Montgomery Blair feared in 1862. Not until after the twin military victories at Gettysburg and Vicksburg did this divisiveness diminish and emancipation gain a clear mandate in the off-year elections of 1863. In his annual message of December 1863, Lincoln acknowledged that his Emancipation Proclamation a year earlier had been "followed by dark and doubtful days." But now, he added, "the crisis which threatened to divide the friends of the Union is past."

Emancipation and War Weariness

Even that statement turned out to be premature and optimistic. In the summer of 1864, northern morale again plummeted and the emancipation issue once more threatened to undermine the war effort. By August, Grant's campaign in Virginia had bogged down in the trenches after enormous casualties, while Sherman seemed similarly stymied. War weariness and defeatism corroded the will of northerners as they contemplated the staggering cost of this conflict in the lives of their young men. Lincoln came under enormous pressure to open peace negotiations to end the slaughter. Even though Jefferson Davis insisted that Confederate independence was his essential condition for peace, northern Democrats managed to convince a great many northern people that only Lincoln's insistence on emancipation blocked peace. A typical Democratic newspaper editorial declared that "tens of thousands of white men must yet bite the dust to allay the negro mania of the President."

Even Republicans like Horace Greeley, who had criticized Lincoln two years earlier for slowness to embrace emancipation, now criticized him for refusing to abandon it as a precondition for negotiations. The Democratic national convention adopted a platform for the 1864 presidential election calling for peace negotiations to restore the Union with slavery. Every political observer, including Lincoln himself, believed in August that the Republicans would lose this election. The *New York Times* editor and Republican national chairman Henry Raymond told Lincoln that "two special causes are assigned [for] this great reaction in public sentiment—the want of military success, and the impression . . . that we *can* have peace with Union if we would . . . [but that you are] fighting not for Union but for the abolition of slavery."

The pressure on Lincoln to back down on emancipation caused him to waver temporarily, but not to buckle. Instead, he told weak-kneed Republicans that "no human power can subdue this rebellion without using the Emancipation lever as I have done." Some 130,000 soldiers and sailors were fighting for the Union, Lincoln noted. They would not do so if they thought the North intended to "betray them. . . . If they stake their lives for us they must be prompted by the strongest motive . . . the promise of freedom. And the promise being made, must be kept. . . . There have been men who proposed to me to return to slavery the black warriors" who had fought for the Union. "I should be damned in time & in eternity for so doing. The world shall know that I will keep my faith to friends and enemies, come what will."

When Lincoln said this, he fully expected to lose the presidential election. In effect, he was saying that he would rather be right than president. In many ways this was his finest hour. As matters turned out, of course, he was both right and president. Sherman's capture of Atlanta, Sheridan's victories in the Shenandoah Valley, and military success elsewhere transformed the northern mood from deepest despair in August 1864 to determined confidence by November, and Lincoln was triumphantly reelected. He won without compromising one inch on the emancipation question.

Alternative Outcomes

It is instructive to consider two possible alternatives to this outcome. If the Democrats had won, at best the Union would have been restored without a Thirteenth Amendment; at worst the Confederacy would have achieved its independence. In either case the institution of slavery would have survived. That this did not happen was owing more to the steadfast purpose of Abraham Lincoln than to any other single factor.

The proponents of the self-emancipation thesis, however, would avow that all of this is irrelevant. If it is true, as Barbara Fields maintains, that by the time of the Emancipation Proclamation "no human being alive could have held back the tide that swept toward freedom," that tide must have been even more powerful by the fall of 1864. But I disagree. The tide of freedom could have been swept back. On numerous occasions during the war, when Union forces were compelled to retreat from areas of the Confederacy where their presence had attracted and liberated

273

contrabands, the tide of slavery closed in behind them. Lee's army captured dozens of black people in Pennsylvania in June 1863 and sent them back South into slavery. Hundreds of black Union soldiers captured by Confederate forces were reenslaved. Lincoln himself took note of this phenomenon when he warned that if "the pressure of the war should call off our forces from New Orleans to defend some other point, what is to prevent the masters from reducing the blacks to slavery again; for I am told that whenever the rebels take any black prisoners, free or slave, they immediately auction them off!" The editors of the Freedmen and Southern Society Project, the most scholarly advocates of the self-emancipation thesis, concede that "Southern armies could recapture black people who had already reached Union lines. . . . Indeed, any Union retreat could reverse the process of liberation and throw men and women who tasted freedom back into bondage. . . . Their travail testified to the link between the military success of the Northern armies and the liberty of Southern slaves."

Precisely. That is the crucial point. Slaves did not emancipate themselves; they were liberated by Union armies. Liberation quite literally came from the barrel of a gun. And who was the commander-in-chief that called these armies into being, appointed their generals, and gave them direction and purpose? There, indubitably, is our *sine qua non*.

Lincoln's Role

But let us acknowledge that once the war was carried into slave territory, no matter how it came out, the ensuing "friction and abrasion" (as Lincoln once put it) would enable thousands of slaves to escape to freedom. In that respect, a degree of self-emancipation *did* occur. But even on a large scale, such emancipation was very different from *the abolition of the institution of slavery*. That required Union victory; it required Lincoln's reelection in 1864; it required the Thirteenth Amendment. Lincoln played a vital role, indeed the central role, in all of these achievements. It was also his policies and his skillful political leadership that set in motion the processes by which the reconstructed or Unionist states of Louisiana, Arkansas, Tennessee, Maryland, and Missouri abolished the institution in those states during the war itself.

Regrettably, Lincoln did not live to see the final ratification of the Thirteenth Amendment. But if he had *never* lived, it seems safe to say that we would not have had a Thirteenth Amendment in 1865. In that sense, the traditional answer to the question "Who freed the slaves?" is the right answer. Lincoln did not accomplish this in the manner sometimes symbolically portrayed, breaking the chains of helpless and passive bondsmen with the stroke of a pen by signing the Emancipation Proclamation. But by pronouncing slavery a moral evil that must come to an end and then winning the Presidency in 1860, provoking the South to secede, refusing to compromise on the issue of slavery's expansion or on Fort Sumter, knitting together a Unionist coalition in the first year of war and committing it to emancipation in the second, refusing to compromise this policy once he had adopted it, and prosecuting the war to unconditional victory as commander-in-chief of an army of liberation, Abraham Lincoln freed the slaves.

VIEWPOINT 2

"No one was more responsible for smashing the shackles of slavery than the slaves themselves."

The Slaves Were the Primary Force Behind Their Emancipation

Ira Berlin (1941-)

Ira Berlin is a professor of history at the University of Maryland. As founder of the Freedmen and Southern Society Project and its director from 1976 to 1991, he coedited the first four volumes of *Freedom: A Documentary History of Emancipation*, a multivolume collection of primary sources that document the transition from slavery to freedom in the American South. The documents featured in these volumes were but a small portion of the more than 50,000 items from the National Archives of the United States that Berlin and other Project historians researched, photocopied, and indexed. Berlin has also written several books on black life in American history, including *Slaves Without Masters: The Free Negro in the Antebellum South*.

The following viewpoint is from an article Berlin wrote in response to a paper presented by noted historian James M. McPherson at a January 1993 American Historical Society panel discussion on the Emancipation Proclamation. In his paper (also reprinted in this volume), McPherson questioned the thesis that the slaves were primarily responsible for their own emancipation during the Civil War—an idea he attributed to Berlin and other historians. McPherson argued instead that Abraham Lincoln should receive primary credit for the slaves' emancipation. Berlin responds here by maintaining that the actions of the slaves during the Civil War were the primary moving force behind their ul-

Ira Berlin, "Emancipation and Its Meaning in American Life," *Reconstruction*, vol. 2, no. 3, 1994.

timate liberation. By escaping to Union military camps during the war and forcing Union armies and government officials to confront the issue of slavery, the slaves set the process of emancipation in motion, he contends. He argues that while Lincoln is due some credit for issuing the Emancipation Proclamation, the president was responding to pressure generated by the actions of slaves and their effect on Northern public opinion. Lincoln and the slaves played complementary roles in the abolition of slavery, Berlin concludes.

On January 1, 1863, Abraham Lincoln promulgated his Emancipation Proclamation. A document whose grand title promised so much but whose bland words delivered so little, the Emancipation Proclamation was an enigma from the first. Contemporaries were unsure whether to condemn it as a failure of idealism or applaud it as a triumph of *realpolitik*, and the American people have remained similarly divided ever since. Few officially sponsored commemorations currently mark the day slaves once called "The Great Jubilee," and, of late, black Americans have taken to celebrating their liberation on Juneteenth, a previously little-known marker of the arrival of the Union army in Texas and the liquidation of slavery in the most distant corner of the Confederacy. Unlike our other icons—the Declaration of Independence and the Constitution, for example—the Emancipation Proclamation is not on regular display at the National Archives. Its [1993] exhibition on the occasion of the 130th anniversary of its issuance was a moment of some note. The exhibit sent thousands of Americans into the streets, where they waited in long lines on frigid January days to see Lincoln's handiwork. At the end of the five-day exhibit, some 30,000 had filed past the Proclamation. As visitors left the Archives' great rotunda, the minions of Dan Rather, Bryant Gumble, and Tom Brokaw waited with microphones in hand. Before national television audiences, visitors declared themselves deeply moved by the great document. One told a reporter from the *Washington Post* that it had changed his life forever. . . .

Mrs. Loretta Carter Hanes, a suburban Washington school teacher whose insistent requests to see the Proclamation had initiated the exhibit, told reporters of her hopes that the display would inaugurate another new birth of freedom.

The public presentation of the Proclamation also brought historians out in force. Meeting in Washington, the American Historical Association—with more than usual forethought—convened a panel entitled "Black, White, and Lincoln." Professor James M. McPherson of Princeton University delivered the lead paper entitled "Who Freed the Slaves?"

For historians, the issues involved in McPherson's question—and by implication Lincoln's proclamation—took on even greater weight because they represented a larger debate between those who looked to the top of the social order for cues in understanding the past and those who looked to the bottom. It was an old controversy that had previously appeared in the guise of a contest between social history and political history. . . .

The debate among historians, although often parochial and self-absorbed, was not without its redeeming features. . . . It . . . addressed conflicting notions about the role of high authority, on the one hand, and the actions of ordinary men and women, on the other, in shaping American society. Both the citizens who queued up outside the Archives and the scholars who debated the issue within the confines of the American Historical Association's meeting found deep resonance in the exhibition of the Emancipation Proclamation. It gave both reason to consider the struggle for a politics (and a history) that is both appreciative of ordinary people and respectful of rightful authority in a democratic society.

The Debate over Emancipation

The debate over origins of emancipation in the American South can be parsed in such a way as to divide historians into two camps, those who understand emancipation as the slaves' struggle to free themselves and those who see The Great Emancipator's hand at work. McPherson made precisely such a division. While acknowledging the role of the slaves in their own liberation, McPherson came down heavily on the side of Lincoln as the author of emancipation. He characterized the critics of Lincoln's preeminence—advocates of what he repeatedly called the "self-emancipation thesis"—as scholarly populists whose stock in trade was a celebration of the "so-called 'non-elite.'" Such scholars, McPherson implied, denied the historical role of "white males"—perhaps all regularly constituted authority—in a misguided celebration of the masses. Among those so denominated by McPherson were Robert Engs, Vincent Harding, and myself and my colleagues on the Freedmen and Southern Society Project at the University of Maryland. While other scholars were implicated, the Freedmen and Southern Society Project—"the largest scholarly enterprise on the history of emancipation"—was held responsible for elevating the "self-emancipation thesis" into what McPherson called a new orthodoxy. If such be the case, I—and I am sure the other members of the Project—am honored by the unanimity with which the Pro-

278

ject's work has been accepted by a profession that rarely agrees on anything. However, McPherson's representation of the Project's position does no justice to the arguments made in *Freedom: A Documentary History of Emancipation*. Indeed, it is more in the nature of a caricature than a characterization.

Lincoln's proclamation, as its critics have noted, freed not a single slave who was not already entitled to freedom under legislation passed by Congress the previous year. It applied only to the slaves in territories then beyond the reach of federal authority. It specifically exempted Tennessee and Union-occupied portions of Louisiana and Virginia, and it left slavery in the loyal border states—Delaware, Maryland, Kentucky, and Missouri—untouched. Indeed, as an engine of emancipation, the Proclamation went no further than the Second Confiscation Act of July 1862, which freed all slaves who entered Union lines professing that their owners were disloyal, as well as those slaves who fell under federal control as Union troops occupied Confederate territory. Moreover, at its fullest, the Emancipation Proclamation rested upon the President's power as commander-in-chief and was subject to constitutional challenge. Even Lincoln recognized the limitations of his ill-defined wartime authority, and, as his commitment to emancipation grew firmer in 1863 and 1864, he pressed for passage of a constitutional amendment to affirm slavery's destruction.

What then was the point of the Proclamation? It spoke in muffled tones that heralded not the dawn of universal liberty but the compromised and piecemeal arrival of an undefined freedom. Indeed, the Proclamation's flat prose, ridiculed as having the moral grandeur of a bill of lading, suggests that the true authorship of African-American freedom lies elsewhere—not at the top of American society but at the bottom. McPherson is correct in noting that the editors of the Freedmen and Southern Society Project seized this insight and expanded it in *Freedom*.

Slaves and the War

From the first guns at Fort Sumter, the strongest advocates of emancipation were the slaves themselves. Lacking political standing or public voice, forbidden access to the weapons of war, slaves nevertheless tossed aside the grand pronouncements of Lincoln and other Union leaders that the sectional conflict was only a war for national unity. Instead, they moved directly to put their own freedom—and that of their posterity—atop the national agenda. Steadily, as opportunities arose, slaves risked all for freedom. By abandoning their owners, coming uninvited into Union lines, and offering their assistance as laborers, pioneers, guides, and spies, slaves forced federal soldiers at the lowest level to recognize their importance to the Union's success. That understanding travelled quickly up the chain of command. In time, it became evident even to the most obtuse federal commanders that every slave who crossed into Union lines was a double gain: one subtracted from the Confederacy and one added to the Union. The slaves' resolute determination to secure their liberty converted many white Americans to the view that the security of the Union depended upon the destruction of slavery. Eventually, this belief tipped the balance in favor of freedom, even among those who had little interest in the question of slavery and no love for black people.

Once the connection between the war and freedom had been made, slaves understood that a Union victory was imperative, and they did what they could to secure it. They threw their full weight behind the federal cause, and "tabooed" those few in their ranks who shunned the effort. More than 135,000 slave men became Union soldiers. Even deep in the Confederacy, where escape to federal lines was impossible, slaves did what they could to undermine the Confederacy and strengthen the Union—from aiding escaped northern prisoners of war to praying for northern military success. With their loyalty, their labor and their lives, slaves provided crucial information, muscle, and blood in support of the federal war effort. No one was more responsible for smashing the shackles of slavery than the slaves themselves.

But, as the slaves realized, they could not free themselves. Nowhere in the four volumes of *Freedom* do the editors of the Freedmen and Southern Society Project claim they did. Nowhere do the editors use the term of "self-emancipation." Slaves could—and they did—put the issue of freedom on the wartime agenda; they could—and they did—make certain that the question of their liberation did not disappear in the complex welter of the war; they could—and they did—insure that there was no retreat from the commitment to emancipation once the issue was drawn. In short, they did what was in their power to do with the weapons they had. They could not vote, pass laws, issue field orders, or promulgate great proclamations. That was the realm of citizens, legislators, military officers, and the president. However, the actions of the slaves made it possible for citizens, legislators, military officers, and the president to act. Thus, in many ways, slaves set others in motion. Slaves were the prime movers in the emancipation drama, not the sole movers. It does no disservice to Lincoln—or to anyone else—to say that his claim to greatness rests upon his willingness to act when the moment was right.

Lincoln and Slavery

Lincoln, as McPherson emphasizes, was no friend of slavery. He believed, as he said many times, that "if slavery is not wrong, nothing is wrong." But, as president, Lincoln also believed he had

Tales of Struggle

Historians Ira Berlin, Barbara J. Fields, Steven F. Miller, Joseph P. Reidy, and Leslie S. Rowland are all past or present members of the Freedmen and Southern Society Project and editors of the multivolume Freedom: A Documentary History of Emancipation. *The following passage on the slaves' role in emancipation is excerpted from the introduction to their 1985 book* The Destruction of Slavery.

After the war, freedpeople and their allies—some newly minted, some of long standing—gathered periodically to celebrate the abolition of slavery. They spoke of great deeds, great words, and great men, praising the Emancipation Proclamation and the Thirteenth Amendment and venerating their authors. A moment so great needed its icons. But in quieter times, black people told of their own liberation. Then there were as many tales as tellers. Depending upon the circumstances of their enslavement, the events of the war, and the evolution of Union and Confederate policy, some recounted solitary escape; others, mass defections initiated by themselves or the Yankees. Many depicted their former owners in headlong flight, and themselves left behind to shape a future under Union occupation. Others told of forced removals from home and family to strange neighborhoods and an enslavement made more miserable by food shortages, heightened discipline, and bands of straggling soldiers. Still others limned a struggle against slaveholders whose unionist credentials sustained their power. More than a few black people shared the bitter memory of escaping slavery only to be reenslaved when the Northern army retreated or they ventured into one of the Union's own slave states. Some recalled hearing the news of freedom from an exasperated master who reluctantly acknowledged the end of the old order; others, from returning black veterans, bedecked in blue uniforms with brass buttons. Those who had escaped slavery during the war often had additional stories to relate. They told of serving the Union cause as cooks, nurses, and laundresses; as teamsters and laborers; as spies, scouts, and pilots; and as sailors and soldiers. . . .

These diverse experiences disclosed the uneven, halting, and often tenuous process by which slaves gained their liberty, and the centrality of their own role in the evolution of emancipation. The Emancipation Proclamation and the Thirteenth Amendment marked, respectively, a turning point and the successful conclusion of a hard-fought struggle. But the milestones of that struggle were not the struggle itself. Neither its origins nor its mainspring could be found in the seats of executive and legislative authority from which the great documents issued. Instead, they resided in the humble quarters of slaves, who were convinced in April 1861 of what would not be fully affirmed until December 1865 [when the Thirteenth Amendment was ratified], and whose actions consistently undermined every settlement short of universal abolition.

a constitutional obligation not to interfere with slavery where it existed. Shortly before his inauguration, he offered to support a proposed constitutional amendment that would have prohibited any subsequent amendment authorizing Congress "to abolish or interfere . . . with the domestic institutions of any state, including slavery." As wartime leader, he feared the disaffection of the loyal slave states, which he understood to be critical to the success of the Union. Lincoln also doubted whether white and black could live as equals in American society and thought it best for black people to remove themselves physically from the United States. Like many white Americans from Thomas Jefferson to Henry Clay, Lincoln favored the colonization of former slaves in Africa or elsewhere. At his insistence, the congressional legislation providing for the emancipation of slaves in the District of Columbia in April 1862 included an appropriation to aid the removal of liberated slaves who wished to leave the United States. Through the end of 1862, Lincoln continually connected emancipation in the border states to the colonization of slaves somewhere beyond the borders of the United States.

Where others led on emancipation, Lincoln followed. Lincoln responded slowly to demands for emancipation as they worked their way up the military chain of command and as they echoed in northern public opinion. He revoked the field emancipations of Union generals John C. Frémont in August 1861 and David Hunter in May 1862, who invoked martial law to liberate slaves in Missouri and South Carolina, respectively. Through the first year and a half of the war, Lincoln—preoccupied with the loyalty of the slaveholding states within the Union and hopeful for the support of Whiggish slaveholders within the Confederacy—remained respectful of the rights of the master.

As pressure for emancipation grew in the spring of 1862, Lincoln continued to urge gradual, compensated emancipation. The compensation would be to slaveholders for property lost, not to slaves for labor stolen. In late September 1862, even while announcing that we would proclaim emancipation on January 1 if the rebellious states did not return to the Union, he continued to call for gradual, compensated emancipation in the border states and compensation for loyal slaveholders elsewhere. The preliminary emancipation proclamation also reiterated his support for colonizing freed slaves "upon this continent or elsewhere." As black laborers became essential to the Union war effort and as demands to enlist black men in the federal army mounted, the pressure for emancipation became inexorable. On January 1, 1863, Lincoln fulfilled his promise to free all slaves in the states still in rebellion. Had another Republican been in Lincoln's place, that person doubtless would have done the same. Without question, some would have acted more expeditiously and with greater bravado. Without question, some would have acted more cautiously with lesser resolve. In the end, Lincoln did what needed to be done. Others might be left behind; Lincoln would not.

Thus, when Lincoln finally acted, he moved with confidence and determination. He stripped the final Emancipation Proclamation of any reference to compensation for former slaveholders or colonization for former slaves. He added provisions that allowed for the service of black men in the Union army and navy. The Proclamation opened the door to the eventual enlistment of nearly 190,000 black men—most of them former slaves. Military enlistment became the surest solvent of slavery, extending to places the Emancipation Proclamation did not reach, especially the loyal slave states. Once slave men entered the Union army, they were free and they made it clear they expected their families to be free too. In March 1865, Congress confirmed this understanding and provided for the freedom of the immediate families of all black soldiers. Lincoln's actions, however tardy, gave force to all that the slaves had risked. The Emancipation Proclamation transformed the war in ways only the President could. After January 1, 1863, the Union army was an army of liberation and Lincoln was its commander.

Lincoln understood the importance of his role, both politically and morally—just as the slaves had understood theirs. Having determined to free the slaves, Lincoln declared he would not take back the Emancipation Proclamation even when military failure and political reverses threatened that policy. He praised the role of black soldiers in preserving the Union and liquidating chattel bondage. The growing presence of black men in Union ranks deepened Lincoln's commitment to emancipation. Lincoln later suggested that black soldiers might have the vote, perhaps his greatest concession to racial equality. To secure the freedom that his Proclamation had promised, Lincoln promoted passage of the Thirteenth Amendment, although he did not live to see its ratification.

The Emancipation Proclamation's place in the drama of emancipation is thus secure—as is Lincoln's. To deny it is to ignore the intense struggle by which freedom arrived. It is to ignore the Union soldiers who sheltered slaves, the abolitionists who stumped for emancipation, and the thousands of men and women who—like Lincoln—changed their minds as slaves made the case for universal liberty. Reducing the Emancipation Proclamation to a nullity and Lincoln to a cipher denies human agency as fully as writing the slaves out of the struggle for freedom.

Complementary Roles

Both Lincoln and the slaves played their appointed parts in the drama of emancipation. From a historian's perspective, denying their complementary roles limits understanding of the complex interaction of human agency and events which resulted in slavery's demise. The Freedmen and Southern Society Project has sought to restore the fullness of the history of emancipation by expanding the terrain upon which it should be understood, emphasizing—and documenting—the *process* by which freedom arrived. While the editors [of *Freedom*] argue that the slaves were in fact the prime movers of emancipation, nowhere do they deny Lincoln's centrality to the events that culminated in universal freedom. In fact, rather than single out slaves or exclude Lincoln (as the term "self-emancipation" implies), the editors argue for the significance of others as well: white Union soldiers—few of them racial egalitarians—who saw firsthand how slavery weakened the Union cause; their families and friends in the North—eager for federal victory—who learned from these soldiers the strength the Confederate regime drew from bonded labor; the northern men and women—most of them with no connection to the abolition movement—who acted upon such news to petition Congress; and the congressmen and senators who eventually moved in favor of freedom. This roster, of course, does not include all those involved in the social and political process that ended slavery in the American South. It omits the slaveholders, no bit players in the drama. Taken as a whole, however, the Project's work does suggest something of the complexity of emancipation and the limitation of seeing slavery's end as the product of any one individual—or element—in the social order.

Emphasizing that emancipation was not the work of one hand underscores the force of contingency—the crooked course by which universal freedom arrived. It captures the ebb and flow of events which, at times, placed Lincoln among the opponents of emancipation and then propelled him to the forefront of freedom's friends. It emphasizes the clash of wills that is the essence of politics—whether it involves enfranchised legislators or voteless slaves. Politics, perforce, necessitates an on-the-ground struggle among different interests, not the unfolding of a single idea or perspective—whether that of an individual or an age. Lincoln, no less than the meanest slave, acted upon changing possibilities as he understood them. The very same events—secession and war—that gave the slaves' actions new meaning also gave Lincoln's actions new meaning. To think that Lincoln could have anticipated these changes—or, more strangely still, somehow embodied them—imbues him with power over the course of events that no human being has ever enjoyed. Lincoln was part of history, not above it. Whatever he believed about slavery, in 1861 Lincoln did not see the war as an instrument of emancipation. The slaves did. Lincoln's commitment to emancipation changed with time because it had to. The slaves' commitment to universal freedom did not waver because it could not.

Complexity—contrary to McPherson—is not ambivalence or ambiguity. To tell the whole story—to follow that crooked course—does not diminish the clarity of an argument or mystify it into a maze of "nuances, paradox, or irony." Telling the entire tale is not a form of obscuration. If done right, it clarifies precisely because it consolidates the mass of competing claims under a single head. Elegance or simplicity of argument is useful only when it encompasses all of the evidence, not when it excludes or narrows it.

In a season when constituted authority once again tries to find the voice of the people and when the people are testing the measure of their leaders, it is well to recall the relationship of both to securing freedom's greatest victory. In this sense, slaves were right in celebrating January 1, 1863, as the Day of Jubilee. As Loretta Hanes noted 130 years later, "It meant so much to people because it was a ray of light, the hope of a new day coming. And it gave them courage." Indeed, the Emancipation Proclamation reminds us all—both those viewing its faded pages and those who studied it—that real changes derive from the actions of the people and require the imprimatur of constituted authority. The Emancipation Proclamation teaches that "social" history is no less political than "political" history—for it too rests upon the bending of wills, which is the essence of politics—and that no political process is determined by a single individual. If the Emancipation Proclamation speaks to the central role of constituted authority— in this case Abraham Lincoln—in making history, it speaks no less loudly to the role of ordinary men and women, seizing the moment to make the world according to their own understanding of justice and human decency. The connection between the two should not be forgotten as we try to rebuild American politics— and try to write a history worthy of that politics.

For Discussion

Chapter One

1. In what way do the views of John C. Calhoun and Daniel Webster differ concerning the history of the founding of the United States? How do these disputes about the past affect their prescriptions for compromise?
2. How are the questions of slavery and secession linked in the viewpoints of Edmund Ruffin and Hinton R. Helper? Do you think, based on these viewpoints, that secession was the only means to preserve slavery in the South? Why or why not?
3. Do you believe Stephen A. Douglas's prescription of popular sovereignty for the western territories could have prevented or delayed war? Could it have been modified enough to satisfy Abraham Lincoln or, had he lived, John C. Calhoun? Explain.

Chapter Two

1. What justifications for secession are given by Robert Toombs and by South Carolina? How similar are they to the arguments of John C. Calhoun found in the first chapter? Explain.
2. Does Alexander H. Stephens in his speech fundamentally oppose secession? Is it surprising, given his speech, that he later became vice president of the Confederacy? Why or why not?
3. The conservative *Albany Atlas and Argus* and abolitionist William Lloyd Garrison probably agreed on few issues. On what main point concerning the possibility of civil war do they agree?
4. What arguments do the *Indianapolis Daily Journal* and *Peoria Daily Transcript* make against letting the Southern states secede? What role do you think the issue of slavery plays in their arguments?
5. Is Abraham Lincoln's inaugural address conciliatory or threatening toward the South? Defend your answer.
6. In what ways do Jefferson Davis and Abraham Lincoln differ in their accounts of the events surrounding Fort Sumter in 1861? What point is each leader trying to make? Who is more convincing?

Chapter Three

1. Joseph E. Johnston, Pierre G.T. Beauregard, George Fitzhugh, Robert E. Lee, and Jefferson Davis all share a certain optimism about a potential Confederate victory. On what factors and assumptions do they base their optimism? What factors does the *Memphis Appeal* stress in its cautionary warning?
2. In what way does the Emancipation Proclamation significantly alter the Civil War, according to Frederick Douglass?
3. What similarities in views about the Emancipation Proclamation, slavery, the war, and other issues can be found in the viewpoints of Jefferson Davis and Clement L. Vallandigham? Do such similarities lend

support for the North's treatment of Vallandigham as a traitor to the Union? Why or why not?

4. Is the clash between the Ohio Democratic Convention and Abraham Lincoln about the fate of one man (Clement L. Vallandigham) or a deeper debate on Lincoln's war policies? Explain your answer.

Chapter Four

1. How does Garrett Davis respond to the argument, made by Frederick Douglass and others, that without the help of black soldiers the North might lose the war? What do you think this suggests about his priorities concerning the Union?

2. Why do you think Alfred M. Green sees an opportunity while R.H. Vashon sees only risk in enlisting blacks to fight for the North?

3. Why do you think the Confederacy finds the use of black soldiers so objectionable and threatening as to warrant the death penalty? Can clues to the answer to this question be found in the viewpoints of Garrett Davis, Frederick Douglass, and Hannah Johnson? Explain your answer.

Chapter Five

1. Why might the soldiers of the Eleventh New Jersey Volunteers have taken personal offense against the resolutions passed by the New Jersey legislature? Are they justified in arguing that the members of the legislature were calling for the North to essentially give up? Explain.

2. What special hardships of war do James M. Calhoun, E.E. Rawson, and S.C. Wells describe? Do you agree with William T. Sherman that such hardships are the inevitable result of war? Why or why not?

3. How might their experiences during the Civil War account for the differing views of Robert E. Lee and Jefferson Davis at the end of the conflict? Based on this pair and other viewpoints in the book by these two leaders, what speculations might one make on the character of these two Confederate leaders?

Chapter Six

1. Do you think it is important to arrive at one specific answer to the question of who freed the slaves? Why or why not?

2. Which primary sources in this volume lend themselves best to defending James M. McPherson's and Ira Berlin's positions concerning the significance of Lincoln's Emancipation Proclamation? Explain your answer.

General Questions

1. Based on the viewpoints of this book, is it fair to say that slavery was the cause of the Civil War? What other causes do you think contributed to the conflict?

2. From the writings and speeches of Abraham Lincoln found in this book, can one draw out a consistent underlying vision or philosophy toward slavery and the United States? If so, how would you summarize this vision?

Chronology

1787	Constitutional Convention meets in Philadelphia to create a new national government. Slavery is a relatively minor issue of debate, but delegates agree on several provisions to protect it. Meanwhile, the Continental Congress meeting in New York passes the Northwest Ordinance. The ordinance organizes the Northwest Territory and officially bans slavery in it, thus setting a precedent.
1819	Missouri applies for admission to the United States as a slave state. Its status concerning slavery becomes an issue because its admission would upset the balance of eleven free states and eleven slave states that now compose the Union. Congress debates whether it can and should allow or prohibit slavery in the territory acquired by the 1803 Louisiana Purchase.
1820	Missouri Compromise passes Congress and is signed into law by President James Monroe. In addition to jointly admitting Missouri as a slave state and Maine as a free state, the law orders slavery excluded in all Louisiana Purchase lands north of 36°30' (except Missouri).
1845–48	The annexation of Texas and victory in the Mexican War spurs debate on whether the newly acquired territories should permit slavery. The Wilmot Proviso is proposed, calling for no slavery in any territory acquired in the Mexican War. While the bill passes in the House, it fails repeatedly in the Senate, where a balance between slave and free states remains.
1849	President Zachary Taylor proposes to admit California as a free state.
1850	Sen. Henry Clay launches the Senate debate on what will become the Compromise of 1850. Despite the opposition of Southerners, including John C. Calhoun, and antislavery partisans, including William H. Seward and Charles Sumner, five separate measures are passed after months of debate and signed by new president Millard Fillmore. California is admitted to the Union as a free state; New Mexico and Utah are admitted as territories, with the power to decide on their own whether to permit slavery ("popular sovereignty"); the slave

trade is abolished in Washington, D.C.; and a new, tougher Fugitive Slave Law is enacted, with heavy penalties for those who interfere with the capture and return of escaped slaves.

1852   *Uncle Tom's Cabin* by Harriet Beecher Stowe is published in book form after first appearing in serial installments in the *National Era*, a Washington newspaper. The book, which indicts slavery and Northern complicity in it, is a great popular success in the North but causes much alarm in the South.

1854   Kansas-Nebraska Act is passed in Congress, voiding the 1820 Missouri Compromise and potentially extending slavery into territories north of the 36°30' under the doctrine of popular sovereignty. The act is sponsored by Sen. Stephen A. Douglas of Illinois and is supported by Southern senators and congressmen but is bitterly opposed by Northerners, including "Sens. Charles Sumner and Salmon P. Chase, as a "slave-holders' plot." Largely in response to the act, a new political organization, the Republican Party, is organized in the Northern states. The Democratic Party loses 66 of its 91 free-state House seats in November midterm elections and becomes increasingly identified with Southern interests.

1855   The Kansas territory becomes a political and military battleground over the issue of slavery's expansion. Armed "Border Ruffians" from Missouri secure election of a proslavery territorial legislature in January. In October, antislavery settlers meeting in Topeka draw up a constitution forbidding both slavery and black immigration. Both slave and free governments of Kansas seek recognition from Washington. President Franklin Pierce and other Democrats support the former; Republicans support the latter.

1856   Violence in Kansas continues; in response to the looting of the free government capital of Lawrence, abolitionist leader John Brown and his followers kill five proslavery settlers in what is called the Pottawatomie Massacre. The incident provokes further armed conflict between proslavery and antislavery forces, both of which receive funding and arms from outside sources interested in securing Kansas's status as a free or slave state.

November 4, 1856   Democratic presidential candidate James Buchanan is elected, but Republican candidate John C. Frémont wins eleven free states despite public threats of secession by Southern politicians if he should win the presidency.

March 6, 1857   The Supreme Court decision of *Dred Scott v. Sand-*

ford is announced; the Court rules that blacks are not citizens and therefore cannot bring suit in federal courts, that since slaves are property they may be taken anywhere in the United States without losing their slave status, and that the Missouri Compromise establishing a border between slave and free territory was unconstitutional. The decision is praised in the South and condemned in the North.

June 16, 1858 Abraham Lincoln of Illinois accepts the Republican nomination for U.S. senator; in his "House Divided" speech he declares that the United States cannot remain divided into slave and free sections.

August 21–October 15, 1858 Lincoln and Douglas engage in seven public debates on slavery and race relations, as they vie for Douglas's Senate seat.

November 1858 In Congressional elections Republicans carry all Northern states except Indiana and Illinois; Douglas defeats Lincoln.

October 16, 1859 John Brown launches an unsuccessful raid on Harpers Ferry, Virginia, in the hope of triggering a general slave revolt. He and his followers are captured or killed by U.S. Marines led by Col. Robert E. Lee. Brown is hanged on December 2 after being convicted of treason and conspiring with slaves to commit murder; he becomes a martyr in the eyes of many Northerners.

May 9, 1860 The Constitutional Union Party nominates John Bell of Tennessee for president; its small platform attacks sectionalism and pledges support for the Constitution but takes no stand on slavery.

May 18, 1860 Lincoln defeats William H. Seward, among others, to win the Republican presidential nomination. The Republican platform opposes slavery in the territories and supports the admission of Kansas as a free state, and a homestead act.

June 1860 The Democratic Party splits into Northern and Southern factions after being unable to agree on a presidential candidate. Stephen A. Douglas is nominated by the Northern faction on a platform supporting a territory's right to choose or reject slavery without interference from Congress. Southerners abandon the party and nominate John C. Breckinridge of Kentucky for president; their platform calls for slavery to be protected in all western territories.

November 4, 1860 Abraham Lincoln wins the presidency with only 40 percent of the national popular vote but captures virtually all the electoral votes of the eighteen free states; Breckinridge wins eleven slave states; Bell wins three border slave states; and Douglas, second to Lincoln in the popular vote, wins only Missouri and part of New Jersey in the electoral vote.

November 10, 1860 On receiving news of Lincoln's election, the South Carolina legislature votes to hold a special state convention to consider secession.

December 3, 1860 Lame-duck president James Buchanan, in his State of the Union message, calls secession illegal but argues that the federal government has no legal power to prevent it by force.

December 18, 1860 The Senate establishes a special committee of thirteen members to examine the secession crisis. Sen. John J. Crittenden of Kentucky proposes to the Senate Committee of Thirteen a compromise whose main features are the restoration of the old Missouri Compromise line dividing slave and free sections (and extending it west to the Pacific Ocean) and constitutional amendments to prevent Congress from interfering with slavery where it now exists. It is rejected on December 31.

December 20, 1860 South Carolina, with a unanimous convention vote, becomes the first state to secede from the Union.

December 30, 1860–February 16, 1861 Federal arsenals and forts are seized by state authorities in South Carolina, Georgia, Florida, Louisiana, Arkansas, and Texas, in some cases before the states officially secede. One federal holdout is Fort Sumter in Charleston, South Carolina.

On December 31, President Buchanan informs commissioners sent from South Carolina that he will not withdraw federal troops from Fort Sumter and initiates plans to send the fort supplies and reinforcements.

January 9, 1861 The merchant ship *Star of the West*, sent by President Buchanan to reinforce Fort Sumter, withdraws without completing its mission after it is fired upon by South Carolina guns in Charleston Harbor.

Mississippi secedes from the Union.

January 10–February 1, 1861 Florida, Alabama, Georgia, Louisiana, and Texas secede from the Union, while Kansas is admitted as a free state.

February 4–23, 1861 Twenty-one states, including most slave states that have not yet seceded, send delegates to Washington, D.C., to a special peace conference called by Virginia. The delegates produce a proposal similar to the Crittenden compromise, but on March 2, the Senate, on the advice of President-elect Lincoln, rejects the measure.

February 4–March 11, 1861 Delegates from the seven seceded states meet in Montgomery, Alabama, to form the Confederate

States of America. They create a provisional Confederate Congress, write a constitution, and elect Jefferson Davis of Mississippi as provisional president and Alexander H. Stephens of Georgia as vice president. Davis is inaugurated on February 18, and selects a cabinet.

February–March 1861	Tennessee, North Carolina, Missouri, and Arkansas reject secession.
March 2, 1861	Congress adopts a proposed Constitutional amendment guaranteeing no federal interference with slavery in slave states; the amendment is never ratified by the states.
March 4, 1861	Lincoln is inaugurated as the sixteenth president of the United States.
March 5, 1861	President Lincoln learns that Fort Sumter is rapidly running short of supplies.
April 6, 1861	Lincoln informs the governor of South Carolina that "an attempt will be made to supply Fort Sumter with provisions only."
April 9, 1861	Confederate president Jefferson Davis, with his cabinet's approval, orders Fort Sumter taken before relief arrives.
April 12, 1861	Confederate guns open fire on Fort Sumter.
April 14, 1861	The American flag is hauled down and the Confederate flag raised over Fort Sumter.
April 15, 1861	President Lincoln issues a proclamation calling 75,000 state militiamen into national service for ninety days. Northern states accept the call for troops; most border states reject it.
April 17, 1861	Virginia joins the Confederacy.
April 19, 1861	Lincoln orders a naval blockade of Southern ports.
April 27, 1861	Lincoln suspends the writ of habeas corpus in portions of Maryland in order to permit the military arrests of suspected secessionists in this border slave state.
May 1861	Arkansas, Tennessee, and North Carolina join the Confederacy. The Confederacy now consists of eleven states with a population of 9 million (including 3.5 million slaves). Twenty-three states, with a population of 22 million, remain in the Union.
May 13, 1861	Great Britain, the leading world power, declares neutrality in the crisis, recognizing the Confederacy as a belligerent under international law but not as an independent nation.
May 24, 1861	Union general Benjamin F. Butler, stationed at Fort Monroe, Virginia, refuses to return fugitive slaves to their owners, declaring them "contraband of

war" and employing them as workers for the Union army.

July 4, 1861
Lincoln in a message to Congress reaffirms that he has "no purpose . . . to interfere with slavery in the states where it exists."

July 21, 1861
Confederate soldiers are victorious at the First Battle of Bull Run (Manassas).

July 24, 1861
Lincoln places George B. McClellan in command of the main Union army of the east. The next months for the Army of the Potomac, as it is now called, are marked by drills rather than battle.

August 5, 1861
Congress levies the first federal income tax in American history.

August 6, 1861
Congress passes the First Confiscation Act, confiscating any property (slaves included) used directly in the Confederate war effort.

August 30, 1861
Gen. John C. Frémont declares martial law in Missouri and confiscates the property and frees the slaves of all Confederate activists in the state; emancipation provisions of the martial law are rescinded by President Lincoln, who later rescinds similar orders by David Hunter and other Union generals.

November 8, 1861
A United States naval ship stops a British steamer, the *Trent*, and seizes two Confederate envoys en route to England, causing a diplomatic crisis. The two envoys are released in December.

February 1862
Union forces under Gen. Ulysses S. Grant score important victories in Tennessee by capturing Fort Henry and Fort Donelson.

March 9, 1862
The world's first battle between two ironclad ships, the Union *Monitor* and the Confederate *Merrimack*, ends in a draw.

March 13, 1862
Congress forbids Union army officers to return fugitive slaves to their masters.

April 4, 1862
The Army of the Potomac is transported by ship to Fort Monroe in Virginia, on the peninsula between the York and James Rivers; the move begins the two-month Peninsular Campaign, conceived by General McClellan, to attack Richmond, Virginia.

April 6–7, 1862
The Battle of Shiloh; Confederates launch a surprise attack against Grant's forces in Tennessee but are beaten back after two days' fighting that kills more people than all previous wars in American history combined.

April 16, 1862
The Confederate Congress enacts the first conscription law in American history.

April 25, 1862
New Orleans, the South's largest city, surrenders to

	a U.S. naval force under David G. Farragut; it is occupied by the North for the rest of the war.
June 1, 1862	Robert E. Lee takes command of the Army of Northern Virginia.
June 25–July 1, 1862	Lee attacks McClellan in the Seven Days' Battles; McClellan retreats to Harrison's Landing, his Peninsular Campaign a failure.
July 12, 1862	Lincoln meets with border state congressmen to urge compensated emancipation.
July 17, 1862	Congress passes the Second Confiscation Act, which frees all slaves whose owners are rebelling against the United States and authorizes the president to "employ" blacks for the suppression of the rebellion.
July 22, 1862	Lincoln informs his cabinet of his intention to issue a proclamation of freedom for slaves; Secretary of State Seward advises him to wait for military success before making a public announcement.
August 14, 1862	Lincoln meets with black leaders in the White House; he tells them that slavery is the "greatest wrong inflicted on any people" but also urges black emigration from the United States.
August 29–30, 1862	The Second Battle of Bull Run results in another embarrassing defeat for the North.
September 7, 1862	The Army of Northern Virginia, under Robert E. Lee, invades Maryland.
September 17, 1862	The Battle of Antietam (Sharpsburg) results in about 12,000 casualties for the North and 13,000 casualties for the South—the bloodiest day of the war. Lee is compelled to withdraw to Virginia, which gives Lincoln an opportunity to act on his emancipation plans.
September 22, 1862	Lincoln issues a preliminary Emancipation Proclamation, to take effect on January 1, 1863.
September 24, 1862	Lincoln suspends the writ of habeas corpus throughout the North and subjects "all persons discouraging voluntary enlistments" to martial law.
November 4, 1862	The Democrats score significant gains in the Northern congressional and state elections.
November 7, 1862	Lincoln, impatient with McClellan's failure to press his advantage following the Battle of Antietam, replaces him as commander of the Army of the Potomac with Gen. Ambrose B. Burnside.
December 13, 1862	Burnside leads his army to a disastrous defeat at the Battle of Fredericksburg, suffering 12,000 casualties. He is later replaced by Gen. Joseph Hooker.
January 1, 1863	The Emancipation Proclamation takes effect. The

proclamation in its final form lays more emphasis on the enlisting of black soldiers; by late spring, recruiting is under way throughout the North and Union-occupied areas in the South.

March 3, 1863	Congress enacts a draft (the Enrollment Act of 1863) to raise troops; the law makes most male citizens aged 20–45 liable for conscription.
May 1–4, 1863	In a brilliant display of military tactics, Lee defeats a larger Union force under Hooker in the Battle of Chancellorsville. Noted Confederate general Thomas "Stonewall" Jackson is accidently shot by one of his own men and dies on May 10.
May 5, 1863	Democratic congressman Clement L. Vallandigham is arrested and tried for treason by military authorities; he is banished to the Confederacy on May 19.
June 3, 1863	Lee leads 75,000 Confederate soldiers in a campaign that will take them to Pennsylvania and culminate in the Battle of Gettysburg.
June 28, 1863	Gen. George G. Meade replaces Joseph Hooker as commander of the Army of the Potomac.
July 1–3, 1863	The Battle of Gettysburg; 23,000 Confederate and 28,000 Union soldiers are killed, wounded, or missing in this Union victory; it marks the end of the last major Confederate offensive of the war.
July 4, 1863	The town of Vicksburg, Mississippi, surrenders to Grant, ending a six-week siege; importance of this victory ranks with that of Gettysburg.
July 13–16, 1863	Antidraft riots erupt in New York City, where mobs of poor white immigrants lynch blacks and burn buildings.
July 30, 1863	Lincoln threatens retaliation on Confederate prisoners if captured black Union soldiers are placed into slavery or otherwise mistreated by the Confederacy.
November 19, 1863	Lincoln delivers his Gettysburg Address.
January 1864	"Free people of color" of New Orleans petition for the right to vote.
March 12, 1864	Ulysses S. Grant is placed in command of all Union armies; William T. Sherman replaces Grant as commander of western forces.
May–June 1864	Armies of Lee and Grant clash in Virginia in the battles of the Wilderness (May 5–7), Spotsylvania Court House (May 8–19), and Cold Harbor (June 1–3). The North suffers much higher casualties than the South, but unlike previous Union generals, Grant nonetheless presses on toward Richmond.

295

June 7, 1864	Lincoln is renominated for president by the Republican Party; to broaden Lincoln's political base, Andrew Johnson, a Tennessee Democrat who remained loyal to the Union, is named his running mate.
June 12–18, 1864	Grant attempts to capture St. Petersburg, Virginia, south of Richmond; the attack fails and the armies of Lee and Grant are locked into siege warfare for the next nine months.
June 15, 1864	Clement L. Vallandigham returns to Ohio from exile to denounce the Civil War as "unnecessary."
August 29, 1864	Democratic Party nominates George B. McClellan for president; in his campaign McClellan repudiates the Democratic Party platform proposing an immediate end to the war.
September 2, 1864	Northern morale rises when Union forces under Sherman capture Atlanta.
	Robert E. Lee writes to Jefferson Davis suggesting the use of black troops in the Confederate army.
November–December 1864	General Sherman marches his army across Georgia to the Atlantic Ocean, destroying Southern economic resources and morale.
November 8, 1864	Lincoln is reelected, carrying all but three states.
January 16, 1865	General Sherman issues Special Field Order 15, setting aside coastal territory in Florida, Georgia, and South Carolina for the provision of 40-acre plots for ex-slaves.
January 31, 1865	Congress approves the Thirteenth Amendment to the Constitution to abolish slavery by a vote of 119–56; amendment is sent to states for ratification.
March 4, 1865	Lincoln is inaugurated a second time; speech emphasizes compassion toward the South; at his reception he signals a change in the political atmosphere by going out of his way to welcome black abolitionist orator Frederick Douglass.
March 13, 1865	Confederate Congress passes a measure authorizing enlistment of black troops, with an implied promise of freedom for slaves who serve.
April 9, 1865	Lee surrenders to Grant at Appomattox Court House.
April 14, 1865	Lincoln is assassinated by John Wilkes Booth, a Confederate sympathizer; Andrew Johnson assumes presidency.
December 13, 1865	Thirteenth Amendment to the Constitution, abolishing slavery, is ratified by the states.

Annotated Bibliography

Historical Studies

William Barney, *The Secessionist Impulse*. Princeton, NJ: Princeton University Press, 1974. A study of the move toward secession that focuses particularly on the states of Alabama and Mississippi.

Richard E. Beringer et al., *Why the South Lost the Civil War*. Athens: University of Georgia Press, 1986. Beringer and three other historians argue that a Southern lack of will led to the Confederacy's defeat.

Ira Berlin et al., *Slaves No More: Three Essays on Emancipation and the Civil War*. New York: Cambridge University Press, 1992. Essays detailing the efforts of the slaves themselves to achieve and exercise their freedom during the Civil War.

Iver Bernstein, *The New York City Draft Riots*. New York: Oxford University Press, 1990. A recent and compelling history of a demonstration against the draft that turned into a race riot and a political attack on the Republican Party.

Mark Boatner, *The Civil War Dictionary*. Rev. ed. New York: McKay, 1988. More than 4,000 entries and 2,000 biographical sketches provide handy information on the military history of the Civil War.

Stanley Campbell, *The Slave Catchers: Enforcement of the Fugitive Slave Law, 1850-1860*. Chapel Hill: University of North Carolina Press, 1970. A study that emphasizes the hostility and violence generated by this controversial element of the Compromise of 1850.

Bruce Catton, *The Centennial History of the Civil War*. 3 vols. Garden City, NY: Doubleday, 1961-1965. A masterly narrative by one of the more prolific writers on the Civil War.

Thomas Connelly, *The Marble Man: Robert E. Lee and His Image in American Society*. New York: Knopf, 1977. A study that is critical of Lee for limiting his military vision too much to the Virginia theater of the war.

E. Merton Coulter, *The Confederate States of America, 1861-1865*. Baton Rouge: Louisiana State University Press, 1950. An unromanticized general history of Southern society during the Civil War.

LaWanda Cox, *Lincoln and Black Freedom: A Study in Presidential Leadership*. Columbia: University of South Carolina Press, 1981. For its time, an important revisionist history that seeks to rescue Lincoln and his party from charges of conservatism and racism.

Avery Craven, *The Growth of Southern Nationalism, 1848-1861.* Baton Rouge: Louisiana State University Press, 1953. A study that implicitly justifies Southern sectionalism as a response to Northern aggression.

David P. Crook, *The North, the South, and the Powers, 1861-1865.* New York: Wiley, 1974. A diplomatic history of the Civil War focusing on the foreign relations of the Union and the Confederacy.

Marilyn Mayer Culpepper, *Trials and Triumphs: The Women of the American Civil War.* East Lansing: Michigan State University Press, 1991. An examination of how the conflict affected the lives of American women, drawing heavily on diaries and letters.

Richard Current, *Lincoln and the First Shot.* Philadelphia: Lippincott, 1963. A dramatic historical account of the events leading up to the Southern attack on Fort Sumter.

Richard Current, *Lincoln's Loyalists: Union Soldiers from the Confederacy.* Boston: Northeastern University Press, 1992. An attempt to assess why some 100,000 whites from the eleven Confederate states decided to fight for the Union.

William C. Davis, *Jefferson Davis: The Man and His Hour.* New York: HarperCollins, 1991. A view of the first and only Confederate president, which proceeds on the assumption (not shared by Davis) that the Confederacy was doomed from the start.

William C. Davis, ed., *The Image of War, 1861-1865.* 6 vols. Garden City, NY: Doubleday, 1981-1984. A photo history of the Civil War with an accompanying historical narrative.

Christopher Dell, *Lincoln and the War Democrats.* Rutherford, NJ: Fairleigh Dickinson University Press, 1975. An account of those War Democrats in Congress who joined with Lincoln and the Republicans to support not only the war but the slaves' emancipation.

Dwight Dumond, *The Secession Movement.* New York: Octagon Books, 1963. A history that stresses the constitutional premises behind secession and presumes that the South had a strong case to make in dissolving the Union.

Robert F. Durden, *The Gray and the Black: The Confederate Debate on Emancipation.* Baton Rouge: Louisiana State University Press, 1972. A study of a Jefferson Davis proposal to initiate emancipation within the Confederacy, from the proposal's introduction in October 1864 through its continued debate to the end of the war.

Paul Escott, *After Secession: Jefferson Davis and the Failure of Confederate Nationalism.* Baton Rouge: Louisiana State University Press, 1978. A history of Jefferson Davis's inability to gain significant support from nonslaveholders in the Confederacy.

Eric Foner, *Free Soil, Free Labor, Free Men: The Ideology of the Republican*

Party Before the Civil War. New York: Oxford University Press, 1970. A pathbreaking history of the Free Soil movement that prepared the way for the advent of the Republican Party in the 1850s.

Shelby Foote, *The Civil War: A Narrative*. 3 vols. New York: Random House, 1958-1974. A graphic military history of the war, written by a novelist-turned-historian.

George M. Fredrickson, *The Inner Civil War: Northern Intellectuals and the Crisis of the Union*. Urbana: University of Illinois Press, 1993. A provocative intellectual history of those abolitionists who were persuaded to support the Civil War and the preservation of the Union.

Louis S. Gerteis, *From Contraband to Freedman: Federal Policy Toward Southern Blacks, 1861-1865*. Westport, CT: Greenwood Press, 1973. A revisionist history that argues that no wartime social revolution occurred in the South, not only because of intransigent Southern whites, but also because of conservative Northern Republicans.

Joseph T. Glatthaar, *Forged in Battle*. New York: Free Press, 1990. An exploration of the often uneasy alliance between some 180,000 black soldiers fighting for the Union and the white officers assigned to command them.

Paddy Griffith, *Rally Once Again: Battle Tactics of the American Civil War*. Marlborough, UK: Crowood Press, 1989. An examination of Civil War military tactics and how they evolved during the conflict.

Holman Hamilton, *Prologue to Conflict: The Crisis and Compromise of 1850*. Lexington: University of Kentucky Press, 1964. The most concise account of this compromise that did not succeed in its ultimate aim of preventing war.

William Hanchett, *The Lincoln Murder Conspiracies*. Urbana: University of Illinois Press, 1983. The best single-volume history of the Lincoln assassination and the theories of what caused it.

Hondon B. Hargrove, *Black Union Soldiers in the Civil War*. Jefferson, NC: McFarland, 1988. A study that disproves the idea that American blacks became free without significant efforts on their own behalf.

Herman Hattaway and Archer Jones, *How the North Won: A Military History of the Civil War*. Urbana: University of Illinois Press, 1983. A volume that seeks the reasons for Northern victory in the Civil War and finds them in the superiority of Northern resources and logistics.

Robert Johannsen, *Lincoln, the South and Slavery: The Political Dimension*. Baton Rouge: Louisiana State University Press, 1991. A series of essays tracing Lincoln's thoughts on the issue of slave expansion between 1854 and 1860 and arguing that his opposition to such expansion grew stronger as the country moved closer to war.

Robert Johannsen, *Stephen A. Douglas*. New York: Oxford University Press, 1973. The definitive biography of the most important Northern Democrat of the 1850s and the chief advocate of popular sovereignty.

299

Frank L. Klement, *Dark Lanterns: Secret Political Societies, Conspiracies, and Treason Trials in the Civil War*. Baton Rouge: Louisiana State University Press, 1984. A study of secret antiwar societies, which sees them not as traitors but as legitimate attempts by Northern Democrats to defend themselves against Republicans.

Bruce Levine, *Half Slave and Half Free: The Roots of Civil War*. New York: Hill and Wang, 1992. An examination of the causes of the Civil War that argues that the war was an irrepressible conflict, but one that carried further the ideals of the democratic revolution of 1775.

Gerald Linderman, *Embattled Courage: The Experience of Combat in the American Civil War*. New York: Free Press, 1987. A story of how the experience of war helped disillusion both Union and Confederate soldiers and call into question any traditional notion of courage.

Leon Litwack, *Been in the Storm So Long: The Aftermath of Slavery*. New York: Knopf, 1979. A general study chronicling the response of slaves to their gaining freedom during and immediately after the Civil War.

Thomas Livermore, *Numbers and Losses in the Civil War in America, 1861-1865*. Bloomington: Indiana University Press, 1957. First published in 1900, it is still used as a reliable compilation of the casualties of the war.

E.B. Long with Barbara Long, *The Civil War Day by Day: An Almanac, 1861-1865*. Garden City, NY: Doubleday, 1971. A detailed reference guide to the major military operations and political developments of the Civil War.

James McPherson, *Abraham Lincoln and the Second American Revolution*. New York: Oxford University Press, 1991. A series of essays around the themes of the Civil War as a revolutionary experience and Lincoln as a revolutionary leader.

James McPherson, *Battle Cry of Freedom: The Civil War Era*. New York: Oxford University Press, 1988. The definitive single-volume history of the Civil War that won a Pulitzer Prize.

James McPherson, *What They Fought For, 1861-1865*. Baton Rouge: Louisiana State University Press, 1994. A short volume examining the personal letters and diaries of Civil War soldiers on both sides.

Grady McWhiney and Perry Jamieson, *Attack and Die: Civil War Military Tactics and the Southern Heritage*. Tuscaloosa: University of Alabama Press, 1982. A military history that attributes Southern military strategy to unique cultural factors in Southern life.

James Moorhead, *American Apocalypse: Yankee Protestants and the Civil War*. New Haven: Yale University Press, 1978. An examination of the attitudes and policies of various Northern Protestant denominations prior to and during the Civil War.

Thomas D. Morris, *Free Men All: The Personal Liberty Laws of the North, 1780-1861*. Baltimore: Johns Hopkins University Press, 1974. A history of the actions of Northern state governments to prevent private citizens from becoming involved in capturing and returning fugitive slaves.

Eugene Murdock, *One Million Men: The Civil War Draft in the North*. Madison: State Historical Society of Wisconsin, 1971. A comprehensive history of the framing and implementation of the American government's first military draft.

Mark E. Neely, *The Fate of Liberty*. New York: Oxford University Press, 1991. An evaluation of the Lincoln administration's wartime handling of civil liberties that reveals numerous presidential inconsistencies but exonerates the president of any charge of dictatorship.

Larry E. Nelson, *Bullets, Ballots and Rhetoric: Confederate Policy for the United States Presidential Contest of 1864*. Tuscaloosa: University of Alabama Press, 1980. A study of Jefferson Davis's attempt to undermine the Lincoln administration by interfering in the campaign of 1864.

Allan Nevins, *Ordeal of the Union*. 4 vols. New York: Scribner, 1947. A multivolume history of the road to war by one of the most prolific writers among American historians.

Allan Nevins, *The War for the Union*. 4 vols. New York: Scribner: 1959-1971. A multivolume military, political, and social history of the war.

Stephen B. Oates, *With Malice Toward None: The Life of Abraham Lincoln*. New York: Harper and Row, 1977. A highly readable, generally praiseful biography of the sixteenth president.

Philip S. Paludan, *Victims: A True History of the Civil War*. Knoxville: University of Tennessee Press, 1981. A study of class tensions between the wealthy plantation owners and small farmers in the South during the Civil War.

David M. Potter, *The Impending Crisis, 1848-1861*. Completed and edited by Don E. Fehrenbacher. New York: Harper and Row, 1976. The best single-volume history of the road to the Civil War.

David M. Potter, *Lincoln and His Party in the Secession Crisis*. New Haven: Yale University Press, 1942. A history guaranteed to offend both Northern and Southern sympathizers because it argues that the Civil War was a tragic war caused by intransigence and lack of understanding on both sides.

Benjamin Quarles, *The Negro in the Civil War*. Boston: Little, Brown, 1953. A general survey of the political-military role played by African-Americans during the war.

Charles Ramsdell, *Behind the Lines in the Southern Confederacy*. Baton Rouge: Louisiana State University Press, 1944. A series of lectures on the general economic and social conditions in the South during the Civil War.

James G. Randall and Richard Current, *Lincoln the President*. 4 vols. Urbana: University of Illinois Press, 1991. A republication of a standard, comprehensive history of the Lincoln administration.

James A. Rawley, *Turning Points of the Civil War*. Lincoln: University of Nebraska Press, 1966. An examination of key events of the Civil War, including Lincoln's treatment of the border states, the First Battle of Bull Run, and the Emancipation Proclamation.

Donald E. Reynolds, *Editors Make War: Southern Newspapers in the Secession Crisis.* Nashville, TN: Vanderbilt University Press, 1970. A study of the critical role played by the press in helping foment the secession crisis.

James Ford Rhodes, *History of the United States from the Compromise of 1850 to the Restoration of Home Rule in the South.* 7 vols. New York: Harper and Bros., 1892-1906. A magisterial early history of the Civil War era.

May Ringold, *The Role of the State Legislatures in the Confederacy.* Athens: University of Georgia Press, 1966. A history of the relationship between the states and the Confederate government that argues that the states generally played a positive and constructive role.

Joel Silbey, *A Respectable Minority: The Democratic Party in the Civil War Era.* New York: Norton, 1977. A history of the Democratic Party as it tried to become a cohesive opposition party during the Civil War.

Dean Sprague, *Freedom Under Lincoln.* Boston: Houghton Mifflin, 1965. An examination of the conflict between federal power and personal liberty during the Civil War.

Kenneth M. Stampp, *And the War Came: The North and the Secession Crisis, 1860-1861.* Baton Rouge: Louisiana State University Press, 1950. A provocative investigation of the growth of war fever in the North prior to the Civil War.

Kenneth M. Stampp, *The Imperiled Union.* New York: Oxford University Press, 1980. A series of essays written between 1945 and 1980 on the background events leading to what the author regards as an irrepressible conflict, but not necessarily an inevitable war.

John M. Taylor, *William Henry Seward: Lincoln's Right Hand.* New York: HarperCollins, 1991. The most recent full biography of Lincoln's secretary of state, who played a crucial role in shaping many foreign and domestic policies during the Civil War.

Emory Thomas, *The Confederate Nation, 1861-1865.* New York: Harper and Row, 1979. An interpretive history of the Confederacy that argues that the Confederacy constituted a revolutionary experience for Southerners who had set out to preserve a conservative way of life.

Hans L. Trefousse, *The Radical Republicans: Lincoln's Vanguard for Racial Justice.* New York: Knopf, 1969. A study of key Republicans, including Charles Sumner and Thaddeus Stevens, who sometimes clashed with Abraham Lincoln in their commitment to emancipation.

Geoffrey C. Ward, *The Civil War: An Illustrated History.* New York: Knopf, 1990. The companion volume to the acclaimed PBS television documentary on the Civil War.

Bell Wiley, *The Life of Billy Yank.* Indianapolis: Bobbs-Merrill, 1952. A popular, yet scholarly history of the ordinary Yankee soldier.

Bell Wiley, *The Life of Johnny Reb*. Indianapolis: Bobbs-Merrill, 1943. A frank, down-to-earth account of the common soldier of the Confederacy.

T. Harry Williams, *Lincoln and His Generals*. New York: Knopf, 1952. A history of Lincoln as commander-in-chief and his efforts to find competent generals and to play a significant role in directing the war effort.

Garry Wills, *Lincoln at Gettysburg*. New York: Simon and Schuster, 1992. A narrative account of the events surrounding Lincoln's Gettysburg Address and a careful analysis of the famous speech itself.

Forrest Wood, *Black Scare: The Racist Response to Emancipation and Reconstruction*. Berkeley and Los Angeles: University of California Press, 1968. A sometimes polemical study of racist thought and activity during the Civil War.

Bertram Wyatt-Brown, *Southern Honor: Ethics and Behavior in the Old South*. New York: Oxford University Press, 1982. A study that seeks to explain the distinctive culture of the South before and during the Civil War.

Agatha Young, *The Women and the Crisis: Women of the North in the Civil War*. New York: McDowell, Oblensky, 1959. A study of twenty-nine leading Northern women and their war-related work.

Primary Source Collections

Roy Basler, ed., *The Collected Works of Abraham Lincoln*. New Brunswick: Rutgers University Press, 1953-1955. The standard primary source for Lincoln's thought and writings.

Ira Berlin et al., eds., *Free at Last: A Documentary History of Slavery, Freedom, and the Civil War*. New York: New Press, 1992. A collection of letters, official reports, and other records depicting how slavery came to an end during the Civil War, emphasizing the role escaped slaves and black soldiers played in achieving their emancipation.

Henry Steele Commager, ed., *The Blue and the Gray: The Story of the Civil War As Told by Participants*. Indianapolis: Bobbs-Merrill, 1950. A massive anthology that seeks to capture how the Civil War affected life in America.

Frederick Douglass, *The Civil War, 1861-1865*. Vol. 3 of *The Life and Writings of Frederick Douglass*, edited by Philip S. Foner. New York: International Publishers, 1952. The wartime writings of America's leading black abolitionist.

Clifford Dowdey and Louis H. Manarin, eds., *The Wartime Papers of R.E. Lee*. Boston: Little, Brown, 1961. The dispatches to Jefferson Davis and other writings of Robert E. Lee, considered by many to be the South's greatest general.

William W. Freeling and Craig M. Simpson, eds., *Secession Debated: Georgia's Showdown in 1860*. New York: Oxford University Press, 1992. The speeches and writings of Georgia secessionists and Unionists in November 1860, which the editors argue were as important for the

South as the 1858 debates between Abraham Lincoln and Stephen A. Douglas were to the North.

Ulysses S. Grant, *Memoirs and Selected Letters: Personal Memoirs of U.S. Grant, Selected Letters 1839-1865*. New York: Library of America, 1990. The highly informative reflections of the general-turned-president who led the North to victory in the Civil War.

Harold Holzer, ed., *The Lincoln-Douglas Debates*. New York: Harper-Collins, 1993. The first complete, unabridged version of the texts of the seven debates of 1858 in Illinois that helped to shape the national debate of 1860.

Louis P. Masur, ed., ". . . *the real war will never get in the books": Selections from Writers During the Civil War*. New York: Oxford University Press, 1993. An anthology of writings on the Civil War by Herman Melville, Walt Whitman, and lesser-known authors.

Frank Moore, ed., *The Rebellion Record: A Diary of American Events, with Documents, Narratives, Illustrative Incidents, Poetry, etc., etc.* New York: G.P. Putnam, 1861-1868. A massive compilation of newspaper articles, speeches, and other documents made during the Civil War.

Paul F. Paskoff and Daniel J. Wilson, eds., *The Cause of the South: Selections from De Bow's Review 1846-1867*. Baton Rouge: Louisiana State University Press, 1982. Selections from one of the leading Southern magazines, with articles from the period prior to and during the Civil War.

Howard C. Perkins, ed., *Northern Editorials on Secession*. Gloucester, MA: Peter Smith, 1964. A compilation of newspaper editorials from the months leading up to the Civil War, providing a diversity of views on secession, the 1860 election, and other issues.

James D. Richardson, ed., *The Messages and Papers of Jefferson Davis and the Confederacy*. New York: Chelsea House, 1966. The official papers, including diplomatic correspondence, of the short-lived Confederate government.

George W. Smith and Charles Judah, eds., *Life in the North During the Civil War*. Albuquerque: University of New Mexico Press, 1966. A sourcebook of writings demonstrating that the North was far from united during the Civil War.

Kenneth M. Stampp, ed., *The Causes of the Civil War*. Rev. ed. New York: Simon and Schuster, 1974. An anthology of primary sources from the 1850s and the Civil War period as well as essays by historians that examine why America plunged into the Civil War.

War of the Rebellion . . . Official Records of the Union and Confederate Armies, 128 vols. Washington, DC: Government Printing Office, 1880-1901. The official records of Civil War military operations, with numerous reports from officers on the field.

C. Vann Woodward, ed., *Mary Chestnut's Civil War*. New Haven: Yale University Press, 1981. A highly informative diary of an important Southern woman who was the daughter and wife of slaveholders and a defender of the Confederate cause, yet who opposed slavery.

Index